Honorable in Business

Honorable in Business

Business Ethics from a Christian Perspective

ANNETTA GIBSON

and

DANIEL AUGSBURGER

WIPF & STOCK · Eugene, Oregon

HONORABLE IN BUSINESS
Business Ethics from a Christian Perspective

Wipf & Stock
An Imprint of Wipf and Stock Publishers
199 W. 8th Ave., Suite 3
Eugene, OR 97401

www.wipfandstock.com

PAPERBACK ISBN: 978-1-5326-6285-0
HARDCOVER ISBN: 978-1-5326-6286-7
EBOOK ISBN: 978-1-5326-6287-4

Manufactured in the U.S.A.   01/11/19

Dedicated to all who follow
the counsel of Jeremiah 9:23–24

This is what the Lord says:
"Let not the wise man boast of his wisdom,
or the strong man boast of his strength,
or the rich man boast of his riches,
but let him who boasts boast about this:
That he understands and knows me, that I am the Lord,
who exercises kindness,
justice and righteousness on earth, for in these I delight."

Table of Contents

Scripture Abbreviations

Gen	Genesis
Exod	Exodus
Lev	Leviticus
Num	Numbers
Deut	Deuteronomy
Job	Job
Ps	Psalm
Prov	Proverbs
Isa	Isaiah
Jer	Jeremiah
Dan	Daniel
Amos	Amos
Mic	Micah
Mal	Malachi
Matt	Matthew
Mark	Mark
Luke	Luke
John	John
Acts	Acts
Rom	Romans
1, 2 Cor	First and Second Corinthians

Gal	Galatians
Eph	Ephesians
Phil	Philippians
Col	Colossians
1, 2 Thess	First and Second Thessalonians
Titus	Titus
Heb	Hebrews
Jas	James
1, 2 Pet	First and Second Peter
1, 2, 3 John	First, Second, and Third John
Rev	Revelation

Introduction

The First Question
You Will Be Asked in Heaven

"Have you been honorable in business?"[1]

Christian ethics is not a set of isolated moral principles but is dependent on a prior Christian view of reality as expressed in the relationship between God and his people. What is expressed in Scripture is not a set of principles or rules, but rather a comprehensive understanding of reality, such as all life originating from God, the nature of God and man, and life's meaning.[2]

WE ARE ALL INTERESTED in the beginning of a story. As Nathaniel Philbrick notes in his book *Mayflower:*

> From the Big Bang to the Garden of Eden to the circumstances of our own births, we yearn to travel back to that distant time when everything was new and full of promise. Perhaps then, we tell ourselves, we can start to make sense of the convoluted mess we are in today.[3]

---

1. Pava, "Developing a Religiously Grounded Business Ethic," 65.
2. Kim et al., "Modernism, Christianity, and Business Ethics," 119.
3. Philbrick, *Mayflower*, xiii.

1

This book, which discusses business ethics from a Christian perspective, begins at the beginning—that is, with the scriptural beginning in Genesis as a starting point for our understanding of the Christian worldview and the Christian's ethical obligations. The authors take the position that not only is the Christian worldview a viable way to look at the world and a satisfactory basis for business ethics, but that a more complete understanding of what was intended when the world was "new and full of promise" can guide businessmen and women in today's business world.

Scripture describes the creation of the world in the first two chapters of Genesis. Here is a description of a beautiful world, fresh from the creator's hand, a garden filled with vegetation and animal life, and human life created to reflect the image of God. Genesis 1:27 states: "So God created man in his own image, in the image of God he created him; male and female he created them." For humans, to be created in the image of God means that God's initial plan was for us to reflect God's character.

God's character is described in Exod 34:6–7 and Jer 9:23–24. In these passages God describes himself as being compassionate and gracious, abounding in love and faithfulness, and exercising justice and righteousness. What these words mean for human life and its interactions with others, especially in business, will be developed in the following chapters.

DOES GOD NOTICE OR CARE?

But first, we need to consider the question: Does God really care about what a person does in business? Is it necessary to mirror the self-described attributes of God in our daily business dealings? Jesus uses a number of business-related examples in his parables (e.g., workers in the vineyard in Matt 20:1–16; the dishonest manager in Luke 16:1–9; the parable of the talents in Matt 25:1–30; the sower of seeds in Matt 13:3–23; the unjust steward in Matt 18:23–35), which indicates that both he and his listeners were acquainted with business activity. Some, however, argue that in these instances Jesus seems to be using familiar examples to teach lessons about the kingdom of heaven rather than critiquing business.

However, when one looks at Scripture as a whole, one notices there is a call for justice and fair dealing in our business relationships (Prov 11:1; Luke 10:7), as well as in all other relationships. The psalmist states: "God has taken his place in the divine council; in the midst of the gods he holds judgment; how long will you judge unjustly and show partiality to the wicked? Give justice to the weak and the fatherless; maintain the right of the afflicted and the destitute. Rescue the weak and the needy; deliver them from the hand of the wicked" (Ps 82:1–4). Further, the psalmist declares: "The LORD is righteous; he loves righteous deeds" (Ps 11:7).

Unfortunately, one cannot consistently find righteous deeds in the business world today. Instead, when the statement "It is simply becoming a business" is made about any organization or profession, it is not generally a compliment. As Max Stackhouse notes:

> Contemporary leaders of law, medicine, education, journalism, and sometimes religion complain that their fields are being "reduced" to "business" decisions. It is not that they are opposed to good management or being solvent, but they do not want life and thought in their fields to be governed by what they understand to be "merely" business criteria or to act in their professions as if material gain were the only goal. And they believe that "good business" means nothing else than greed, a congenital blindness to the needs of others and to justice, health, wisdom, honesty, and the common good. People often view business with suspicion, in other words, because it is thought to be constitutionally unethical in some regard or another. The "good" of "good business" is not thought to be a moral good.[4]

Stackhouse goes on to argue that unless one takes seriously a scriptural foundation for one's ethics and one's understanding about what is right and good and fitting, one will be unable to avoid the "temptations to self-interest, greed, possessiveness, and opportunism" that are so easily worshipped as today's economic idols. He notes:

> This is what the Bible warns about when it preaches against Mammon, the raising of business, acquisition, or profit into the idol of our lives. All profound religion, after all, has at its depth a celebration of giving and not getting, of sharing and not possessing, of sacrificing and not only accumulating. Theological ethics thus stands in a constant tension with Mammon's temptation to make success in a purely material sense the goal of life and the rule of behavior. It cannot save humanity, even if it pretends to by drowning souls and civilizations in commodities and services. Indeed this is the greatest threat to modern business life and contemporary business professionals.[5]

4. Stackhouse, "Foundations and Purposes," 16.

5. Stackhouse, "Foundations and Purposes," 33.

This book takes the position that what one does in business matters to God, that God has defined what is right and wrong, and that he has given us moral principles and rules that we can follow.

BACK TO THE BEGINNING

Beginning at the beginning will provide a better understanding for the purpose of one's life, the framework for one's actions in business, and how these actions can mirror the image of God. But while we may be interested in the beginning of a story, we are equally interested in the end of a story. In fact, at times we are so interested in how the story will end that we cheat just a little, and read the last chapter first! From the Christian perspective, insight about the end of the story is available from the Babylonian Talmud, Shabbat 31a, which suggests that the first question asked in the world to come is: "Have you been honorable in business?"[6]

The suggestion that we may be asked about our business dealings in the next world may come as a surprise to many, given the Christian church's struggle with understanding, let alone affirming, people who engage in business. Initially the early Christian church questioned whether it was even possible to be in business and still please God. With the coming of John Calvin and the Protestant perspective on business, the pendulum swung toward not only affirming people who engage in business, but even asserting that financial success in business was proof of the blessing of God. Ironically, this belief has, from time to time, led to the justification of greed in the name of piety and religion.

Genesis 1 not only tells us that in the beginning we were created in the image of God, but it also gives humans a benediction that informs us of our role as humans while we are living our lives—a role that moves us from the beginning to the middle of the story. We know from Genesis 1 that God created the material world and pronounced it "good." Thus the material world around us matters to God. We also know that human beings were tasked to be stewards of God's creation, not owners. As stewards, humans were asked to act on God's behalf. God's instructions were: "Be fruitful and increase in number; fill the earth and subdue it. Rule over the fish of the sea and the birds of the air and over every living creature that moves on the ground" (Gen 1:28).

---

6. Pava, "Developing a Religiously Grounded Business Ethic," 65.

The work to "subdue" and "rule" and be "fruitful" mean that humans are to extend God's creativity across the entire world through their own creative actions. Human creative work is derived from the work of God. But humans are subject to limits; they cannot create out of nothing (*ex nihilo*) like God can. The Tree of the Knowledge of Good and Evil was planted in the garden to remind Adam and Eve that they were made to live within limits. What does this mean for business people today?

Van Duzer suggests:

> In business terms God made the initial capital investment. He richly endowed the earth with resources. Adam and Eve were the initial managers called to creatively organize (name the animals) and manage these resources (take dominion), to enhance the productivity of the Garden (be fruitful and multiply) in a sustainable (guard creation) manner. Creativity is not just a gift given to some artists or design engineers. It is inherent in the very meaning of being human.[7]

If we accept God's initial creation of humans in his image, and his ownership over creation as outlined in Genesis, then his interest in what we, as stewards, have done with the investment he has made seems like a natural expectation. From that natural expectation comes the subsequent question to be asked at the end of the story: Have you been honorable in business?

WHAT FOLLOWS

While this book discusses ethics topics similar to those found in other business ethics textbooks, it is designed to be neither the sole business ethics text used in an ethics class nor a theological treatise on Scripture. Rather it references commonly available business ethics texts in areas where they very adequately describe specific business ethics subjects. The contribution this book makes to the field of business ethics is that it takes seriously the integration of the Christian worldview with business ethics discussions in order to provide a Christian with a mental framework from which to answer the question: How can I be honorable in business?

This book is primarily designed for undergraduate business students who are enrolled in Christian colleges and universities and who plan shortly to enter a career in business. Because it is not intended to

7. Van Duzer, *Why Business Matters*, 33.

be the *only* business ethics text used in a class, it does not cover every possible business ethical issue nor does it exhaustively discuss the various ethical philosophies. It is assumed that the reader is already somewhat familiar with both ethical philosophies and major business topics. From a teaching perspective, the instructor might choose to provide additional material if he or she wishes to discuss the major ethical philosophies in greater depth or go into more detail on any given business topic when in a classroom situation.

Rather than providing a series of action steps to follow to achieve ethical decision-making, this book seeks to introduce the reader/student to the possibility that a Christian worldview provides the principles upon which one may make Christian ethical choices in a primarily non-Christian-oriented business environment. Accordingly, the book approaches the subject from a philosophical perspective. It is written to encourage and support readers as they seriously consider how to live their personal and professional lives as Christians, whether within or outside the workplace. It is also hoped that the book may be helpful to those already employed in business who struggle with how to engage in their daily work life in a business environment while maintaining the vision that what they do every day is meaningful and important to God.

The book is divided into eleven chapters. Each chapter begins with an opening story from the business world which illustrates that chapter's topic. The topics discussed include the environment and economic growth, the dignity of work and employee workplace rights, discrimination, product safety, technology, advertising, whistle-blowing, accounting fraud and insider trading, and business ethics in the international arena. Included in each chapter are numerous biblical texts which provide the Christian perspective on the issue at hand. At the end of each chapter there is a short "Thinking It Through" section, where the reader is reminded of the ethical issue outlined in the opening story and then invited to consider the story from the perspective of two major philosophical theories (which are discussed in chapter 1), as well as the Christian perspective. In the "Thinking It Through" sections the two philosophical theories presented are utilitarianism, a teleological theory, and Emmanuel Kant's Categorical Imperative, a deontological theory. Teleological theories focus on the results or consequences of the decision (*telos* is Greek for "end"), while deontological theories focus on what is one's duty, based on broad ethical principles such as honesty, loyalty, and fairness (*deon* is Greek for "duty").

The final chapter, "What Difference Does a Christian Make?" discusses the value added to business relationships by being a Christian businessperson. It would be foolish to believe that all who claim the name "Christian" act in a Christ-like manner. But even while recognizing that some may fall short, this chapter outlines the difference that a Christian businessperson *can* bring to the table in his or her business dealings, above and beyond what an ethical person without a Christian worldview might provide.

Foundational to the entire book are two major scriptural passages. First, Genesis 1–3, which outlines what God intended the world to be when he created it, and what happened to the world and the human race when mankind chose to walk away from God's plan. Second, the Ten Commandments as given in Exodus 20.

Why the Ten Commandments? What is unique about this portion of Scripture? In Deut 4:13–14, Moses makes an important and clarifying statement regarding the role of the commandments and the statutes in Scripture:

> And he declared to you his covenant, the Ten Commandments, which he commanded you to follow and then wrote them on two stone tablets. And the Lord directed me at that time to teach you the decrees and laws you are to follow in the land that you are crossing the Jordan to possess.

In this passage Moses distinguishes clearly between the Ten Commandments which the people, it appears, can be expected to know and keep, and the statutes and ordinances which will have to be taught. There is little in common between the giving of the Decalogue and the issuing of the statutes and ordinances. The dramatic scene of the proclamation of the Ten Commandments, their being written on tables of stone by the very finger of God, the solemn oath of fidelity by the people, all give that document a unique appearance of absoluteness and permanence. The same scene is not repeated when the statutes and ordinances are given to Moses.

Does this not lead us to deduce that the Ten Commandments express universal moral principles written on the heart of humans at creation, while the statutes and ordinances are the application of the principles of those commandments to the Jewish theocracy? An attempt to build a society on the principles of the Ten Commandments would result in a

remarkable design for political, social, and economic life. David Gill calls
the Ten Commandments "the atlas of ethics."[8] We will therefore rely on
them for direction in our discussion of business ethics in this book.

ACKNOWLEDGMENTS

Initially this book was a dream in the minds of the two authors as they
team-taught the Christian business ethics class at Andrews University in
Berrien Springs, Michigan. The book began to take shape while Gibson
was on sabbatical in 2000–2001. During this time Daniel Augsburger
compiled his teaching notes which outlined the scriptural basis for the
class, while Gibson worked on the business examples. The support of
Andrews University during that sabbatical is gratefully acknowledged.

With Augsburger's untimely passing in February 2004, the book
returned to its dream-like state, although it certainly continued to define
and refine Gibson's business ethics lectures at Andrews University done
solo until the present time. Much has occurred in the business world
since the early 2000s, particularly in the area of unethical business activity. The business ethics students' responses to these real-world examples,
which are almost too numerous to list, included many questions. The
resulting class discussions have focused Gibson's understanding of the
issues as she and the students struggled together to formulate what it
means to be a Christian in today's business world. A sabbatical in the fall,
2013, at the Center for Christian Bioethics and the School of Religion
at Loma Linda University provided the opportunity to move from the
classroom to the book format, from the dream to reality. Gibson wishes
to thank the Center for Christian Bioethics and the School of Religion at
Loma Linda University, and, in particular, the following individuals, for
their support of this project: Roy Branson, PhD, Director of the Center
for Christian Bioethics and Associate Dean of the School of Religion
(now deceased); Jon Paulien, PhD, Dean, School of Religion; the faculty
of the School of Religion; Gerald R. Winslow, PhD, Vice President for
Mission and Culture, Loma Linda University (now Director of the Center
for Christian Bioethics); Alice Kong, Coordinator, Center for Christian
Bioethics; and John Brunt, PhD, Senior Pastor, Azure Hills Seventh-day
Adventist Church (now retired).

8. Gill, *Doing Right*, 52.

No book is written without the support of numerous people, and to begin to mention the friends who assisted (whether through conversations or through their writings) risks not only extending the length of this book, but also omitting important players whose ideas have greatly enriched mine. However, three people in particular must be mentioned. One is my colleague Betty Gibson, who assisted me selflessly with any and all formatting or software-related questions. Her expertise was invaluable and greatly appreciated. The second is Terry Robertson, Associate Dean of the James White Library, whose love of detail and infinite patience made referencing and footnoting possible, and even close to fun! Finally, my unending gratefulness must be given to my husband, Lawrence W. Onsager. His willingness to listen to numerous readings of the chapters, provide honest feedback, go without meals, offer unnumbered expressions of support, including many hugs along the way, and in general, constantly reassure me that "you can do this," can never be sufficiently acknowledged. My appreciation to him knows no bounds. He went far beyond what was either asked or expected.

Ann Gibson

Chapter 1

How *Does* One Make Business Decisions?

Ethical Decision-Making Tools

No regulatory system, however stringent, can provide against the consequences of human greed, folly or corruption.

—TIM YEO, SHADOW SECRETARY FOR THE UNITED KINGDOM DEPARTMENT OF TRADE AND INDUSTRY

THE WALMART[1] CORPORATION'S STATEMENT of ethics (as revised on January 1, 2005) reads as follows:

Improper Payments:

> You should not offer anything of value, directly or through third persons, to anyone (including governmental authorities) to obtain an improper advantage in selling goods and services, conducting financial transactions, or presenting the Company's

---

1. Wal-Mart Stores, Inc., changed its legal name to Walmart Inc., in February 2018 (see https://news.walmart.com/2017/12/05/walmart-changes-its-legal-name-to-reflect-how-customers-want-to-shop). For the sake of consistency, outside of directly quoted material, the name "Walmart" will be used throughout.

interests. All countries prohibit bribery of their own public officials, and many also prohibit the bribery of officials of other countries. Wal-Mart's policy goes beyond these legal requirements and prohibits improper payments in all activities, both with governments and in the private sector.

Bribes, Kickbacks, Or Payoffs:

The US Foreign Corrupt Practices Act, other US laws, and similar laws of other countries, prohibit you, on behalf of Wal-Mart, from directly or indirectly making, promising, authorizing or offering anything of value to a government official or employee, political party, or any candidate for political office. A governmental official includes any person acting in an official capacity on behalf of a government, agency, department or instrumentality, such as a business with government ownership (e.g., a national oil company).[2]

In September 2005, Maritza Munich, at that time the general counsel of Walmart International, was informed by a former executive of widespread bribery at the Walmart subsidiary, Walmart de Mexico. Based on this information, a team of investigators was sent to Mexico City from the company headquarters in Bentonville, Arkansas, in November 2005. Unfortunately for Walmart, the information provided by the whistle-blower, Sergio Cicero Zapata, was confirmed by the evidence found on site in Mexico.

The total amount of the suspect payments was more than $24 million. These payments, made to mayors, city council members, urban planners, and to the lower bureaucrats who issued permits, were not created in a vacuum. Top Walmart officials in Mexico were aware of these payments, made for the purpose of securing zoning approvals, cutting through government paperwork, and gathering support for the establishment of new stores in various locations across Mexico. It worked. In 2005, Eduardo Castro-Wright, the chief executive at Walmart, Mexico, was promoted to Walmart headquarters and put in charge of all US Walmart stores, and in 2008, was further promoted to vice chairman of Walmart International, all because of his stellar accomplishments in the enormous growth of Walmart de Mexico. In fact, today Walmart is Mexico's largest private employer.

2. Smith, "Wal-Mart Sets New Policy on Ethics."

The whistle-blower, Sergio Cicero Zapata, was personally involved in the scandal. He assisted in getting the bribes to the fixers (known as "gestores"), and he provided the approvals for Walmart de Mexico's payments to the gestores. He decided to become a whistle-blower because he felt underappreciated for his role in fueling the growth of Walmart de Mexico. He had been passed over for the job of general counsel of Walmart de Mexico in early 2004, a job he anticipated to be his in recognition of his work in dealing with the "greedy" officials who jacked up bribe demands.[3] When he did not get the promotion, he began to document the bribes so that he had evidence in case he was accused of wrongdoing in the future.

The bribes were placed in operation in response to the very aggressive growth goals set by the leaders at Walmart de Mexico. The goal was to open new Walmart stores before the competition entered the market. But to get new stores open, permits were required, which ordinarily took months to obtain. In addition, there were zoning laws and other regulatory safeguards to circumvent. However, by using two "gestores" (who were lawyer friends of Mr. Cicero), and asking them to deliver the payments to the local official or person of influence (thus distancing Walmart from the bribes), these obstacles were swiftly overcome.

To cover up the payments, which were in violation of the Foreign Corrupt Practices Act of 1977, it was necessary to employ fraudulent accounting procedures. A vaguely-worded invoice would be submitted to Walmart de Mexico by the "gestores" which contained a code that specified the "irregular act" that had been performed, such as a bribe for a permit, or a bribe for confidential information, or a bribe to eliminate a fine. These invoices were then posted to the account "legal fees" in order to hide the payments from the auditors. However, the payments had been uncovered in an internal Walmart de Mexico audit in March 2004, and were brought to the attention of the executives through an internal memo that highlighted the growth in these payments which corresponded with the growth in Walmart de Mexico's stores. The internal audit memo recommended that Walmart International in Bentonville, Arkansas, be informed of these payments for new store permits. This recommendation was removed by Walmart de Mexico's chief auditor, and the internal auditor who suggested it was subsequently fired.

3. Barstow, "Vast Mexico Bribery Case," 4.

When the internal audit memo was shown to Mr. Castro-Wright, he was primarily concerned about the use of only two "gestores" and suggested that more should be hired so that Walmart de Mexico was not dependent on so few assistants. The general counsel of Walmart de Mexico, Jose Luis Rodriguezmacedo Rivera, was also consulted about the plan to increase the number of "gestores." His recommendation was that they no longer be called "gestores," but "external service providers."

When the news of bribery at Walmart de Mexico broke in Bentonville, the internal investigation was first given to Walmart International's Corporate Investigations Unit, not to the outside investigators that Walmart International had used in other internal investigations. This unit was too small to take on such a major international corruption investigation and had already seen earlier internal corruption investigations suffer because of top administration's interference. However, Ronald Halter, of the Corporate Investigations Unit, went to Mexico in November 2005 to investigate the whistle-blower's allegations. He found that what Mr. Cicero had reported was verifiable. He also noted that the payments to the "gestores" ceased in 2005 when Mr. Castro-Wright left Walmart de Mexico for the United States.

When Mr. Halter interviewed Jose Luis Rodriguezmacedo Rivera, Rodriguezmacedo indicated that based on the results of the internal audit of 2004, concerns were raised by top administration at Walmart de Mexico about Mr. Cicero, including an accusation that Mr. Cicero's wife worked for one of the "gestores" (a fact he did not disclose) and that Mr. Cicero had stolen the gestor payments himself from Walmart de Mexico and then given them to the "gestores" to be used as bribes. If such were the case, the finger would point only to Mr. Cicero and not to any of Walmart de Mexico's administrators. However, if this were true, why hadn't Mr. Rodriguezmacedo notified Bentonville of the theft and taken action against Mr. Cicero? Mr. Cicero had not, in fact, been fired; he had resigned with severance benefits and a $25,000 bonus. In addition, the accusations by Mr. Rodriguezmacedo were not supported in the documents reviewed by Mr. Halter and were vigorously denied by Mr. Cicero. Mr. Halter returned to Bentonville and recommended that Walmart International undertake a deeper investigation, which should include interviewing the two main "gestores" and Mr. Castro-Wright, who by this time was at Walmart International.

In January 2006, Bentonville received an anonymous email that indicated that "Wal-Mart de Mexico's top real estate executives were receiving kickbacks from construction companies. 'Please you must do something.' the e-mail implored."[4] But Walmart International's executives did not act. On February 1, 2006, Ms. Munich submitted her resignation as general counsel for Walmart International, while continuing to urge the Bentonville team to follow through with Mr. Halter's recommendation for expansion of the investigation of the bribery charges at Walmart de Mexico.

Four days after Ms. Munich's resignation, H. Lee Scott, chief executive of Walmart International, called a meeting to review the effectiveness of the Corporate Investigations Unit. After the meeting, Scott recommended that new protocols be drawn up for internal investigations. Four days later, with the new protocols in place which gave senior Walmart executives more control over internal investigations, the bribery investigation of Walmart de Mexico was in the process of being transferred to Mr. Rodriguezmacedo. The files that Mr. Halter had developed were shipped to Mr. Rodriguezmacedo, who chose to do no further investigation, despite Mr. Halter's recommendations that his findings were only preliminary and that additional interviews should be conducted. Mr. Rodriguezmacedo closed the case within a few weeks with a report to Bentonville that included the following statement: "There is no evidence or clear indication of bribes paid to Mexican government authorities with the purpose of wrongfully securing any licenses or permits."[5] His findings, he indicated, were supported by denials of bribery by the executives of Walmart de Mexico. He did, however, include in his report questions about the integrity of Mr. Cicero and repeated his allegations that Mr. Cicero may have personally benefitted from the payouts. His report was accepted by Bentonville.

The report may have been accepted, but the case was not closed. In its 2018 10-K (annual report), Walmart stated that "the Audit Committee of our Board of Directors has been conducting an internal investigation into, among other things, alleged violations of the Foreign Corrupt Practices Act (FCPA) and other alleged crimes or misconduct in connection with certain of our foreign subsidiaries, including Wal-Mart de Mexico . . . and whether prior allegations of such violations and/or misconduct were appropriately handled by the Company." Footnote 10 to the 2018 financial statements stated that while the financial impact of

4. Barstow, "Vast Mexico Bribery Case," 10.

5. Barstow, "Vast Mexico Bribery Case," 12.

these investigations was still unknown, Walmart had already incurred costs of $157 million in fiscal 2013, $282 million in 2014, $173 million in 2015, $126 million in 2016, $99 million in 2017, and $40 million in 2018. It also noted that in 2018 the probable loss would be $283 million. The 2018 footnote concluded: "The Company does not presently believe that these matters . . . will have a material adverse effect on its business, although given the inherent uncertainties in such situations, the Company can provide no assurance that these matters will not be material to its business in the future."[6]

The 2013 Walmart statement of ethics continued to affirm Walmart's anti-bribery policies, as had been true in 2005. The 2013 statement reads:

> We believe in fair, free and open markets, and in promoting good government. We do not tolerate, permit, or engage in bribery, corruption, or unethical practices of any kind. Bribery of public officials in the US and abroad is illegal under both US law and the local law of the countries in which we operate. Walmart's policy goes beyond these legal requirements and prohibits corrupt payments in all circumstances, whether in dealings with public officials or individuals in the private sector . . .
>
> Specifically, the Global Anti-Corruption Policy prohibits us from paying, promising, offering, or authorizing a payment, directly, indirectly, or through a third party, money or anything of value to a government official or political party for the purpose of influencing an official act or decision in order to obtain or retain business or secure an improper advantage. The term "government official" includes any person acting in an official capacity for or on behalf of a government or governmental agency or department, including a business with government ownership (for example, a national oil company); a public international organization (for example, the UN or World Bank); or a political party or candidate for political office. Even when local practices or customs allow behavior that violates our Anti-Corruption Policy, it is not acceptable for us to do so.[7]

6. Walmart, "Annual Report, 2018, Notes to the Consolidated Financial Statements," 10.

7. Walmart, "Statement of Ethics," 22.

HOW ARE ETHICAL DECISIONS MADE?

As you read the Walmart de Mexico story, what thoughts went through your mind? Perhaps you thought about the competitive market demands that required Walmart de Mexico to grow quickly and place their stores in advantageous locations before the competition did. Similar market demands exist in almost all areas of business. Does that fact justify the decision to bribe the officials who granted building permits and zoning variances for the new stores? What about the fact that Walmart's own corporate code of ethics stated that offering bribes to officials in any country for any reason was wrong? How did Walmart's corporate office determine that offering bribes was "wrong"? How did Walmart de Mexico decide that, under the current circumstances, offering bribes was "right"?

When we enter into the discussion of "right" or "wrong," we enter into moral decision-making and into the field of ethics. Steve Wilkens notes in his book *Beyond Bumper Sticker Ethics* that such discussions center on the "ought" questions rather than the "is" questions. We are not asking in what year the bribery occurred. We are asking whether or not bribery ought to be the course of action for a corporation like Walmart. Wilkens states: "In ethics, *right* means something different from *correct*. *Correct* is the label we attach to information that is factually true, while *right* is oriented to moral truth. Because the type of question is different, the means by which we look for and test answers in ethics will differ."[8]

Whenever philosophers attempt to explain how moral decisions are made, they usually refer to several well-known moral philosophies or theories.[9] We will briefly discuss four of these major theories below. But before discussing the theories, it is important to consider one additional concept—that of *worldview*. One's worldview will shape the decision about which moral theory is acceptable for any given situation. As we will discover, each philosophy or theory incorporates a particular worldview. It is therefore important to consider one's personal worldview first so that there is consistency between one's own worldview and the worldview expressed by the ethical philosophy under consideration.

Wilkens defines *worldview* "[as consisting] of our beliefs and assumptions about how the world fits together."[10] What do you see as the

8. Wilkens, *Beyond Bumper Sticker Ethics*, 16.

9. See Trevino and Nelson, *Managing Business Ethics*, 80–84, and Kidder, *How Good People Make Tough Choices*, 23–29, 154–76.

10. Wilkens, *Beyond Bumper Sticker Ethics*, 19.

origin and purpose of the world? Did the world come from a "big bang" long ago, or was it created by a master designer whom we call God? If we assume that the world was created by a master designer, then the ultimate reality is God, and we look to what God has revealed about himself to best understand the purpose of the world and what God desired it should be. If we believe the creation story as recorded in the Hebrew Scriptures, we understand that God created the world and pronounced it "good." Thus we look to God as the ultimate origin of right and wrong and we seek from his revelations to humans the understanding of good and evil. If, on the other hand, we assume that the world came from a "big bang" long ago, we eliminate the possibility of God as the designer of the world and as the ultimate origin of right and wrong. We must then set up other standards of right and wrong—perhaps human pronouncements or the laws of nature. Under this worldview, the definitions of right and wrong may change over time, depending on who is engaged in the conversation. For example, sixty or seventy years ago, premarital sex was considered wrong, and if engaged in, marriage was immediately expected, even if the marriage was likely to be unhappy. It was considered essential that the bride be wed before the baby was born. Today many people believe that premarital sex can no longer be defined as "wrong" and that entering into marriage or subsequent divorce is merely a matter of choice or convenience. However, some human actions are considered wrong both across time and across cultures, even by those who leave God out of the equation. For example, stealing and murder are considered wrong. By whose standard is this distinction made? Why are these actions (stealing and murder) consistently considered wrong by so many everywhere in the world, while other actions humans choose to do may be considered right or wrong, depending on both time and culture?

One's *worldview* must also take into account the role of human beings in the world. We ascribe morality and ethics to human actions. It is human behavior that we expect to follow the lines of "right" and "wrong." Interestingly, all the moral philosophers acknowledge that humans need help in the area of correct moral behavior, which implies that something must have gone wrong with our understanding of "right" and "wrong," or at least with our ability to act in a right manner as opposed to a wrong manner. Christians call what went wrong "sin." Others may call it "lack of willpower" (Kant) or "lack of knowledge" (Plato). What you think regarding the origin and purpose of the world and what you think about what went wrong and how it can be made right will influence which of the various theories below you choose as your preferred ethical theory for decision-making.

THE PHILOSOPHICAL THEORIES

Utilitarianism: What Are the Consequences?

The first ethical philosophy we will consider can best be understood by the question: What are the consequences of the decision? Philosophers call this philosophy "utilitarianism." This theory seeks to maximize the benefits of the decision's outcome while minimizing the harms that occur, recognizing that not everyone will be happy with the outcome. Cost/benefit analysis is a business example where a businessperson considers how much a proposal for a product or a project costs, and what the benefits are likely to be. One will generally move forward with the proposal if the benefits outweigh the costs. For philosophers, the corresponding question is: does the moral action maximize benefit (or "happiness," expressed as a state of overall being, not as an emotion) and minimize harm *for the greatest number of people*? If so, it is the appropriate moral action to take. The rightness of the selected action can be determined by the results, which are subject to measurement.

Of course, this philosophy assumes that one can both see and measure the benefits and the harm. In the case of Walmart de Mexico, the benefits were a large number of new stores in areas of Mexico where Walmart did not already have a presence, thus providing the population with shopping options which were not previously available. These new stores not only benefitted the population as a whole, but also provided increased sales for Walmart and profits for Walmart's stockholders. The harm was a loss of Walmart's favorable reputation due to the use of illegal methods, the overriding of the elected and appointed officials and procedures that ensured that the stores were placed in locations that maximized the economic growth of the entire community, and, ultimately, fines for breaking the law. If one believed that "no one will ever know" about the bribes, one might not consider the consequences for breaking the law as part of the benefit/harm equation. But as often happens, the news gets out. At the time of this writing, Walmart is faced with huge potential fines. While Walmart's reputation as an asset is difficult to measure, the cost of diminishing that reputation is an even more difficult measurement to quantify. Once reputation is diminished, it is difficult to recover. Cost/benefit analysis, or utilitarianism, works best when we can easily quantify and foresee both the costs and the benefits.

Utilitarianism also ignores the consequences for the minority—i.e., those who are not part of the "greatest number" but who are still recipients of the decision. One of the Walmart de Mexico stores was in Teotihuacan, which is also the location of ancient artifacts which are considered to be of both historical and cultural value to the people of Mexico. After the town's mayor and other decision makers were bribed, Walmart was permitted to build a store on an ancient site. During construction, many artifacts were dug up and destroyed. Some townspeople protested the presence of the building equipment and attempted to stop the construction. However, the voices who valued the cultural and historical importance of the site and the artifacts were in the minority, as compared with those who had been bribed and who apparently valued the store, the shopping convenience, the economic growth, and the profits more than the artifacts.[11]

While utilitarianism demands that the decision-maker consider the consequences of the decision, they are the consequences for the majority—not for the minority. Utilitarianism does not consider the voices of those who are in the minority because it seeks the greatest good for the greatest number. For Christians, it is helpful to remember Paul's warning to the church at Corinth about failing to consider the minority position when he wrote about eating meat which had been offered to idols (1 Cor 8:4–13). While Paul argued persuasively that for the majority (i.e., those who know that idols are "nothing at all in the world") it was fine to eat food which had been sacrificed to idols, he urged the Corinthians to consider those in the minority—the "weak brother"—who still believed that eating such food was engaging in worship of the idol. As Paul put it: "Be careful, however, that the exercise of your freedom does not become a stumbling block to the weak" (1 Cor 8:9).

Utilitarianism leaves these questions hanging: Should morality be based *solely* on the results of an action? Does the actor's motive count at all? What about the concept of fairness? Finally, is happiness (well-being) attainable by seeking it, or is happiness a *result* of right choices and following prescribed duties? In the Sermon on the Mount, Jesus described people who are happy as those who are simple in spirit, because they are satisfied with what God gives them. They are happy because they

---

11. Barstow, "Bribery Aisle."

are willing to admit that they make mistakes. They are happy because they are meek; they are not compelled to assert themselves arrogantly to safeguard a shaky self-esteem. Because they are meek, they can be peacemakers. They do not find any thrill in crushing others. They are pure in heart. Their words can be trusted. They are willing to be persecuted for righteousness' sake. This means they are willing to espouse unpopular causes when justice and truth are involved. This description of how to be happy speaks more to the spiritual life of the individual than to a method of decision-making calculated to result in the greatest good.

Kant's Categorical Imperative: It's Your Duty!

The second philosophy we will consider recommends that the decision-maker forget about the consequences of the decision and just do what is right based on duty and obligation. Immanuel Kant (1724–1804) is the father of this philosophy, often known as the *Categorical Imperative*, which outlines unconditional moral laws that depend on the reason and the rationality of humans. For Kant, reason and rationality are the qualities that make humans moral beings. It is through reason that the will is directed; thus the intention (or will) to fulfill our duty meets our ethical obligations and the result is expected to be standards that everyone, including yourself, would be happy to operate under.

For example, Kant argued in his first *Categorical Imperative* that we know our duty because we know how we want others to act. We understand the basic principles of morality (honesty, promise keeping, fairness, respect) because we know what kind of society we want to live in—that is, we want to live in a society where people tell the truth, keep promises, respect others, act with fairness. Therefore it is our duty to act in accordance with what we want everyone else to do. Kant also stated that one must never use others (or themselves) as a means to an end. In Kant's view, people are inherently valuable. The person in the minority position is just as valued as the person in the majority position and therefore must be equally considered. Utilitarianism, as we noted, would give the most weight to the perspective of those in the majority when making an ethical decision.

Faced with Walmart de Mexico's situation, Kant would ask: Does Walmart want to do business in a country where officials accept bribes and payoffs when engaged in business and where promises made to the voters and the town constituency are broken because there is money on the table available for the mayor's personal gain? Do they want other companies to act like they did? If the answer to those questions is "no," then according to Kant, Walmart should not engage in such actions themselves. Neither should Walmart use elected and appointed officials as a means to the end of achieving greater profit for their shareholders. Kant might point to the example of the servant in Luke 17 who works in the field all day and then comes into the house to prepare the meal for the master, expecting no recognition and no thanks because he has "only done [his] duty" (Luke 17:10). In the described situation, Kant might ask Walmart's management: What was your duty? Did you do it?

If these basic principles of morality sound a lot like the Ten Commandments and the Golden Rule, it is because they are similar. Kant was raised in a household that held to the Pietist branch of the Lutheran Church and he was familiar with both the Old and New Testament. So while Kant does not mention God or Christianity in his theory, one can hear echoes of Scripture in his arguments. There is, however, one point in his philosophy with which Scripture would disagree, and that is Kant's reliance on reason as the moral authority for humans. Human reason is created and, like all of creation, subject to sin and the consequences of the fall. As a result, humans may be unable to discern right and wrong, as discussed more fully later in this chapter. In addition, Kant does not recognize the availability of God's grace for the strength to do moral actions. "Do your duty" is a humanly achievable statement from Kant's perspective. In reality, however, mankind has found that human will alone is insufficient for moral action.

Rawls and the "Theory of Justice": Is It Fair?

The third philosophy is most often applied when there are disputes among individuals regarding whether the proposed course of action is fair to all parties concerned. For example, when someone is accused of "unjust" discrimination or "unjust" favoritism in the workplace, such accusations are often comparative in nature. To respond adequately, the claims of the parties involved must be understood and compared in order to determine whether *justice* or fairness has occurred.

This comparative approach is also used when there is some scarce good to distribute or some financial burden, such as a tax, to be imposed.

This situation, commonly occurring in business, requires *distributive justice*. The issue at hand is whether all are treated equally. If in the past people were not treated equally, justice may require some compensation to make up for the harm that occurred. This is known as *compensatory justice*, and on occasion, business encounters this type of situation as well.

In his book *Theory of Justice*, John Rawls proposed a method for choosing principles that would answer the questions raised in *distributive justice* situations. Manuel Velasquez summarizes Rawls's principles as the *principle of equal liberty, the difference principle*, and *the principle of fair equality of opportunity*.[12]

Under *the principle of equal liberty*, each person's liberties must be safe from erosion and must be equal to those of others. This principle takes priority over the other two principles in case of a conflict between principles. The *difference principle* recognizes that while there will be inequalities in society, for justice to occur the position of the most needy members of society must be protected and improved as much as possible. Finally, under *the principle of fair equality of opportunity*, the privileged positions in society should be accessible to everyone through equal opportunities. Velasquez illustrates this last principle with a business example:

> This means not only that job qualifications should be related to the requirements of the job (thereby prohibiting racial and sexual discrimination), but that each person must have access to the training and education needed to qualify for the desirable jobs. A person's efforts, abilities and contribution would then determine his or her remuneration.[13]

Rawls suggested that the best way to make decisions under these principles is to imagine ourselves as a group of rational persons who value our own good and who voluntarily use the concept of a "veil of ignorance" as we create our policies. Because we operate under the "veil of ignorance" we do not know what position in society we occupy—whether we are rich or poor, talented or untalented, handicapped or not. We also do not know our race, gender, or social status. In this situation, Rawls argued that we would demand the distribution of benefits or burdens using his three principles: his *principle of equal liberty*, his *difference principle*, and his *principle of fair equality of opportunity*. For example, when

12. Velasquez, *Business Ethics* (6th ed.), 96–97.
13. Velasquez, *Business Ethics* (6th ed.), 97.

creating a hiring policy to ensure non-discrimination in our workplace, we would use the "veil of ignorance" to ensure that the created policies are fair to all, including ourselves, because our race, gender, or social status are unknown. If we do not consider the policy creation from this perspective, Rawls argued that we might create an unjust policy, perhaps even a policy that discriminates against others while providing benefits to ourselves.

Rawls's theory of justice fits the political and economic systems of much of the Western world. We are familiar with the concepts of freedom, equality of opportunity, and concern for the disadvantaged. We also concur with his proposal that benefits and burdens are distributed according to ability and contribution. We are familiar with biblical passages such as those in Isaiah 1 where God states that he desires justice and the defense of the fatherless and the widow, and finds the offered prayers and gifts to be a burden when given without considering the needs of those who are weakest in society. But even though we understand the importance of justice, does justice, as defined by Rawls, give us the best philosophy for making an ethical decision?

The three philosophies we have discussed thus far emphasize different sides of the diamond of ethical decision-making. Utilitarianism considers the effect of the action on the majority. Kant's appeal to duty addresses the importance of the individual and the necessity of always choosing the right action, irrespective of the consequences. Rawls's standards of justice consider how to distribute scarce goods or share societal burdens. None of these perspectives considers what is left out, such as the minority or the distribution questions in utilitarianism, the consequences of actions in Kant, or the effect on the individual or the aggregate social welfare in Rawls. None of these philosophies incorporate God into their theories, even though, as we have noted, there are scriptural examples where each of these philosophies has been considered. Perhaps we need to look further to find a philosophy that better appears to match a Christian worldview.

Aristotle: Who Is the Person in the Mirror?

Sometimes ethical decisions are made by asking: Would I like to see my action described in the headlines of tomorrow's *Wall Street Journal* or *New York Times*? Do I want to explain my action to my mother? Do I want this action to be the public definition of who I am? No doubt Eduardo Castro-Wright of Walmart de Mexico, if asked, would have indicated that the bribes he was authorizing were not the actions he wished to publicize. However, his actions *were* publicized in the *New York Times*—open to all who either received the paper or read the story on the Internet.

Philosophers call the acts we *would* like to see in the headlines virtuous actions. They refer to the person who does virtuous actions as a good or virtuous person—a person who has cultivated specific virtues. The underlying assumption is that a virtuous person does virtuous acts because of *who they are*. Virtue theory does not focus on what act was performed or its consequences, but on the person who performed the act. The major philosophers who argued for virtue ethics were Plato and Aristotle. Both believed that it takes time to develop virtue, but it is because one takes the time to become a virtuous person that one makes appropriate ethical decisions.

Plato identified four ideal virtues: courage, temperance, justice, and practical wisdom. Note that these virtues are not personal preferences; they are ideals to which an ethical person strives. Aristotle, Plato's student, further defined virtue as "a mean between two vices, that which depends on excess and that which depends on defect."[14] For example, Plato's virtue of courage would be at the mean or center of the continuum with the endpoints being cowardice (the lack of courage) and foolhardiness (unwise excess of courage). Temperance would be at the center of the continuum with the endpoints being gluttony (excess of appetite) and abstinence (refraining from needed food). For Aristotle, virtue lies in the middle; either extreme is vice, i.e., not virtuous. Because Aristotle believed that one must not just study what virtue is, but must *be* a virtuous person, it is needful for one to engage in virtuous actions so that over time one's actions are a reflection of who one really is. Just doing a virtuous action once or twice does not make the person a virtuous person. Becoming a virtuous person takes time. To assist with this process, Aristotle recommended that one identify a virtuous person, a person of character, and then imitate that individual. One can easily see how this counsel was translated for Christians into a recommendation to imitate Jesus Christ, the ultimate virtuous person.

As commendable as it is, virtue theory does not answer all the ethical questions that one can raise. For example, what does one do if virtues

---

14. Aristotle, *Nicomachean Ethics*, 1107a.

conflict? It is virtuous to be loyal. It is also virtuous to be honest. What should you do if your friend steals an item from a store and the store owner asks you if your friend took the item without paying for it? Do you tell the truth (honesty) or do you "cover" for your friend because of your loyalty?

Scripture gives us lists of virtues, but they do not match the virtues of the ancient philosophers. Micah 6:8 lists the triad of virtues that God requires: to do justice (which matches Plato); to love mercy (not in Plato's list); and to walk humbly with God (also not in Plato's list). Perhaps most important is Paul's list of virtues in 1 Corinthians 13: faith, hope, and love, with the greatest of these being love. The ancient Greeks did not see love as a virtue, but as an unstable emotion. The ancient Greeks also saw the development of virtues as only available to those who were educated, thus placing virtue development solely as a result of human effort and confined only to the most fortunate of humans. In Scripture, the development of virtues is associated with the fruits of the Spirit (see Gal 5:22–23). As humans, we are reminded that we cannot become virtuous without the aid of a power outside ourselves. Perhaps it is time to look to Scripture for answers about why we search for virtue and goodness with such limited success.

CREATION PERSPECTIVE: THE ORIGINAL PLAN

As noted above, one's worldview affects one's decisions and one's decision process. If one subscribes to modernism as their worldview, reality, knowledge, and morality are answered through science, human reasoning, and evidence that one can observe through the physical senses. Modernism looks to human activity and the scientific method for ways of knowing. If one subscribes to postmodernism as their worldview, one questions whether anything is certain.[15] But prior to the nineteenth century, worldview was not founded on either modernism or postmodernism. For most of Western history, one's worldview, one's belief about how the world is put together, was tied to Christianity and Scripture. During the early days of the Enlightenment, scientists believed that because God created nature, nature is good and is governed by rational laws, and therefore it can be studied and understood by man through his reasoning process.[16] But

15. Kim et al., "Modernism, Christianity and Business Ethics," 115–21.
16. Kim et al., "Modernism, Christianity and Business Ethics," 117.

as science progressed through the eighteenth and nineteenth centuries, modernism taught us that science could explain everything and that God was no longer necessary—not even to explain creation. As Kim et al., in their article in the *Journal of Business Ethics*, state:

> Since God was no longer needed to explain creation, he was no longer needed to determine moral laws. Reason would replace God to establish morality. Ethics would be discussed increasingly in philosophical and scientific terms, as opposed to theology. Without God or transcendent truth to establish one's values, modernism turned to science and philosophy along with tradition and cultural norms as the basis of what is good or right. However, attempts to resolve ethical issues without God could only result in moral relativism where ethical standards were relative to a particular culture, individual, or time in history.
>
> Besides moral relativism, modernism helped to shape the meaning and purpose of one's vocation or business. The rejection of God and the Biblical view of creation meant that human beings were no longer God's handiwork but instead were merely a part of nature, driven by self-interest and expediency. The Protestant work ethic was separated from its Christian context of stewardship and service and viewed only as a means to material success. . . . Without God, the purpose of work or vocation changed to personal achievement, material possessions, and status.[17]

The move to rely on science and philosophy for ethical principles and direction in determining what is good or right has left us with no clear moral standard. All decisions become relative to time and place. Effectively, without consideration of Scripture, we lack sufficiently dependable moral standards to instruct us as to what is right or wrong. In fact, without such standards, the idea of right and wrong hardly makes any sense at all.[18] Recognizing this dilemma, let us turn to Scripture to meet the God of the Bible and to understand the nature of human beings.

The first two chapters of Genesis frame the Christian worldview by informing us that what is ultimate in the world is one's relationship to God; that humans were created for relationships with others; that humans were given the role of being the stewards of creation; and that humans have the responsibility to care for the earth upon which they

17. Kim et al., "Modernism, Christianity and Business Ethics," 118.

18. Kim et al., "Modernism, Christianity and Business Ethics," 119.

were placed. Understanding these relationships and roles as provided by Scripture frames our understanding of life and our values.

Genesis 1 and 2: Meeting the God of Creation

In Genesis 1, God appears as a person, not as a force. As a person, God can relate, plan, and act. The universe is the expression of his thoughts and will. For he spoke, says Ps 33:9, and it came to be. As a person he reacts with joy at the results of his creative acts. "It was good" is repeated several times in the first chapter of Genesis (Gen 1:4, 10, 12, 18, 21, 25, and 31). Thus we see that God enjoys one of the most exhilarating experiences of a person—the joy of creativity.

There is found everywhere in the world an order that can be explained only by a mind. The Greeks used the word *cosmos* for the universe, a word that originally means *a collar*. Just as in a jewelled collar, pearls or precious stones are held together in a certain willed order, so the world gives the impression of having been put together to achieve a certain purpose. The world reveals a creator who is infinitely wise and inventive.

The personality of God expresses itself in the element of beauty that is present everywhere. God could have turned off light suddenly at the end of the day the way we do it with our electric switches, but there is too much of an artist in him to do that. He made provision for the fireworks of light and color that accompany the rising and the setting of the sun. Color, fragrance, sound may be expendable from a practical standpoint, but they make everything good. God is a person who loves what is good and beautiful and he wants his children to love what is good and beautiful.

When describing himself, God said: "The Lord, the Lord, the compassionate and gracious God, slow to anger, abounding in love and faithfulness, maintaining love to thousands and forgiving wickedness, rebellion, and sin. Yet he does not leave the guilty unpunished" (Exod 34:6–7). Further, in Jer 9:24, God says: "I am the Lord, who exercises kindness, justice and righteousness in the earth, for in these I delight."

In these passages, God describes himself in a series of pairs: in Exodus, compassion and graciousness, love and faithfulness; and in Jeremiah, justice and righteousness.

What do these words tell us about God? Compassion, which is translated from the Hebrew word *rachum*—the womb, the seat of feelings—reveals God's capacity to empathize with the sufferings of others. It is the spirit of Jesus, weeping over the fate of doomed Jerusalem or his feeling of compassion for the multitude that had not eaten for a whole day. Graciousness is the readiness to take the initiative in accepting even the outcasts of society. It is the spirit that drives the father of the prodigal son to run to meet his son who is coming home. Grace is the essence of the plan of salvation, where God seizes the initiative in forgiving sinners. "While we were yet sinners Christ died for us" (Rom 5:8).

Steadfast love (from the Hebrew: *chesed*) and faithfulness (from the Hebrew: *emeth*) constitute the second pair. These two virtues are the virtues of responsibility. *Chesed* describes an attitude of fidelity to a pledge. Few virtues characterize God so well. He is the one who cares for us even when we do not care for him, because he has pledged to be our Father. It is the virtue that is the basis of a solid marriage, a love that is not grounded on feelings but on a covenant. *Emeth* is the quality of being true to oneself. Persons who are true to themselves are predictable. They refuse to be controlled by circumstances. The way they have acted in the past is a guarantee of how they will act in the future. God is *emeth* because he does not change.

Justice (from the Hebrew: *mispat*) and righteousness (from the Hebrew: *tsedeqah*) constitute the third pair. They bring to light the importance for God of the rights of beings whom he created as persons, who were given the opportunity to be free moral agents. Justice and righteousness describe two different aspects of character. Justice (*mispat*) is the respect for law and order that must reign in an orderly society. It is the quality that protects the rights of all, but also assures us that those who do not respect law and order will also receive their due. The text from Jeremiah, however, couples justice (*mispat*) with righteousness (*tsedeqah*), a magnificent biblical concept. God is not only concerned with everyone enjoying the rights that are recognized (which is just), but also the rights that are not granted. These are the rights of the weak, the poor, the widows, the orphans, whose voices are not heard in legislative assemblies or even courts of justice. They live practically beyond the protection of the laws designed to shield the advantages of the rich and powerful. *Tsedeqah* is the quality of those who empathize with the weak. That justice is also called restorative justice. It is a justice that vindicates and affirms (Ps 82:1–4).

These self-described qualities give evidence that God is a person who cares intensely for what he has created. The God of creation is not the Supreme Being, as believed by the Deists of the Enlightenment, who creates but afterwards lets his creation continue essentially on its own. God not only cares, exhibits compassion, and is gracious, trustworthy and fair, but he also wants to maintain a relationship with his creatures. What a difference there is between the impersonal *logos* of the Greeks and the personal *logos* of the Gospel of John, who used the logos term to introduce Jesus Christ as the one who is with God and is God but who came and dwelt with us humans! "In the beginning was the Word and the Word was with God, and the Word was God. . . .The Word became flesh and made his dwelling among us" (John 1:1, 14).

This relational aspect of God is initially expressed in himself, as described in Genesis. Christians are monotheists, who believe there is one God, but Christians know that this one God is a Triune God. Genesis 1:1 introduces God as the creator of the heavens and the earth. John 1:1–3 introduces the word (i.e., Jesus Christ, the Son of God) as with God in the beginning and the one through whom all things were created. Genesis 1:2 introduces the Spirit of God as "hovering over the waters." Genesis 1:26 identifies God as saying, "Let Us make man in Our image," further indicating the relational aspect of God as described in Scripture. Thus it is not surprising that a God who "is a community in a profound sense"[19] would desire a relationship with those he created in his image.

God's desire for a relationship with humans has a unique expression in the institution of the Sabbath. Because the creator feels a bond with his creation, he is the one who took the initiative of stopping his work to enjoy what he had done. God relates to us much more as a friend than as a distant potentate. Thus the Sabbath is not a legal requirement imposed by God upon mankind. It is his gift of quality time, his way to bring us nearer to him.

The Sabbath also reminds us that because God is the creator, he is worthy of our worship. As the one worthy of our worship, we are commanded (in the first of the Ten Commandments) to give our undivided loyalty to God: "You shall have no other gods before me" (Exod 20:3). This makes the God of Genesis totally distinct from all forms of pagan worship. The Jews could not build a Pantheon in which to place and adore all the gods of the conquered nations. Likewise we cannot divide our lives between the worship of God and the worship of things. The Sabbath reminds us that God created the world and all that we receive is a gift from

---

19. Gill, *Becoming Good*, 48.

God, not an achievement of our own. Our role is to give thanks and worship God as Father, Son and Holy Spirit.[20] David Gill, in his book *Doing Right: Practicing Ethical Principles*, reminds us that "a god is whatever we bow down to and worship."[21] Martin Luther gave us some practical examples: mammon (money and possessions), great learning, wisdom, power, prestige, family, and honor. Others have noted that of particular power today are technology, sex, power, beauty, health, careers, children and family.[22] Gill notes that "probably the greatest rival to God in our era is the self. The gospel of self-satisfaction, personal autonomy and self-determination is wowing and wooing thousands of converts today."[23]

Coupled with the thought that God as described in the creation story is a person comes consideration of the second commandment—that God cannot be represented by a material image. "You shall not make for yourself an image in the form of anything in heaven above or in the earth beneath or in the waters below. You shall not bow down to them or worship them" (Exod 20:4). A person has both a will and potential for action. These qualities are used in our relationships, both with others and with God. Specifically with God, we can converse with him and share our problems with him. We can love him and let him know that we love him. Worship and prayer are the heart of a Christian's life. When our ultimate objects of worship are visible and material, we have created "a god by means of making it for myself."[24] When we lower our conception of God, we are perilously close to spiritual shipwreck. The only image of God that God has shown to us, which we are invited to worship, is Jesus Christ.[25]

Finally, because God is a person, he relates to us by sharing his name, and with that name, his character. We noted six of these character traits above: compassion and grace; steadfast love and faithfulness; justice and righteousness. Scripture also tells us that as Christians, we bear the name of Christ (Acts 11:26). The third commandment (Exod 20:7) forbids misusing the name of God whether by the use of profanity or by swearing falsely by it. God's name can also be misused when we fail to reflect his character by showing a lack of compassion when dealing

20. Wilson, *God's Good World*, 28–29.

21. Gill, *Doing Right*, 84.

22. Gill, *Doing Right*, 85.

23. Gill, *Doing Right*, 86.

24. Gill, *Doing Right*, 98.

25. Gill, *Doing Right*, 106.

with others, acting without graciousness, love, or faithfulness, or failing to practice justice and righteousness. David Gill states: "To pray and not to practice, to believe and not to obey, to praise and yet at heart to rebel, is to take the name of the Lord in vain. . . . In an act of love for us, God gives us his name. It is our act of love to wear it with pride and to speak it with respect and warmth."[26]

The Uniqueness of Human Beings

The creation account also provides the answer to one's major query: Who am I? To a great degree one's conduct and self-esteem are determined by the answer to that question. According to the creation account, humans are unique creatures because of a unique creation. They are persons. They have a sense of responsibility.

In the second chapter of Genesis we are told that God fashioned man out of clay and breathed his breath into him, thereby transforming a lump of dust into a living being. These words clearly define man's relation to nature. He was made out of natural substances and his life in many ways mirrors the life of other living creatures. But it is the breath of God that makes that parcel of dust a living being, created in the image of God. Much discussion has been devoted to the meaning of the expression, "image of God." It implies a parallelism between God and man, a parallelism in the capacities of man and his functions with God's capacities and functions.

As God is a God of truth, human beings are able to seek and understand truth. As God is a God of love and justice, men and women are endowed with a disposition to love others and to treat them fairly. The God of beauty shared his capacity to enjoy beauty with humans. The God who cares and rejoices gave humans the ability to care and rejoice. He gave them a "will" and endowed them with the capacity to choose and decide. Perhaps most amazing of all, the creator shared with man his creative capacity when he endowed him or her with the gift of imagination. Just as God thought and spoke and it was so, the engineer beholds in his mind a daring new bridge and builds it. The composer hears a melody and writes it down. The author thinks of a story and through imagination makes the story more real than reality itself. Technology, art, and industry all depend upon the imagination of the creator.

26. Gill, *Doing Right*, 131, 135.

The God who wants to communicate with his creatures gave them capacities for communication. The relational God who exemplifies community created humans as "them" (Gen 1:27)—a partnership. Man was created a social being. The most important demonstration of man as a social being is the fashioning of woman. God said: "It is not good for the man to be alone. I will make a helper suitable (some translation read "comparable") to him" (Gen 2:18). Woman was not provided as a servant but as an *ezer*, a help. In the Old Testament, that word is most often applied to God. For example, it appears in the verse, "My help cometh from the Lord" (Ps 121:2). Far from indicating subordination or inferiority, the term suggests capacities akin to God's capacity to give assistance and advice in difficult situations. Woman's role, according to the creation account, is not primarily to have and raise children, but to be a divine-like help. This suggests a great closeness, a sharing not only of bodies but also of ideas and dreams. Thus from the very beginning we see the existence of the principle of mutuality. Man and woman were created with different gifts, not only physiologically but in all dimensions of being a person. As a result they enrich each other's lives. The Bible notes the existence of different gifts in their descendants. One is a fruit grower, another a shepherd. One is a musician, another a metal worker. Just as we can perceive distance because we have two eyes, so humans can act better when there are many different gifts. This fact makes each individual indispensable and valuable to the group. Because of mutuality, one cannot use one's gift selfishly. It must be, so to speak, offered to the community.

It is important to note that the one item mentioned as "not good" in the Creation story of Genesis 1 and 2 is solitary existence. David Gill notes:

> Our need for community is woven into the fabric of our being, our nature. There is a distinction between man (*ish*) and woman (*ishah*), but they are made of the same stuff and even the similarity of their names emphasizes their commonality. The tasks of being fruitful, multiplying, filling and subduing the earth, receiving and caring for the earth, are given to man and woman in their community and partnership. It is only sin and its curse that alienated and separated man and woman in these tasks (Genesis 3). Hard-core, rugged, "Lone Ranger" individualism violates our nature and contradicts God's purposes.[27]

27. Gill, *Becoming Good*, 49.

Finally, Scripture gives an unshakable ground for human dignity by virtue of the declaration that humans were created in the image of God. This dignity does not depend on rank or the size of one's bank account. Anyone created in the image of God deserves respect and concern and should be treated accordingly. The insistence of the Bible upon the fact that human beings are persons who have equal dignity is of immense importance in the world of business. It rejects the business decisions that only take into account the profit line in the financial statements. It demands that people not be exploited like tools, but treated as persons who can think and feel, who have family obligations, who are our brothers and sisters. It condemns sweatshops. It requires administrators to provide for as much involvement of the workers in the life of the company as possible. It sets an ideal of creating a real community in factories and offices, but eliminating as far as possible class distinctions, and reducing the huge financial gap between workers and managers. Essentially it means that a Christian businessperson will deal with others as sons and daughters of God.

WHAT HAPPENED TO THE ORIGINAL PLAN?

The creation account gives us the explanation for the most puzzling aspect of our universe: the existence of evil. Throughout history many explanations have been offered. The Manicheans taught that evil was a power just as eternal and just as powerful as good. Some have denied the reality of evil while others use the fear of punishment for evil deeds as an incentive to practice good behavior. Some, especially after the Holocaust, suggested that the presence of evil is evidence that God's power is limited; others talk as if God needs evil to reveal his power and his justice.

According to Scripture, evil is a stark reality but not part of the fabric of the universe created by God. It is neither willed nor brought into existence by God. It is a direct result of the misuse of the freedom that God granted to those whom he wanted to be real persons. God did not want mechanical love and obedience. Love is meaningful only as it expresses itself in actions. The love of his creatures, God purposed, must be a genuine feeling, and their obedience a real expression of their trust in his wisdom. Human beings, therefore, were created with the power of choice. Although the capacity to choose freely entailed immense perils, it was so important to God that Christ, according to Heb 7:22, accepted the role of guarantor for that free relationship between God and man. Christ assumed the risk and the responsibility of the results of giving such latitude to creatures.

The Bible introduces a very unique concept: the concept of sin. Sin is different from moral error because sin implies disobedience to a clear command of God. Moral error stems from ignorance or thoughtlessness. Sin is a form of rebellion on the part of creatures who attempt to become equal with their creator. God is the creator of the world; he is the one who spoke and it stood fast (Ps 33:9). God is beyond the world which he created. As creator, only God is without limits. Adam and Eve, however, were not created as gods; they were subject to limits. These limits were set in the command not to eat of the Tree of the Knowledge of Good and Evil. God said to our first parents, "You are free to eat from any tree in the garden; but you must not eat from the Tree of the Knowledge of Good and Evil, for when you eat of it you will surely die" (Gen 2:16–17). But Eve saw that "the fruit of the tree was good for food and pleasing to the eye, and also desirable for gaining wisdom" and so she took it, ate it, and gave some to her husband, who also ate it (Gen 3:6). The serpent, named in the Bible as Satan (Rev 12:9), told Eve that she could never fully be herself until she became autonomous. Turning God's command into mockery, he advised her to use her freedom and to refuse to allow God to keep her from what would give her true happiness. Only then, he said, could she experience complete fulfillment.

Van Duzer states in his book *Why Business Matters to God*:

> By disobeying God and eating of the tree of the knowledge of good and evil, Adam and Eve asserted their unwillingness to live within limits (or to be less than God). This is what theologians refer to as the Fall. Not only did this disrupt their relationship with God but it tore a hole through the whole fabric of the "good" creation. Nothing has been the same ever since.[28]

History has shown that very soon the misuse of God's gift of freedom led to slavery of the worst kind—slavery to the senses, slavery to greed, slavery to the need to control, slavery to all that destroys human relationships and even the environment over which man was to be the steward. Sin is essentially self-centeredness—out of which grows lust for power, greed, violence, deception, and the manipulation of others. In the Bible, sin has a cosmic dimension. It is the expression of the spirit of one called

28. Van Duzer, *Why Business Matters*, 55.

Satan, who, because of pride, tried to wrest ultimate power from God. Admittedly, the idea of a personal evil being is less and less popular in our secular culture, but Jesus acted on the assumption of the reality of Satan's existence and his struggle against God. Because it has its root in a person (Satan), sin is a very dynamic reality. It enslaves and blinds its subjects. According to Jesus, everyone who sins is a slave to sin (John 8:34). The misuse of freedom leads to the loss of freedom. The purpose of the gospel is to restore true freedom (Luke 4:18).

It is only in understanding the Scripture story of the original plan and what went wrong that one can explain actions like those described in the opening story about Walmart de Mexico. The "hole that was torn in the fabric of the 'good' creation" (Van Duzer) broke the relationships between humans and God and between humans and humans. After he sinned, Adam was afraid of God. He hid. Following his indictment by God, Adam blamed his wife for what had happened. Eve, in turn, excused her act by what the serpent had urged her to do. Their sense of responsibility was warped. They found themselves unwilling and unable to face honestly the consequences of their act. They claimed that their decisions were the product of circumstances or their environment. They were the unfortunate victims.

Their personal dignity also suffered. When they separated from God, they saw that they were naked. The covering of glory which was probably part of the image of God was gone. They did not lose their reason but now they used it to rationalize their evil deeds. They did not lose their sense of beauty, but now their gaze was warped by lust. They did not lose their speech capacity, but too often it became a tool of deception or anger. They did not lose their imagination and their creativity, but now it was often devoted to evil fantasies and acts or products designed to hurt or kill.

Perhaps worst of all was the degradation of the will, which now became the choice servant of greed and selfishness. It is the will that often propels people to actions which ultimately bring suffering and grief. It is the will that drives people to self-destruct in their quest for power. It is the will that causes individuals to make unethical decisions, such as those described in the opening story—to bribe officials for business purposes that will ultimately increase personal power, but then to refuse to accept responsibility for the results of their actions when they are discovered.

We saw the management of Walmart de Mexico, like Adam, attempt to hide the payments of the bribes through clever accounting tricks. The

New York Times article describes how they sought to smear the names of those who attempted to tell the truth about the actions which violated even Walmart's own code of ethics. When the perpetrators of the bribes were promoted to Walmart headquarters because of the growth of Walmart de Mexico, we observed further cover-up activity as the bribery practices came to light through the *New York Times* articles. Their actions are reflective of those initially taken in the garden by Adam and Eve. They are repeated again and again throughout history because as Van Duzer said, when the hole was torn in the fabric of the "good" creation, nothing has ever been the same since.

Chapter 2

What Resources Are Free for Business Use?

Ethical Issues and the Environment

The world has enough for everyone's needs, but not enough for everyone's greed.
—MOHANDAS GANDHI, 1937

ON SEPTEMBER 1, 1914, Martha, the last Passenger Pigeon, died at the Cincinnati Zoological Garden, thus making certain what had been feared for several years—the Passenger Pigeon was indeed extinct. When Europeans first came to North America in the seventeenth century, they commented on the "countless numbers" and "infinite multitudes" of these birds, but by the early twentieth century, they had totally disappeared. Their story illustrates a case of business greed, coupled with technological advance that made overuse, or in this case, overkill, possible. As a result, one of the most beautiful resources in the North American environment was lost.

The Passenger Pigeon, a larger and more brightly colored bird than our current-day mourning dove, had a wide-ranging migratory pattern that covered the central and eastern sections of the United States. Its preferred habitat was the mixed hardwood forests of these regions where the birds could feast on beechnuts, acorns, chestnuts, seeds, and berries. The birds traveled in huge colonies and roosted so crowded together that often the tree limbs broke under their weight. While completely accurate data is unavailable, it was reported that a large nesting area in central Wisconsin, north and west of the Wisconsin Dells, covered 850 square miles, with 136,000,000 birds nesting there.[1]

Ultimately the birds' colonization pattern clashed with human activity that destroyed the habitat through clearing of forests for farmland, killing the birds for food by striking them when the birds were in flight, and by disrupting their nesting areas. By the 1860s, two technological advances hastened the birds' extinction: the national expansion of the telegraph and the railroad. Professional hunters joined the locals in netting and shooting the birds by locating their nesting sites through telegraphed messages. They then shipped the dead birds by rail to various cities such as Milwaukee, Chicago, St. Louis, Cincinnati, Philadelphia, New York, and Boston. When the early conservationists began protesting the mass killings, people either stated that there was no possibility that humans could destroy a species so plentiful, or that to end the killings would cause the people who both shipped and marketed the dead birds to lose their jobs.[2]

As a result of the extinction of the Passenger Pigeon, in 1900 the US Congress passed a bill banning interstate shipping of unlawfully killed game. Other legislation followed, including the Migratory Bird Treaty Act in 1917 that protects birds and their nests, eggs, and feathers.[3] But these acts were too late to save the Passenger Pigeons. Their colonization was not only their protection from most predators, except for man, but it was also their incubator for reproduction. Even though conservationists preserved a few captive breeding flocks, the birds did not breed successfully in small groups. Today the only Passenger Pigeons one can see are the stuffed ones in museums, such as the Smithsonian.

Because of the loss of the Passenger Pigeons and other environmental disasters, such as Union Carbide and its mistakes in Bhopal, and the energy giant BP and its Deepwater Horizon spill in the Gulf of Mexico, business today recognizes its responsibility for the environment. For example, Patagonia, an outdoor clothing and equipment company, states its mission as follows: "Build the best product, cause no unnecessary harm, *use business to inspire and implement solutions to the environmental*

1. Smithsonian, "Passenger Pigeon."
2. Yeoman, "Why the Passenger Pigeon Went Extinct," para. 25–26.
3. Yeoman, "Why the Passenger Pigeon Went Extinct," para. 15.

crisis"[4](*italics mine*). Management textbooks have added a chapter on sustainability to their tables of contents, recognizing the importance of creating "a good quality of life for both current and future generations of humans and nonhumans by achieving a balance between economic prosperity, ecosystem viability, and social justice."[5]

One company noted for its sustainability practices is Herman Miller, a furniture company established over one hundred years ago in Zeeland, Michigan. In 2017 Herman Miller received the inaugural "SEAL Organizational Impact Award" for overall corporate sustainability performance. In 2016, for the twelfth consecutive year, it was selected for inclusion in the 2016 RobecoSAM Sustainability Yearbook. In 2015 the company achieved its twelfth consecutive listing on Dow Jones Sustainability World Index.[6] Why? What has it done?

Herman Miller is named in honor of the father-in-law of the founder, D. J. De Pree, although Herman Miller himself never actually worked at the organization that bears his name. However, he was responsible for assisting his son-in law in purchasing the business, originally known as Star Furniture Company, in 1923.

While initially specializing in the same type of furniture as its competitors did (that is, reproductions of whatever period furniture was in style at the moment), the company went out on a limb during the Great Depression to create something new. Management had noted that following the pack was leading the company swiftly toward bankruptcy.[7] De Pree, then president of Herman Miller, furnished the "House of Tomorrow" at the 1932 Chicago World's Fair with furniture designed by Gilbert Rohde. De Pree then sat in the room, listening to the comments of the people who passed through his exhibit of modern furniture designs. Based on that experience (and against his father-in-law's advice), he dropped period furniture and began to offer new designs from designers such as Gilbert Rohde, George Nelson, Charles and Ray Eames, and Alexander Girard.[8] Herman Miller's classic products include the Aeron chair, designed by Bill Stumpf and Don Chadwick in 1994 and named the

---

4. Patagonia homepage.

5. Carroll and Buchholtz, *Business & Society*, 432.

6. Herman Miller homepage.

7. Ruch, *Leaders & Followers*, 117.

8. Herman Miller homepage.

Design of the Decade (1990s) by *Business Week*, and the office cubicle, created in 1968 and originally known as "Action Office II."

One of Herman Miller's best known products is the Eames Lounge Chair, designed by Charles and Ray Eames in 1956. This chair is "a cradle of molded wood veneer holding calfskin cushions" and is included in the collection held at the New York Museum of Modern Art.[9] The wood veneer was rosewood, as specified by the designers. However, by the late 1980s, it was clear that Herman Miller's use of rosewood and Honduran mahogany to manufacture the chair was resulting in the destruction of the rain forests. Because Herman Miller is a company that practices "roving leadership," a management style which empowers independent decision-making by all employees irrespective of their title or position, top management was informed of the problem by the research manager.[10]

The company had a sustainability problem that would require a change in the way they did business. As the chief executive Richard H. Ruch wrote in 2002: "My first reaction was, we can't do that (i.e., change the wood) because Charles Eames (then deceased) specified that it be made only in rosewood. 'Ah,' they said, 'but rosewood is not a sustainable veneer.' That was my first real introduction to the destruction of the rain forest and the issue of sustainability, which has since become a cornerstone of Herman Miller's environmental policy. Shortly thereafter, we were influential in getting BIFMA, the trade association of the office furniture industry, to adopt an industry policy of using sustainable woods and veneers."[11] But Ruch was only following what D. J. De Pree had said in 1953: "Herman Miller will be a good corporate neighbor by being a good steward of the environment."[12]

In 1994 Herman Miller started a program called "Earthright," which had the goal of reaching a zero operational footprint. This program had three parts. The first was "positive transparency," which meant that the company would share information about its environmental impact. A look at their website demonstrates their willingness to inform all stakeholders, including the public, of their record. The second part was "products as living things." The company's goal was to create better products and processes to protect everyone's health and well-being, restore the

9. Birchard, "Herman Miller's Design for Growth," 56–67.

10. Woodruff, "Herman Miller: How Green Is My Factory."

11. Ruch, *Leaders & Followers*, 98.

12. Herman Miller homepage.

ecosystem, and give back more than they extracted. Finally, the third part, called "becoming greener together," focused on engaging everyone, from the employees to the larger community, in considering the environment when making decisions.

The results? On their website in the fall of 2014—the tenth anniversary of the "Earthright" program—the company announced the following achievements: waste down from all facilities by 91.8 percent; air emission down by 87 percent; hazardous waste down by 90 percent; materials to landfills down by 97 percent; process water uses down by 84 percent.[13]

Interestingly, Herman Miller is equally focused on being a good corporate citizen in other ways. For example, it demands the same high environmental actions on the part of its suppliers through its supplier code of ethics.[14] It was one of the first companies to provide profit sharing to its employees through the Scanlon plan, developed by Jack Frost in 1950. This plan was initially offered to all employees working in production, but as changes in production occurred, many of the company's employees moved into other-than-production positions. In order to include all employees, the profit-sharing plan was revised and offered to everyone in 1979—long before employee profit sharing became popular.[15]

BUSINESS RECOGNIZES ITS ENVIRONMENTAL RESPONSIBILITY

In the latter part of the twentieth century, businesses, sometimes on their own like Herman Miller and sometimes with the encouragement of government, began to consider the possibility that the earth's resources might not be infinite. The question, "What resources are free for business use?" led people to examine concepts that had previously been assumed—that the air, water, and land were truly free for all, including business, to use with impunity. Negative consequences, such as the pollution of these generally available and used resources, were labeled *externalities*—unintended side effects of actions, and generally ignored in the pricing structure of the product. However, with the strengthening of the environmental movement, governments adopted environmental protection laws to mandate that businesses protect these externalities and other

13. Herman Miller homepage.
14. Herman Miller homepage.
15. De Pree, *Business as Unusual*, 123.

resources from destruction. Businesses responded to public and governmental pressure and litigation by joining the environmental movement and then publicizing their environmental accomplishments on lists that can be found on the Internet by Googling "Green Companies" or "Environmentally Friendly Companies." Lists of "top companies" are compiled annually by a variety of organizations such as *Newsweek, Forbes, Working Mother, Mother Earth*, the *EPA*, and *Inc.com*. Once public opinion ran pro-environment, there was much to be gained for a business by demonstrating voluntary compliance.

Organizations such as the Coalition for Environmentally Responsible Economies (Ceres) have developed goals for business with respect to environmental performance and provided annual updates on progress toward these goals. Ceres also created a "roadmap for sustainability," with the subtitle: "A strategic vision and practical framework for sustainable corporations in the 21st century economy." This roadmap has four broad categories and twenty expectations that companies should seek to meet by 2020.[16]

The first category Ceres identified is *governance for sustainability*. This category includes five expectations relating to board oversight and management accountability designed to set the organization on a path toward sustainability. The challenge is for the organization to create specific policies and provide stated positions in the public square on their sustainability commitments and strategies.

The second category is *stakeholder engagement*, which stresses communication with a diverse group of stakeholders, including investors and senior executives. The goal of this category is to integrate stakeholder feedback on sustainability issues into corporate strategic planning, risk management, and decision-making.

Ceres's third category is *disclosure*. It is anticipated that companies will not only announce their sustainability strategy, but will also provide performance data and information on their targets in various reports, including financial reports, and through other communication vehicles, such as corporate websites.

The fourth category is *performance*. Ceres challenges organizations to improve their operations, products, and services to ultimately reach environmental neutrality with respect to climate change stabilization and the conservation of natural resources. Ceres also includes in this category

16. Ceres, "Ceres Roadmap for Sustainability."

the necessity of protecting the human rights of employees, suppliers, and clients by maintaining safe and fair workplaces.

As previously noted, most textbooks provide recognized and accepted reasons for business organizations to be concerned about environmental issues and sustainability. For example, businesses are encouraged to be socially responsible in order to gain a competitive advantage over other companies. Acting in a socially responsible manner will strengthen customer loyalty. Economic and environmental performance enhance the bottom line because costs may be reduced and/or revenues increased through socially responsible decisions. As one author explains:

> Better environmental performance can reduce costs by improving risk management and stakeholder relationships, reducing the amount of materials and energy used, and reducing capital and labor costs. Improved environmental standards should prevent major environmental disasters in the future. For those disasters that cannot be avoided, the firm can at least show it applied due diligence with its environmental performance, which may reduce the company's culpability in the public's eye. Companies can decrease the costs of compliance with governmental regulations and reduce fines if they become more energy efficient.[17]

As was true in the early twentieth century with the demise of the Passenger Pigeon, increased technology and public disbelief contribute to the environmental discussion. As noted above, technology has so enhanced worldwide communication that what happens anywhere in the world is quickly communicated everywhere. Technology can help business create better ways to manage its resources, while also increasing its ability to recycle and re-use resources that in the past would have been delegated to the landfill. However, it can also give large corporations the option of going far beyond their former boundaries to exploit resources in parts of the world where governments are not yet aware of, or do not care for, their own environmental needs. Some businesses respond to environmental concerns with a low commitment to act, often due to a hope that nothing really bad will happen or a disbelief that human activity can really cause so much harm. They question whether the pollution of a river can really be caused by such a small spill or whether we are really sure that human activity causes global warming.

17. Ferrell et al., *Business Ethics*, 367.

ONE'S ATTITUDE TOWARD THE ENVIRONMENT INFLUENCES BEHAVIOR

Often one's attitude toward the environment reflects one's attitude toward the material world in general. Centuries ago it was believed that the material world was either evil (as compared with the heavenly realms) or subject to use and misuse for the sole benefit of the owner. Plato taught that the unseen, rather than the seen, was the ultimate reality, and espoused a hierarchy of society which dictated who would deal with the material world. Philosophers were to be the thinkers, and therefore above the material world around them. Soldiers were the fighters, and the slaves dealt with matter. To some extent, Plato's hierarchy influences our thinking even today. We honor those who educate themselves for jobs using their minds, while we often look down on those who work with their hands and deal with matter and the material world.

The Christian, however, views the environment and matter in a different light. The creation account in Genesis 1 and 2 paints a very different picture of the world than the one Plato painted. The Bible teaches that matter is good and that working with matter is not an inferior mode of living. We can be sure that matter is good because God created it and declared it good. In fact, there is something sacred about the whole world. Its beauty and its perfection lift our sights to an all-wise and all-powerful author. We can see why the psalmist proclaims: "The Heavens declare the glory of God" (Ps 19:1). When they behold nature, humans feel a unity with God and with all of his creation.

Because God created matter and called it good, a businessperson never has to feel that if he or she truly wants to serve God, they should leave their work and enter the pastoral ministry. There are great possibilities for doing good in the market place. Money is a divinely given talent that can be used for good purposes. The opportunity to provide work, especially the opportunity to employ people who are often victims of poverty or discrimination, is a challenge and a blessing. For a Christian there is also an opening for shedding joy and hope where so often there is only competition and fear.

A Christian businessperson remembers, however, that his or her use of matter is conditioned by the fact that he or she holds a stewardship role. As noted in the first chapter, humans were not created as gods, nor was their rule or dominion over nature to be that of a god. It is God who gives the ability and the right to rule over nature and to exploit its resources. God said, "Rule over the fish of the sea and the birds of the air and over every living creature that moves on the ground" (Gen 1:28). In the account of creation found in the second chapter of Genesis, God's command includes the duty to take care of it (Gen 2:15).

Unfortunately, the concept of "ruling" (or in some translations, "dominion") that was given to humans in the garden has been often used to justify environmental destruction in the name of meeting human needs and wants. That is why it is important to bring both Gen 1:28 and Gen 2:15 together so that ruling and serving are combined. This concept is also illustrated in Jesus' words to the disciples when they argued among themselves as to who was the greatest. Jesus responded: "The kings of the Gentiles lord it over them; and those who exercise authority over them call themselves Benefactors. But you are not to be like that. Instead, the greatest among you should be like the youngest, and *the one who rules like the one who serves*" (Luke 22:24–26, *italics mine*).

We have further evidence of the stewardship role assigned to humans when we note that immediately after telling humans that they are to "rule over the fish of the sea and the birds of the air and over every living creature that moves on the ground," God gave to humans "every seed-bearing plant on the face of the whole earth and every tree that has fruit with seed in it" for food (see Gen 1:28–29). In commenting on these verses, Jeff Van Duzer, dean of the School of Business and Economics at Seattle Pacific University, notes that "God did not intend to relinquish the ongoing productive capacity of God's creation to human beings. They could eat the fruit, and the plants would continue to grow more fruit. In effect, Adam and Eve were invited to enjoy the income from God's trust without invading the principal. God remained the owner."[18]

Because God is the owner, he provides ongoing care for the creatures he has made. Psalm 104, for example, speaks of the daily care of God for *all* his creatures, not just humans:

> He waters the mountains from his upper chambers; the earth is satisfied by the fruit of his work. He makes grass grow for the cattle, and plants for man to cultivate—bringing forth food from the earth: wine that gladdens the heart of man, oil to make his face shine, and bread that sustains his heart. (Ps 104:14–15)

---

18. Van Duzer, "Why Business Matters," 29.

> These all look to you to give them their food at the proper time.
> When you give it to them, they gather it up; when you open your
> hand, they are satisfied with good things. (Ps 104:27–28)

In the Sabbath commandment (Exod 20:8–11) God speaks of rest for the
animals as well as humans, and in his instructions for the sabbatical year
(Lev 25:1–7) is included the statement: "The land is to have a year of rest."
In Gen 9:8–17, God makes a covenant with Noah "and with your descendants after you and *with every living creature that was with you—the birds,
the livestock and all the wild animals, all those that came out of the ark with
you—every living creature on earth*" (*italics mine*). God promises that he
will never again destroy the earth with a flood. The rainbow that shines
after rain is a sign of God's care, not just for mankind, but for all living
creatures on the earth.

HUMAN RESPONSIBILITY FOR THE ENVIRONMENT

Today, in the quest for income and comfort, we may trample heedlessly
upon other creatures as if we were gods, as if these creatures belonged to
us. Waste of natural resources or any of the gifts of God that are present
in our world reflects one's forgetting the basis of his or her rights in the
natural world. God warned Adam and Eve that they had the power of
choice and with that the responsibility for their actions. If they failed the
test and ate of the Tree of the Knowledge of Good and Evil, they would
die. The message was clear: with freedom of choice comes responsibility,
and the responsible one cannot avoid his or her responsibility for the
subsequent consequences.

Human actions have consequences because God created humans to
be persons, with the power of choice. Adam and Eve suffered the consequences of their actions. They lost the garden. Their capacity for human
relationships was broken. After they sinned, they hid from God. When
questioned as to what happened, they blamed each other and the serpent,
and ultimately even God himself. They did not want to face the consequences of their choices.

We, too, are persons, created with the power of choice and with the
responsibility for our actions. We cannot blame others for the results of
our own decisions. Thus, because humans have been granted stewardship
over the resources of the earth, the question arises: How should these
resources be used? A Christian businessperson will be a conservationist,

not because of the laws of the country, but because of a deep sense of stewardship to God, and an understanding that what one chooses to do has consequences for which one bears responsibility. The Christian will remember the warning in Revelation: "The time has come for judging the dead and for rewarding your servants the prophets and your saints and those who reverence your name, both small and great, and *for destroying those who destroy the earth*" (*italics mine*) (Rev 11:18).

Given that we live after Adam and Eve chose to eat of the Tree of the Knowledge of Good and Evil, how do we know what being a steward really means? What is a Christian's obligation or duty with respect to others, to the environment and the natural resources which we have been given, and to life in general? How can we know the best choices to make when we are faced with these decisions every day? We may "feel" that we have an obligation or duty to do something, but what action should we take? How does one choose?

UNDERSTANDING OBLIGATION AND DUTY

Conscience

Traditionally humans have looked to conscience as one's guide to understanding one's duty or obligation. The Stoics first described the experience of obligation, and explained it as the result of the presence of a divine spark in every human soul. In modern times psychologists can be divided between those who explain conscience as the internalization by the individual of the moral tenets of their society, and others who give a unique supernatural account for its existence. The shortcoming of the explanation of conscience as the internalized voice of the community is that historically the most powerful manifestations of conscience have been when it demanded painful changes and actions against the voice of the community.

Never was conscience more powerful than when it protested against the treatment of orphans, of prisoners, of slaves, or of women. It took on century-old attitudes and called them wrong, often in the name of a higher moral authority. Knowing this, can we leave the decisions regarding the use of the earth's resources up to the conscience of business? Might we not risk seeing results similar to the fate of the Passenger Pigeon, when the combined pressures of technological advances which permitted actions which were not previously possible partnered with greed for profits?

While conscience is not mentioned by name in the Old Testament, its activity is often recognized. Perhaps the first and best known manifestation of conscience is found in Genesis 3, where Adam and Eve sought to hide themselves from God when they transgressed his command to not eat of the Tree of the Knowledge of Good and Evil. It is eloquently described in Genesis 4 in the flight of Cain after his crime. It is also described most poignantly by David in Psalm 51, where he pours out his feelings as one accused by his conscience and who wishes to confess his sin.

In the New Testament, the word *conscience* is used thirty-one times, usually by Paul, who most likely borrowed the term from the Stoics, but gave it a different dimension. For Paul and other New Testament writers, conscience is not the absolute knowledge granted by a spark of the divine. It is a witness that can be powerful, but can be made ineffective when its messages are neglected.

Paul noted that the conscience can approve (Acts 23:1; 2 Tim 1:3; Acts 24:16). In 1 Cor 8:12, however, the apostle talks about a "wounded conscience" and in Titus 1:15 he speaks about a "defiled conscience." In Heb 10:20 we hear about an "evil conscience" and in 1 Tim 4:2, a "seared conscience." The term used in the Greek for seared is *kauterizo*, from which we derive *cauterize*. Thus, for Paul, conscience is not the final moral authority. Rather, it is like a compass that does not set the north but informs the traveler of their position in relation to that point of the compass. Just as a compass loses its accuracy if one places it where there is iron, so conscience loses its reliability little by little if one dwells in the world of impurity and dishonesty.

As the image of God in man was distorted but not fully erased by the entrance of sin, so conscience can never be totally deleted. Jesus said: "If you, then, though you are evil, know how to give good gifts to your children, how much more will your Father in heaven give good gifts to those who ask him!" (Matt 7:11). Paul speaks of the law written in the hearts of the Gentiles (Rom 2:15). Even in cases of extreme moral corruption, it is impossible to completely silence the voice of conscience. It is therefore morally very dangerous to act against the warnings it gives when we plan a course of action. However, the word of condemnation from conscience is always more reliable than its word of approval.

Love

A second suggested ground for knowing one's obligation or duty is to follow the command of love—and choose to do the loving action. In his second letter to the Corinthians, Paul writes: "For Christ's love controls us [many translations have *constrains*]. . . . Therefore, if anyone is in Christ, he is a new creation" (2 Cor 5:14–17). In this text we have the essential characteristics of the love that constrains all the children of God, a love that has roots far beyond the level of human relations. It is illumined by the thought of Christ's example of self-sacrifice which leads humans to return to a community mode of living. Christians do not live for themselves; they have shed the self-centered approach to life. The change is so deep that those who are in Christ are a new creation. Christ lives in them. The spiritual constraint of such love is unbelievable. It has led people to give away their fortunes, to leave home and go to far-off lands for the remainder of their lives, to live entirely by trust in God in very dangerous circumstances.

A modern school of ethics known as situational ethics makes love the ultimate rule; anything is right if done for the sake of love. It could be argued under this theory that adultery, murder, theft, and lying are justified if they are for the sake of another fellow human being. This approach, however, raises very serious questions. If I commit adultery to help someone rediscover self-esteem, what about my marriage partner whose trust I betray? Is this really the way love acts? Does it command me to break solemn promises? What about my lying to a person who is unlikely to recover from his or her sickness? Is it helpful to hide the truth when the person is in a state of denial but should get his or her estate ready for the future? As the disease follows its course, will not that individual lose trust in my word? Would I have been more supportive if I had spoken words of hope and trust in God while attempting to prepare him or her, as well as the family, for the unavoidable?

On March 24, 1989, the Exxon *Valdez*, a giant oil tanker, ran aground on Bligh Reef, south of Valdez, Alaska. The tanker was sailing outside the normal shipping lanes in order to avoid ice, which was probably wise, but that decision produced another navigational challenge. Outside of the usual shipping lane, the tanker was headed toward Bligh Reef. Bligh Reef was well identified by the navigation lights at Busby Island, but the Captain, Joseph Hazelwood, was not at the bridge to see the lights. He had gone below, ostensibly to do some paperwork, and left the third mate,

Gregory Cousins, on the bridge alone—a violation of normal protocol. Cousins was exhausted and was supposed to have ended his shift and headed for bed. He thought he had put the vessel into the turn maneuver so that it might return to the shipping lane. But the ship did not turn. Instead it struck the reef and spilled eleven million gallons of oil into Prince William Sound. After ten days, the spill covered one thousand square miles and affected not only the ocean life, but also life along the beaches, including seabirds, otters, and eagles.

During the trial in the Ninth Circuit Court of Appeals, it was revealed that Hazelwood had a drinking problem, had been in rehabilitation in 1985 and subsequently had attended Alcoholics Anonymous, but had quit attending its meetings. Unfortunately, at the time of the accident, he was drunk. When tested ten and one-half hours after the spill occurred, his blood-alcohol level was 0.061—a level that indicated intoxication.[19]

For an individual on the ship that night, what would have been the appropriate ethical action based on love and concern for the captain, the crew, the ship, the environment, and the company? Should one have demanded that Captain Hazelwood, who was the only person on board the tanker to have the required license to navigate in this part of Prince William Sound, stay sober so that the multiplicity of wildlife would not be harmed and the ship not be damaged? Perhaps love would have demanded that Hazelwood be removed from the command of the vessel, given that he was drunk. Maybe the best action would have been to send Cousins to his bed and remain in port until the entire crew was capable of sailing. Would confrontation, even in a loving and gracious way, have worked? Clearly something needed to be done before the ship ran aground. But what?

Situational ethics brings to light the very important realization that love is a great imperative but not a very good indicative. The more I love, the more I need help in determining my response. I can kill a fly without much moral debate. It is much more difficult to have a pet dog put to death. When it comes to major decisions, whether in personal life or on the job, I find that my love raises formidable questions as to what I should do. Love tells me I must act, but not *what* I must do. I need guidance that is more specific.

19. Jennings, *Business Ethics* (7th ed.), 405–11.

Scripture: A Superior Source of Guidance

If conscience works best at condemnation (but not at approval), and if love strongly demands action (but without providing guidance as to the best course to pursue), to what source can one turn to understand one's ethical obligation? Most Christians would suggest turning to the Scriptures for moral guidance, particularly to the Decalogue, the messages of the prophets, the Sermon on the Mount, and the moral sections of the epistles of the New Testament. Rae and Wong note that the Scriptures are "biblical resources (i.e., moral instruction given in the form of laws, commandments, and principles to individuals and communities on topics such as justice, stewardship, and duties to others) that enable critical and constructive engagement with . . . questions (of corporate purpose and duties)."[20]

What principles for environmental use can one find in the Old Testament, which was written for an economic system, an agrarian society, so different from what most experience today? George Monsma Jr. contends that Scripture is clear that the earth's resources should be used to provide justice (or equity) for all and provide for all people the necessities for life and opportunities to care for their own needs through their labor and the resources available to them. In his article "Biblical Principles Important for Economic Theory and Practice" he states:

> The Mosaic laws . . . provided all people with access to food at all times through limitations on the rights of farmers to completely harvest their own crops, with the right to what remained given to the poor (Lev 19:9–10) . . . through tithes that were partly for the poor (Deut 14:28–29), through the right given to the poor to whatever the land produced in the sabbatical year (Exod 23:10–11), and through the right to eat in a neighbor's field or vineyard (Deut 23:24–25). The poor were also given access to necessities in the short-run by means of interest-free loans which were to be canceled every seventh year (Deut 15:7–10). . . . There were also restrictions against keeping a cloak or a mill stone (or by implication any necessity) as security for such a loan, and provisions to safeguard the dignity of the borrower (Exod 22:25–27; Deut 24:6, 12–13).[21]

He also noted:

20. Rae and Wong, *Beyond Integrity*, 173.

21. Monsma, "Biblical Principles," 39.

If they became poor and had to temporarily serve another they were to be treated as hired servants or sojourners rather than as slaves. In addition, the land could not be sold in perpetuity; rather it was to stay with the family to whom it had been entrusted by God when the land was settled. . . . In the long-run none would be forced to live from the charity of others, or even to earn a living by working under the orders of others. Rather each family was given an opportunity to respond to God's call to be a steward over the world's resources by being given control over their own labor and a share of the land and working-capital needed to produce a living in an agrarian society.[22]

A CHANGE OF FOCUS

What does this mean for business in today's generally capitalistic societies? Van Duzer, following his discussion of Genesis 1 and 2, suggests:

From this I would conclude that at this time in history, there are two legitimate, first-order, intrinsic purposes of business: as stewards of God's creation, business leaders should manage their businesses (1) to provide the community with goods and services that will enable it to flourish, and (2) to provide opportunities for meaningful work that will allow employees to express their God-given creativity.[23]

In further developing these purposes, Van Duzer suggests that rather than primarily determining what products or services would result in the highest profit, business managers should consider what products or services God might want their business to make at this time, given the goal of enabling one's community to flourish. He suggests that service to employees and customers are the actual ends of the business, rather than profit. He places the role of profit as a means of attracting sufficient capital to allow the business to sustain itself and to generate economic capital to sustain society, not as an end in itself.[24] This idea, of course, flies in the face of the most commonly cited article identifying the purpose of

22. Monsma, "Biblical Principles," 40.
23. Van Duzer, *Why Business Matters*, 42.
24. Van Duzer, *Why Business Matters*, 45–47.

business—that of Milton Friedman who argued that the primary responsibility of business is to maximize profits.[25]

Rae and Wong support Van Duzer's perspective and argue that Friedman's view "runs counter to a Christian understanding of human nature as fallen/selfish but still bearing a reflection (of) God's image and thus capable of other motivations."[26] In further commenting on the purpose of business to be supportive of human flourishing, Rae and Wong propose that it is the responsibility of business to *both* protect and serve the garden.[27] They identify three ways in which this can be done:

> 1. Reframe the issues. Rather than placing business and the environment in opposite camps, understand and act on the reality of the interconnectedness of human interests with natural ones.

> 2. Engage in a paradigm shift in what economic activity fits into larger natural systems. What is sustainable growth? How can sustainable growth both serve to enhance economic growth so that the poor share in its benefits while at the same time reducing waste and misuse. The story of Herman Miller illustrates this goal of both continuing economic development while reducing the company's environmental footprint.

> 3. Bring business to the table. Only business (teamed with government) is big enough to make a difference in how the world approaches the use of the resources provided by God. Business can shape the decisions regarding capital and market influence. But consumers have a role to play as well. To speak forcefully to business and government, consumers must change their lifestyles to refuse to vote with dollars "for products and services that may be cheap and convenient in the short term but are destructive to the environment and to human health down the road."[28]

Carroll and Buchholtz define sustainability as using the resources required for the present without compromising what is needed for future purposes or by future generations.[29] Van Duzer expands on this concept by insisting that a business should do no harm to *any* of its stakehold-

25. Friedman, "Social Responsibility of Business," 122–26.

26. Rae and Wong, *Beyond Integrity*, 175.

27. Rae and Wong, *Beyond Integrity*, 442–48.

28. Rae and Wong, *Beyond Integrity*, 448.

29. Carroll and Buchholtz, *Business & Society*, 432.

ers, whether investors, employees, suppliers, customers, communities, or the natural environment. He fleshes out his position with the following examples:

1. Investors should receive a reasonable, risk-adjusted return on their investment.

2. Employees should be treated as having intrinsic value, not just as a means of production. This means they should not be required to work in dangerous or demeaning situations, nor be required to work 24/7, thus ultimately destroying their ability to engage in relationships with God and with others. Finally, because the business is using the employee's productive capacity as a business resource, the employee should be paid a living wage in return.

3. Suppliers are entitled to honest and transparent dealings, not harassed to provide goods and services at unreasonably low prices.

4. Customers should not be deceived by insufficient information about the product, or sold products which are unsafe or priced in an unfair manner.

5. Communities should be dealt with in a trustworthy manner, understanding that social capital is as important as economic capital if the business desires to be successful in the long run.[30]

Herman Miller's management recognized that to continue to use the same wood products in their furniture as had been used in the past would result not only in major environmental destruction, but ultimately would lead to these resources disappearing from the earth, just as the Passenger Pigeons have vanished. If they were going to be a good steward of the environment they had to change their manufacturing procedures. They did. Today they use sustainable woods and veneers. They took responsibility for their actions and changed the consequences for the benefit of everyone—their employees, their stockholders, their customers, their suppliers, the community, and the environment. Their decisions show wisdom in answering the question: What resources are free for business use? Only those decisions which advance sustainability in the broadest sense of the word, as described by Van Duzer, are the safe answers for a Christian to consider when asking questions that deal with the use of

30. Van Duzer, *Why Business Matters*, 158–60.

the earth's resources. What God has gifted to us is not only for us, but for those who will follow us far into the future.

THINKING IT THROUGH: THE PASSENGER PIGEON CASE

While the case of the Passenger Pigeon is now a matter of historical interest, the issue of what technological advances do to the environment and human life continues to raise ethical questions.

From a utilitarian perspective, the inventions of the telegraph and the railroad expanded travel, jobs, and economic growth for the population of the United States. While it is unfortunate that the Passenger Pigeons were decimated by the use of these technologies, such use should not change the fact that the technologies brought much good to many people. Thus, while the loss of a species of birds is regrettable, the overall benefit of these inventions to human life exceeded the cost of losing the Passenger Pigeons.

From Kant's perspective, because one does not wish to live in a world where species die as a part of the cost of economic growth, it was unethical for people to destroy the Passenger Pigeons in order to provide food and desirable feathers for fashion purposes. The facts that the inventions of the telegraph and the railroad enhanced the ability to both obtain and get the "product" to distant markets, and in the process, provided jobs, are insufficient to justify the destruction of the species. While not recommending that the creation of products be stopped, Kant would argue that the ethical decision does not rest on whether or not sufficient good will result from the invention to counterbalance any evil, but whether or not the evil use can be stopped (e.g., through regulation).

To be honorable in business, the Christian worldview would require that all of God's creatures, including the Passenger Pigeon, and God's creation be protected from the results of greedy decisions and actions taken by those who think only of themselves and the profits they may accrue from their inventions, or from subsequent actions that focus only on their own benefit. The mandate for the protection of creatures would be considered a fundamental part of the stewardship responsibilities given to humans at creation.

Chapter 3

How Much Do I Owe My Employees?

The Dignity of Work and Employee Workplace Rights

We can invest all the money on Wall Street in new technologies, but we can't realize the benefits of improved productivity until companies rediscover the value of human loyalty.

—FREDERICK REICHHELD, DIRECTOR, BAIN & COMPANY

ON DECEMBER 11, 1995, fire broke out in a factory in Lawrence, Massachusetts, a mill town located on the Merrimack River. There had been numerous fires in Lawrence in the early 1990s[1] as the town struggled with abandoned buildings and loss of businesses during the recession. This fire, however, was at Malden Mills, one of the few remaining large employers in town. Malden Mills was best known for manufacturing Polartec, a lightweight fabric made from recycled plastic that is used in winter clothing and blankets sold by companies such as L.L.Bean, Patagonia, Lands' End, and Eddie Bauer. At the time of the fire, Malden Mills employed about 2,400 people, 700 of whom were working at the time the boiler exploded and ruptured the gas mains. The wind-whipped fire destroyed three of the company's four factories and injured thirty-three employees, but fortunately, there was no loss of life. Conventional

1. Jimenez, "New Rash of Fires."

wisdom said that the owner of Malden Mills, Aaron Feuerstein, being seventy years old at the time, would take the insurance money and retire to a warmer climate.

Instead of following conventional wisdom, Feuerstein shocked the community by stating that he would rebuild his factory in Lawrence rather than moving it south or overseas. He also stated that he would pay his employees their full salaries for the next sixty days. In fact, he kept the salary payments going for many months longer than initially promised, spending about $25 million in the process. At the end of six months, about 90 percent of his employees were back to work. Those who were displaced due to the new buildings and updated technology were transitioned to other jobs through Feuerstein's job training and placement center.

It cost about $430 million to reconstruct the plant with state-of-the-art equipment, with insurance covering only about $300 million. As a result of this shortfall, Feuerstein had to borrow money, which ultimately led, in 2001, to Malden Mills declaring bankruptcy and Feuerstein losing control of the company to its creditors. He was replaced as CEO as a result of the bankruptcy. While the company declared bankruptcy again (in 2007), it continued to operate under the name Polartec. In December 2015, the new owners announced that they would move the factory to Tennessee,[2] citing "Tennessee's 'business friendly environment' including lower energy and tax costs compared with Massachusetts" as the reason.[3] In 2018 the city announced that the former factory would be used by IndusPAD as a business incubator site for start-up companies.[4]

When asked why he chose to rebuild the mill in Lawrence, Feuerstein stated:

> We insist the business must be profitable . . . but we also insist a business must have responsibility for its workers, for the community and the environment. It has a social obligation to figure out a strategy, which will be able to permit workers to make a living wage. There's a responsibility to the workforce, to this community.[5]

2. Moser, "Polartec Moving Operations South."

3. Associated Press, "Polartec Moving 150 Jobs from Mass."

4. Conti, "Manufacturing Poised for a Comeback."

5. "Fire Destroys Malden Mills December 11, 1995."

As a devout Orthodox Jew, Feuerstein explained that he "drew on Jewish tradition when faced with the crisis: 'When all is moral chaos, this is the time for you to be a mensch,' the Yiddish word for an honorable, decent, compassionate person who embodies justice and strives for righteousness."[6]

The employees at Malden Mills expected that they would lose their jobs following the fire, since no factory remained in which to work. With the loss of their jobs there would be a commensurate loss of personal income, which would affect their families in a negative way. The city expected that they would lose a major employer, with the result that unemployment numbers would rise, and perhaps as a consequence, people would move out of the area in search of alternative employment. While that would lower the demand for city services in the long run, it would also mean a loss of taxable property, the income on which the city built its budget. But this is not what happened. Their expectations did not come true. Instead, they were amazed and pleased by Feuerstein's decision to rebuild the factory in Massachusetts, and during rebuilding, to keep employees on the payroll.

No one would have faulted the employees of Malden Mills for their initial expectations. In fact, people would have thought the employees unrealistic if they had expected to retain their personal income levels and get their jobs back following the fire. But this raises the questions: What are appropriate expectations, perhaps even rights, for employees to anticipate from their employers? What expectations should employers have of employees? Finally, what Aaron Feuerstein decided to do exacted an enormous personal cost, including ultimately the loss of ownership control of Malden Mills. Were his actions an illustration of what is expected for an ethical businessperson?

THE CONCEPT OF RIGHTS

The usual list of employee rights includes the following: The right of due process and fair treatment; workplace safety and the right to a healthy workplace; the right to privacy in the workplace, including the collection and use of employee information by employers; and fair compensation.

Where does the concept of rights come from?

6. Story of Malden Mills adapted from Jennings, *Business Ethics* (7th ed.), 356–57, and Leung, "Mensch."

There is very little agreement on how to explain the existence of rights. The interpretations go from pragmatism to idealism. Many explain rights in a very pragmatic way. They believe that you have the rights that you can enforce. In other words, might is right and the strongest wins the day. We often note that the rights of the poor and the weak are easily overlooked or trampled by the stronger ones. For example, in America, without the clout of unions, especially in the late nineteenth and early twentieth centuries, workers' rights were mostly an illusion.

Without question there is a pragmatic dimension to the task of securing one's rights. But can we say that might is right? Constantly rights are invoked against might. People have died to protect their rights against very powerful opponents because they refused to admit that force gives special rights. In fact, when conquering soldiers go around raping women or carrying out ethnic cleansing, no one justifies their acts as being right just because they have the might to carry out these deeds.

The legal view is quite close to the pragmatic. It teaches that a right is a legally created and protected capacity to exercise a privilege. In that case the authority that gives the right is the state which has the power to enforce its will. It can extend new rights, such as affirmative action, and it can withdraw rights from some people. A criminal loses his or her right to freedom, and a reckless driver loses his or her right to drive. However, the same questions can be raised concerning the legal view as were raised concerning the pragmatic one. Revolutions are the deeds of people who are convinced that the state is threatening or neglecting their rights. Thus we cannot identify the source of rights with legal pronouncements.

In the sociological view, rights are acquired in the context of a social contract. Originally, according to this interpretation, the creation of rights resulted from a trade of services. For example, labor and taxes would be given in exchange for police and army protection. Historically the person chosen as the defender of the community had the right to certain services from others in the community. Ultimately these rights became the privileges of the nobility. Today this view is used to indicate that rights arise from promises (or contracts) that employers give to employees, such as the right to have one's job defined or the right to a "just cause" for dismissal.

This view properly calls our attention to the fact that rights reflect a relationship. Certainly a doctor's relationship with a patient is quite different from the same doctor's relationship with a friend. Sometimes in a relationship certain civil rights may be limited if their use interferes with

the attainment of the grantor's objectives. Take, for example, the relationship between the school and the student. In the past, some colleges and
universities did not permit freshmen to have cars on campus until the
end of the first academic year. This was done because it was felt that having easy access to cars conflicted with the acquisition of the discipline of
study required for academic success.

Many thinkers, rather than accepting a pragmatic interpretation of
rights, have advocated for an idealistic view of rights. In this view, rights
are grounded in natural or divine law. They are parts of the moral fabric
of the universe and indissolubly bound with human dignity. People have
rights because they are persons who feel, think, want to worship, and
desire to associate with others without impediment. In the idealistic view,
people sink to the level of animals or machines when they do not have
rights. One must have the freedom of speech because a human being
has ideas and is able to speak. One must have the freedom of association
because he or she is a social being who finds in the company of others the
true dimension of human life.

The study of the creation account shows that God gave rights to his
creatures that enabled them to be truly persons—rights we still consider
to be essential human rights. The first right given is the right of association. Adam and Eve can associate with the serpent; God does not curtail
their freedom of association. Second is freedom of speech. Adam and Eve
can talk to the serpent. Even if Satan's words are lying words, the freedom
of speech is complete. Third, the prohibition to eat the fruit of one tree
certainly suggests a sense of property rights. There are things which are
not ours, available resources which we are not supposed to touch or to
use. The concept of property rights is further enforced by the Old Testament laws which forbade the removal of boundary stones as an attempt to
acquire property that was not one's own (Deut 19:14 and 27:17). Fourth,
the diet of seeds and fruits which God gives to humans does not require
the destruction of plants or the slaughtering of animals. This implies a
respect for life, a concept reinforced in Lev 19:16, which states: "Do not
do anything that endangers your neighbor's life." Finally, Adam and Eve
are essentially free to determine for themselves their relationship to God,
and thus they have religious freedom. In the idealistic view, rights are not
granted by a human authority but have a divine foundation.

EMPLOYEE RIGHTS

How do these various concepts regarding rights operate in today's business environment? As noted above, the usual rights granted to employees include the right of due process and fair treatment; workplace safety and the right to a healthy workplace; the right to privacy in the workplace, including the collection and use of employee information by employers; and fair compensation.

The Right of Due Process and Fair Treatment

There are two conflicting views regarding the employer's right to fire an employee. The first view, known as "employment-at-will," states that either the employer or the employee may terminate the employment contract at any time without giving a reason for termination. This practice does not cover any firings that fall under the discrimination laws of the Civil Rights Act of 1964, nor can an employer fire an employee in violation of a union contract. But just as an employee can leave a job without having to give a reason, so an employer can fire an employee without having to give any reasons.

The other view, known as "good cause" or "due process," states that employees can only be fired for good reasons and these reasons must be documented. This view insists that employees be granted the right to due process and fair treatment, including the opportunity to have an impartial review of any complaints or decisions that are made that are detrimental to the employee. In order to ensure fairness in their employee-related decisions, some companies use an ombudsman or a peer review panel to review any complaints. One of the favorable results of these measures is that companies may experience a decrease in employment-related litigation.[7]

Workplace Health and Safety

Workplace safety hazards usually relate to issues involving physical damage to the employee as a result of either malfunctioning workplace equipment or some physical danger present in the workplace. The International Labour Organization states that work-related accidents and

7. Carroll and Buchholtz, *Business & Society*, 495–502.

diseases cost approximately 3.94 percent of the Global Domestic Product each year. In 2018 they reported 2.78 million work-related deaths and 375 million accidents.[8]

In the United States, the primary government organization charged with workplace safety is the Occupational Safety and Health Administration (OSHA), established by government regulation in 1970. Many of the safety regulations in the United States owe their birth to the Triangle Shirtwaist Factory fire which occurred on March 25, 1911, in Greenwich Village, downtown Manhattan, New York. One hundred and forty-six people died in this fire, primarily because the owners locked the exit doors during working hours and because the factory was located on the eighth, ninth, and tenth floors of the building—beyond the reach of the fire ladders of that day.[9] Following that fire, many safety laws were enacted in an effort to make certain that a similar tragedy would not occur again. Such extensive loss of life did not occur again in New York City until the bombing of the World Trade Center in 2001. However, workplace safety laws are not enacted everywhere around the world, and, unfortunately, the news reports often carry stories of workplace fires and building collapses in other countries, even to this day.

A more recent problem arises with workplace violence, which can come either from outside the workplace or from violence between co-workers. Unfortunately, such violence, which has been job-related in certain industries, appears to be increasing and extending into traditionally safe places, such as schools and theaters. The prevalence of workplace violence is a matter of much political debate in the United States as it is related to the population's views on gun control and the strength of the gun lobby in influencing legislation.

Workplace health issues arise from factors present in the workplace that make people ill because of long-term exposure to unhealthy conditions. Historically these health hazards included black lung disease among miners, silicosis among stone cutters, skin cancer among chimney sweeps, and phosphorus poisoning among matchmakers. More recent workplace hazards include asbestos, various gases, certain chemicals and cigarette smoke. Many of these effects appear only after years on the job, or perhaps not even until the employee retires. As a result, tracing these

8. International Labour Organization, "Safety and Health at Work."

9. Von Drehle, *Triangle*, 48.

effects back directly to the workplace is difficult, and often the business is not blamed for the resulting illness.[10]

Scripture supports the human right to a safe and pleasant environment. At creation, God placed humans in a garden. We can imagine that there were trees, flowers, creeks. The air was pure, the water safe and all was very peaceful. God said that it was very good. Even in a world of sin, God continues to pour out the beauty of the sunset, the refreshing cool of the morning air, the striking display of all the colors of the rainbow, and the many fragrances of flowers and plants. God does not want his creatures to suffer in unpleasant and unsafe working conditions.

Numerous studies[11] have shown that a pleasant physical work environment goes far toward producing a more productive workforce. Employees need good lighting and aeration. Employees cannot function effectively if they are squeezed together; adequate work space is required, as well as well-designed office spaces. Beyond the physical environment, employees need good relationships with coworkers and supervisors, and training and development to do their jobs well.[12] Teresa Amabile's research, composed of experiments, interviews, and surveys, identifies six important work environment practices that boost employee creativity: challenge, freedom, resources, work-group features (specifically diversity), supervisory encouragement, and organizational support.[13]

The Right to Privacy, Including the Collection and Use of Employee Information

While there are laws covering what information the government can collect and use regarding individuals (e.g., the Privacy Act of 1974 and the USA Patriot Act of 2001), there are fewer laws specifically covering what information employers can collect and use regarding their employees. For hiring purposes, businesses will collect personal information that relates to the job, including information required to ensure that the employee is qualified for and can perform the job for which they are

---

10. Boatright, *Ethics and Conduct of Business*, 244–45.

11. Ajala, "Influence of Workplace Environment," 141–49; Haynes, "Evaluation of Impact," 178–95; Ollukkaran and Gunaseelan, "Study of Impact of Work Environment," 71–85.

12. Awan, "Impact of Working Environment," 329–45.

13. Amabile, "How to Kill Creativity," 77–87.

applying. Employers will also collect information required for meeting any government regulations, such as information for taxes, social security, and discrimination reporting.[14] The most common information collected that may be considered questionable in terms of privacy comes from background checks, integrity or other types of personality tests, and drug tests. Information collected on the employee is generally held in the Human Resources Department in the employee's personnel file. This information cannot be said to be the property of either the employer or the employee, as the employer must justify the collection and use of the employee's personal information. However, the employee has relinquished some rights to this information by entering into the employment relationship. Thus exceptional care must be maintained over this information so that it is not misused by either party.[15]

Employers may monitor employee activity on the job, particularly what websites are visited and email content. Still to be decided on a national basis is whether the employee has legal privacy protection with respect to Facebook usernames and passwords, although some states are beginning to enact laws in this area in favor of the employees' privacy.[16] More will be discussed on employer monitoring of employees through the use of technology in chapter 6.

The Right to Fair Compensation

Most people choose to work because the compensation they receive from their employer is needed to meet their own financial obligations. However, once in the workplace, employees often compare their compensation with that received by others in an effort to determine if their compensation is both just and fair. This comparison process often results in questions on the part of the employees and defensiveness on the part of the employers.

From the employer's perspective, compensation includes wages, bonuses, profit sharing arrangements, and benefits, including health care and pensions. Some companies may also offer employee stock options. The level of compensation selected may also reflect the company's strategy with respect to employee retention. Some companies may pay less

14. Boatright, *Ethics and Conduct of Business*, 149–51.

15. Boatright, *Ethics and Conduct of Business*, 152.

16. Carroll and Buchholtz, *Business & Society*, 517–28.

and hire a large number of part-time employees because turnover is not considered to be detrimental to the company's business (e.g., Walmart), while other companies may pay higher wages in order to retain experienced staff to better serve the hopefully repetitive customer (e.g., Starbucks).[17]

From an economic perspective, wages are set by the market, with labor being one input into the productive process, in the same manner as materials and equipment are inputs into the process. Under this perspective, a shortfall of desired labor (which may be influenced by the population growth or by the need for educated and/or experienced employees) will increase the price offered for labor, whereas a surplus of workers (especially a surplus of unskilled labor) will result in a lower price for this input into the production process. For the economist, workers are considered to be free to choose the most lucrative employment possible. In fact, this may not always be true because workers may not be able to move to wherever the market is offering the best compensation. As a result, the question of justice in compensation arises. Most governments answer the question of a sticky labor market with legislation mandating a minimum wage to be paid for labor, hoping that a legislated minimum wage will provide a living wage.

Scripture supports the concept of justice with respect to compensation. The Hebrew economy was an agricultural society where one's livelihood was often dependent on the daily provisions provided to the worker. Accordingly, the people were instructed to pay their worker's wages each day "because he is poor and is counting on it" (Lev 19:13; Deut 24:14–15). Likewise, when dealing with others in business transactions, the Hebrews were forbidden to secure a loan with any item that was needed to sustain life, such as clothing needed to keep a person warm while sleeping (Exod 22:26–27), or a millstone required to grind the grain so that food could be obtained (Deut 24:6).

Executive compensation for the CEO and other top corporate officers has drawn special ethical attention over the past few years in the United States. In an effort to obtain data on the pay of the chief executive as compared to the median compensation of other employees in the company, the 2010 Dodd-Frank banking regulation law included a provision that publicly-traded corporations in the United States must reveal their pay ratios. This law went into effect in 2017. As reported in the *New York*

17. Boatright, *Ethics and Conduct of Business*, 225.

Times, an employee at Walmart "earning the company's median salary of $19,177 would have to work for more than a thousand years to earn the $22.2 million that Doug McMillon, the company's chief executive, was awarded in 2017."[18] While this ratio is startling, the article warned that the newly-available information was incomplete and perhaps inaccurate because not all companies reported their pay ratios, and some companies relied on overseas workers who receive significantly lower pay than workers in the United States. For example, Mattel, a toy company, employs workers in overseas factories, resulting in a pay ratio for the CEO of 4,987 times that of the median employee, while Incyte, a drug maker, outsources its factory work and has a small, highly-paid domestic work force, resulting in a pay ratio of 64 times.[19]

The median pay for CEOs for the 100 largest companies in 2017 was $15.7 million, up from the previous high in 2016 of $15 million. This is 235 times the salary of the median paid worker in these companies.[20] By way of contrast, in the 1950s, the ratio between CEO pay and that of a typical worker was about 20 to 1.[21] Since CEO pay is approximately one-third cash, one-half stock and stock options, and the remainder composed of pensions and perks, the relationship between CEO pay and the average worker's pay fluctuates, depending on the stock market. When the stock market is high, the difference between CEO pay and the worker's pay is higher than when the stock market has tumbled, as it did in 2008.

Usually the justification for high CEO pay is that it encourages the CEO to align his or her goals with those of the company. Critics state, however, that CEOs who focus on high stock prices for their companies are focusing on the short-term instead of the long-term, which is ultimately detrimental to the organization. These critics often point to the bad behaviors exhibited by the CEOs of Enron and WorldCom as examples of short-term strategies used to obtain high stock prices, which ultimately led to fraudulent financial reporting.[22] Other critics argue that the current practice of buying back their own stock, which raises the price of the stock and increases the company's earnings per share, results in pleas-

18. Gelles, "Want to Make Money?," para. 1.

19. Gelles, "Want to Make Money?," para. 11–12.

20. McGregor, "Median CEO Pay," para. 5.

21. Koehn, "Great Men," para. 2.

22. Boatright, *Ethics and the Conduct of Business*, 230–31.

ing the market without changing the actual earnings of the corporation. These critics note that money spent on stock buy-backs might better have been invested in research and development for new products and growing the company's markets, thus focusing on the long-term health of the company. A focus on the short-term stock price benefits the stockholders and the CEO's pay, but not the future of the organization or the job security of the average worker.[23]

Nancy Koehn, a historian at Harvard Business School, argues that CEO pay "rests on the Great Man theory of history, a school of thought that attributes virtually all important developments through time to heroic individuals."[24] This theory, initially made popular by Thomas Carlyle in the mid-nineteenth century, has been strengthened by the media's attention to individuals in business, sports, and Hollywood, and its recognition of these people through such mediums as *Time* magazine's Man of the Year award (e.g., Ted Turner [1992], Jeff Bezos [1999], and Mark Zuckerberg [2010]). In fact, success in any endeavor, whether a sports team, a successful movie, or a corporation, requires many people working together to achieve the desired result. From the perspective of the Great Man theory, one individual, usually the CEO, is given the credit and compensation, with the tacit understanding that he or she was the sole driver, and therefore the primary beneficiary, of the corporation's financial achievement. When one person is given the credit for the work that the group has done, it is possible to overrate that person's contribution, and thus assign to one person the accolades and rewards that perhaps should be more equally distributed. The human tendency to gather offered rewards to oneself because of greed or selfishness can make it difficult to refuse rewards when praise is heaped on one individual rather than the team.

Scripture speaks harsh words to the rich who engage in greed, enjoy big houses and lush vineyards while the poor go hungry (Amos 5:11–12; Jer 22:13), or who have failed to pay the workmen their wages in order to live in self-indulgence (Jas 5:1–6). James states: "Your wealth has rotted, and moths have eaten your clothes. Your gold and silver are corroded. Their corrosion will testify against you and eat your flesh like fire" (Jas 5:2–3). Deuteronomy cautions: "Do not take advantage of a hired worker

23. Brill, *Tailspin*, 60–63.
24. Koehn, "Great Men," para. 5.

who is poor and needy, whether that worker is a fellow Israelite or a foreigner residing in one of your towns" (Deut 24:14).

Robert J. Samuelson would add his own critique. He states:

> But they [CEOs] have contrived a moral code that exempts them from self-control—a moral code that justified grabbing as much as they can. They unduly enrich themselves at shareholders' expense and set a bad leadership example. Because almost everyone else sees their code as self-serving and selfish, CEOs have undermined their moral standing and their ability to be taken seriously on other issues. They are slowly becoming a threat to the very system they claim to represent.[25]

THE DIGNITY OF WORK

Scripture also sheds light on the role of work in the lives of those God created. In the garden of Eden, God gave his new creatures both authority and responsibility. They were to have dominion over the realm of creation and they were to maintain the garden in which they had been placed. Thus authority was balanced with responsibility. In the biblical perspective, work is a major expression of human dignity. In the context of Genesis, work is a gift of God to mankind, not a punishment or a chore. It is a provision for the use of talents and creativity that has an immense impact on human growth. It is also a command (Exod 20:9).

This understanding is very important in the business world. The creation account sweeps away any concept of different levels of dignity of workers. Work is more than a necessity to provide food, lodging, and raiment. It is the arena in which the worker develops his or her capacity for achievement and responsibility. What gives dignity to a laborer is not whether he or she works with their hands or at a desk, but whether they are faithful or not. In the parable of the talents, the one who has developed five talents receives the same commendation as the one who has developed ten talents. The rebuke to the one who had received only one talent is due to his failure to use it (Matt 25:14–29).

In the creation account the work that is given is work God values, that is, manual work. God worked the clay with his hands and Adam also worked with his hands. This is particularly significant since historically manual work has been considered as very inferior. Plato placed manual

25. Samuelson, "Delinquency of CEOs."

workers at the very bottom of the social ladder. During the Middle Ages, society was divided between nobility, clergy and serfs. The serfs were the ones who did manual work and were looked upon as having no dignity. In some countries in Europe, the nobility refused to allow their children to be baptized in the same water as the common workers because of the view that those who worked with their hands were in some manner inferior people.

Equal dignity, however, does not mean that all are gifted with the same talents. There are people who have unique gifts of intelligence, creativity, and energy. Because of their capacity to inspire, they can lead others. They seem to revel in juggling problems and can take a failing company and make it successful. Where others see insurmountable obstacles, they find opportunities. There are also different levels of responsibility. Some workers can punch a clock at 9 a.m. and at 5 p.m. and go home to do whatever they please. Others must stay late in the office and bring work home for the weekend. These have not the weight of one machine but of an entire enterprise on their shoulders. Some have to answer only to a foreman; other have to deal with the state, the stockholders, the community, the employees, and with the retired workers. Recognizing the equal dignity of all does not require equal remuneration. A true Christian can recognize multi-talented individuals and rejoice in their success without losing his or her self-esteem, because they know that in the end they will be judged on the basis of their faithful use of the talents they had and not on the position they reached.

In the creation story we also find the characteristics of the work which God planned for his creatures. It involved much more than getting a paycheck. It was creative work, not a mind-numbing repetitive task. It called for imagination and decision. It required a sense of responsibility. It resulted in a sense of satisfaction and achievement. It is the responsibility and the challenge of a Christian manager to organize work in such a way that when it is completed, the worker can say: "It is good."

Through the institution of the Sabbath we discover the most unique characteristic of the biblical concept of work. Man must dominate his work, not be ruled by it. One's attitude toward work must be such that it can be interrupted for a totally different and indispensable experience, the experience of communion with God, the experience of worship. The Sabbath is the concrete expression of Jesus' famous saying: "Man cannot live by bread alone" (Matt 4:4). The Sabbath provides a stringent condemnation of individuals who are workaholics. No one can be totally obsessed with his or her work and live. Even the most successful person will eventually wither away if he or she spends all their existence on the horizontal level. To be a worker according to God's will, one must inject the vertical dimension into his or her life. The labor of the week must lead to the joyfulness of the Sabbath.

Mankind has responded to God's gift of the stewardship of the earth by using and abusing nature to their own glory and as a resource which supports their achievements. To a large extent, business reflects this same response through the use of natural and human resources to generate commerce and economic activity in all of its forms, with the end goal of making a profit. Abraham Joshua Heschel, in his book *The Sabbath*, describes how humans have focused on the creation of things to fill space.[26] Perhaps that is to be expected, since at creation mankind was given the task of subduing the earth (Gen 1:28). But this focus results in a worship of things, even to the extent where we are willing to trade time for things. The Sabbath is a reminder that God saw the gift of time—the gift of the Sabbath—as the capstone of creation.

Back in the 1950s and early 1960s the labor-saving devices which had then been recently invented for the home and factory were promised to guarantee excessive quantities of leisure time in the immediate future. There were published expectations that everyone would probably only work twenty-five to thirty hours a week, with the remaining hours being available for leisure. The question for the philosophers and futurists was: What would the population do with such a large quantity of leisure time?

Today we know that there was no need to be so concerned. What we have done is trade away all the expected leisure time for more work and greater pay, so we can afford more and more things. In his book *Sabbath: Finding Rest, Renewal, and Delight in Our Busy Lives*, Wayne Muller notes:

> In 1947, the average American adult spent $6,500 on material possessions, goods, and services. Today [1999], adjusted for inflation, we spend an average of over $14,000 per adult. We spend twice as much for a larger house, and fill it with twice as many appliances, cars, clothes and televisions. When we are not using our time to get money, we are using time to spend money. Compared to Europeans, American spend three to four times as many hours per year shopping. Shopping has become a primary use of leisure time. With our few remaining free hours

26. Heschel, *Sabbath*, 3.

we scurry about in monstrous malls where we spend on goods and services we secretly hope will bring us peace, nourishment, or relief.[27]

Heschel notes that as humans we are "infatuated with the splendor of space, with the grandeur of things of space."[28] As a result, we spend our lives, our time, our efforts, and our labor on things which can be seen and touched. We have allowed work to rule our lives; we quickly trade time for things. In fact, in the business world we insist that "time is money" and we describe not being productive in terms of things as a "waste of time." We refer to people who have a lot of money and no time as being "rich" while we describe people who have a great deal of time but no money as "poor." We do not know what to do with time except, as Heschel says, "to make it subservient to space."[29]

In the Sabbath, God gave us time so that we would not be ruled by things of space, but would always have time for relationships with other humans and with God. God refused to associate himself with things of space, but always insisted on being present in time. The Bible tells us the history of God's dealings with people through the description of events in which he acted, not in describing a specific geographic location where he resided. Heschel notes that the first time the word *qadosh* (or holy) is used in the Bible is when it is applied to a day—to time—to the Sabbath. Only later, when the word is applied to the tabernacle in the wilderness, is it used to denote a holy place. Heschel further describes the Sabbath as a "palace in time" and notes:

> Three acts of God denoted the seventh day: He rested, He blessed and He hallowed the seventh day (Gen 2:2–3). To the prohibition of labor is, therefore, added the blessing of delight and the accent of sanctity. Not only the hands of man celebrate the day, the tongue and the soul keep the Sabbath. . . . The seventh day is a palace in time which we build. It is made of soul, of joy, and reticence. In its atmosphere, a discipline is a reminder of adjacency to eternity.[30]

27. Muller, *Sabbath: Finding Rest*, 99.

28. Heschel, *Sabbath*, 5.

29. Heschel, *Sabbath*, 5.

30. Heschel, *Sabbath*, 14–15.

THE BIBLE AND THE USE OF RIGHTS

In the Old Testament, rights, however sacred they were, always had to be used in the context of the needs of others. For instance, property rights were not an absolute. Owners had to recognize the needs of those who did not own property. "When you reap the harvest of your land, do not reap to the very edges of your field. . . . Leave them for the poor and the alien" (Lev 19:9–10). The Hebrew was prohibited from greedily extracting everything possible from his property. Some of it was to be shared with the indigents. That attitude is the result of acknowledging the fact that whatever we have comes from God. It is a public recognition of the reality of the unity of all human beings as children of God. It is also an expression of the responsibility to care for others. Where God's will is understood, no one can feel totally isolated.

God taught the true dimension of property by the institution of the tithe. The Hebrew people were commanded to give a tenth of all their profit to the temple personnel. That reminded them of God's right when they enjoyed their rights. Their income was not exclusively their own. Part of it must be returned to God.

In his letter to the church at Corinth, Paul stated that our rights must be used responsibly and that we must take into consideration the effect of our actions upon others. His counsel is given in the context of discussing eating the meat of animals that had been offered in sacrifices in the temples and was then sold for general consumption. He stated: "Everything is permissible but not everything is beneficial. . . . If an unbeliever invites you to a meal, eat whatever is put before you without raising questions of conscience. But if anyone says to you, 'This has been offered in sacrifice' . . . then do not eat it both for the sake of the man who told you and for conscience' sake. . . . Do not cause anyone to stumble" (1 Cor 10:27–33). Paul shows great concern for the weaker brother, the new convert who wants nothing to do with his old lifestyle, or the man who is easily led astray by the attraction of his past pagan ways. Seeing a respected Christian eating the meat offered to idols will scandalize the new member or encourage the one who is fighting the temptation to yield. While eating that meat has no religious or moral significance, it is of great import for those who are weak in the faith (1 Cor 10:23–33).

For fear of being misunderstood, Paul did not use some of his rights as an apostle. Because he knew that some questioned his motives for becoming a Christian and suggested that he left the synagogue for the remuneration he would receive as a minister of the new faith, he worked as a tentmaker to earn his living rather than depend upon the support of the church. As he tells the Corinthians, he did not want any to be able to say that this crafty fellow had taken advantage of them (2 Cor 12:13–18).

To the same group Paul suggested that rather than going to court against a brother, it was better to be wronged. "The very fact that you have lawsuits among you means you have been completely defeated already. Why not rather be wronged? Why not rather be cheated?" (1 Cor 6:7–8).

In the Sermon on the Mount Jesus made it clear that we must not be guided by the spirit of the courtroom and its insistence upon enforcing our rights. Referring to the Old Testament precept, "An eye for an eye and a tooth for a tooth," Jesus said: "Do not resist an evil person. If someone strikes you on the right cheek, turn to him the other also. And if someone wants to sue you and take your tunic, let him have your cloak as well. If someone forces you to go one mile, go with him two miles. Give to him who asks you, and do not turn away from one who wants to borrow from you" (Matt 5:36–42).

In this passage Jesus mentioned several situations where one's personal rights were invaded and one might have felt like fighting for one's due. Scripture offered: "An eye for an eye and a tooth for a tooth" (Exod 21:24) as a basic principle of justice. The penalty must be proportionate to the offense. It is the epitome of the spirit of the courtroom. For the Romans, the great legislators, it was "To each his own."

Jesus was not demanding that his followers be wimps. He was not afraid to speak his mind and to refuse to grant his opponents' demands. He uncovered their wicked intentions, their pride, and their arrogance. They knew what God expected from them. As religious leaders they betrayed their sacred responsibilities. Jesus uttered frightening woes upon them. There is nothing dishonest in seeking "one's own," but Jesus does not want his followers to be controlled by the spirit of the courtroom.

The people whom Jesus had in mind in this passage were most likely people who did not know God. They may have been soldiers or thugs who believed that might made right. They knew nothing about a loving Father in heaven. They expressed what their nature demanded—the love of control and their greed. Fighting with them with the adversarial spirit of the courtroom would only lead to greater damage. Jesus advocated the attitude of goodwill, of conciliation. He urged the spirit of God who sheds the rain on the just and the unjust. Resistance would be of little avail, but goodwill may touch hearts and change things. Perchance an enemy may become a friend.

When a Christian has the choice of either destroying an enemy or attempting to make a friend, he or she will always try to make a friend, even if it entails some personal loss. The Christian knows that their Heavenly Father will more than make up for the loss. Thus, this passage urges us to display the power of love rather than the authority of law.

It is of extreme importance, however, to note that it is Paul who decided when to use his freedom and when not to use it. It was the owner of the field who decided where not to reap. It is the wronged individual in Jesus' illustrations who chooses his or her actions. It was Aaron Feuerstein who made the decision to remain in Massachusetts rather than moving his company overseas, and to keep his employees on the payroll while the factory was being rebuilt. It was his right to take the insurance money and retire. No one would have faulted his decision. In the years since the fire, many have criticized Feuerstein for his business decision because in the end, he lost control of Malden Mills to its creditors, and even though the company has survived, it is no longer his company. When asked, however, Feuerstein credits his decision to his belief in Jewish law. He said: "I have a responsibility to the worker, both blue-collar and white-collar. I have an equal responsibility to the community. It would have been unconscionable to put 3,000 people on the streets and deliver a deathblow to the cities of Lawrence and Methuen. . . . I think it was a wise business decision, but that isn't why I did it. I did it because it was the right thing to do."[31]

The use and the non-use of one's rights can never be forced upon anyone. In many ways, the decision not to use one's freedom is the supreme expression of being truly free, and no one has the right to impinge upon that! Jesus wants his followers to be truly free when it comes to rights and possessions, free to surrender them, especially if that is the way to create a new relationship, or when we believe that it is the right thing to do. This perspective summons us to demonstrate the spirit of the Heavenly Father.

31. Kile, "Feuerstein."

THINKING IT THROUGH: THE MALDEN MILLS CASE

While the case of Aaron Feuerstein and Malden Mills demonstrates a well-recognized decision that is considered to be admirably ethical, the issue of what responsibilities employers have to their employees continues to raise ethical questions and stimulate considerable discussion on the part of both employers and employees.

The utilitarian is likely to question Aaron Feuerstein's thinking process when he decided to rebuild his factories in Massachusetts. While recognizing that a move would be unfortunate for the town of Lawrence, the utilitarian would argue that the benefit to all of his customers and stockholders around the world would have been greater if he had immediately moved to a lower-cost area. If he had done so, his customers would have been able to obtain his products at a lower cost, and probably more quickly because the factories might have been restored at a faster pace than in Massachusetts, given the immense clean-up and other necessary steps to rebuild at the same location. If business could be restored faster, higher profits would likely be realized. In addition, a move would have permitted Feuerstein to bring employment opportunities to another location, which would have benefitted the economy in another locale, thus merely trading benefits in one place against losses in Lawrence. Finally, rebuilding his factory in Lawrence resulted in considerable debt, which ultimately cost him control of his own company. How did that outcome benefit anyone, except perhaps the creditors?

Kant would argue that Aaron Feuerstein made the ethical decision because he followed the categorical imperative that we choose the actions that mirror how we want others to act. He treated his employees as he would choose to be treated; he saved the jobs for his loyal workers; he kept the company in a town where he had found a home over the years; he rebuilt his factory and while the rebuilding process was taking place, he provided for the livelihood of his employees. The fact that ultimately the debt he incurred would cost him the control of his company was immaterial to the ethical decision he made immediately after the fire.

To be honorable in business, the Christian worldview would applaud Feuerstein's decision to practice the Golden Rule with respect to his employees and the town where he lived. Recognizing that he experienced a high personal cost as a result of his decision would, for the Christian, make his decision more ethically admirable. However, like Feuerstein, the potential for a personally unfavorable end would not be a part of the initial consideration undertaken when the decision was made.

Chapter 4

What If He Is Really Handsome—or Not?

Workplace Discrimination and Sexual Harassment

Every human being, of whatever origin, of whatever station, deserves respect. We must each respect others, even as we respect ourselves.

—RALPH WALDO EMERSON

DISCRIMINATION IS "ANY ACT or failure to act . . . that adversely affects privileges, benefits, working conditions, or results in less favorable effects for one group than another or inconsistent application of rules and policies to one group over another."[1] In the United States, certain classes of employees are considered to be potentially at risk for discriminatory actions by others, particularly in business situations. Individuals in these classes are therefore protected by the Civil Rights Act of 1964 from discriminatory actions based on their race, color, religion, sex, national origin, age, or mental or physical disability.[2] Thus, in the United States both discrimination and sexual harassment, which is included under the Civil Rights Act, are illegal.

Despite the illegality of discrimination for more than fifty years, in early 2014 a lawsuit brought by George McReynolds and 1,400 other

1. *Merriam-Webster*, s.v. "discrimination."
2. Equal Employment Opportunity Program, "EEO Terminology."

black brokers against Merrill Lynch for discrimination was settled in favor of the plaintiffs for $160 million, the largest cash award in a racial bias employment case. McReynolds and his fellow black brokers composed only 2 percent of Merrill's full brokers and had smaller books of business. Merrill Lynch argued that this allotment of employment and business was a reflection of society—i.e., white brokers had stronger and richer social networks from which to draw business. McReynolds argued that Merrill Lynch compounded the problem by forming teams to boost their books of business and that black brokers were less likely to be asked to join the teams. In addition, when brokers left the firm, Merrill transferred more of and the better accounts of those who left to the remaining white brokers rather than to black brokers, even if the white brokers were newer to the firm.

In 2011, in a lawsuit related to the outcome of the McReynolds case, the US Supreme Court ruled against the plaintiffs in the *Dukes v. Walmart* discrimination lawsuit, stating that Walmart's corporate headquarters could not be responsible for actions by individual managers across the wide Walmart network of stores. This ruling put a damper on class action suits, leaving it up to individuals who suffer from discriminatory actions by an employer to fight the employer on their own. Therefore, the ruling of the Seventh Circuit Court of Appeals that the McReynolds class action suit could go forward was a breakthrough, even though the court did not rule as to whether Merrill Lynch's policies were in fact unequal—a matter to be decided by another trial. Following this ruling however Merrill Lynch decided to proceed with a record out-of-court settlement. In addition to the settlement, Merrill Lynch agreed to adjust how the firm distributes accounts to trainees and create new coaches for black brokers, a process to be overseen by a committee of black brokers, including McReynolds.

While McReynolds noted that the preliminary settlement was announced around the fiftieth anniversary of Martin Luther King Jr.'s "I Have a Dream" speech, the fact that fifty years had passed since the Civil Rights movement was itself evidence that even though discrimination is illegal in the United States, there are still continuing issues of discrimination in the workplace.[3]

---

3. Weise, "Judge Approves Merrill Lynch Settlement."

DISCRIMINATION AND THE CHRISTIAN

As noted in chapter 3, rights are gifts of God given to all humans when he created mankind in his image, thus granting every human being dignity, and requiring that each should be treated with respect. It was in the garden of Eden that God gave his creatures fundamental rights, including the right to determine their course of action, to associate with others, freedom of speech, a basic sense of property rights, religious freedom (i.e., the right to determine for themselves their relationship to God), and respect for life.

For a Christian, discrimination in all of its forms is wrong because it is the denial of rights granted to humans at creation. It is evidence of the failure to reflect God's concern for all his creatures. It is a transgression of the Golden Rule that commands us to treat others as we wish to be treated. It is a negation of the new order that the gospel has brought into the world, which makes it quite clear that there is no difference in the value or worth of any person, irrespective of gender, ethnicity, or status in life (Gal 3:26–29). It fails to follow God's command in Mic 6:8: "What does the Lord require of you but to do justice." While the Christian recognizes that people have varying degrees of attractiveness, intelligence, and social appeal, the Christian also remembers that all humans depend upon divine compassion and grace for success. Love often transforms the unlovely into human jewels and brings out of the unpromising rich potential and much talent. It is with this perspective that a Christian businessperson deals with other human beings.

The most eloquent witness to God's concern for rights are his demands for justice. The idea of justice appears over eight hundred times in Scripture. As he addresses the judges of Israel, God commands: "Justice and only justice you shall follow" (Deut 16:20). In a prayer for the king, David says: "Give the king thy justice, O God" (Ps 72:1–2). Isaiah states: "The Lord loves justice" (Isa 61:8) and describes God as "the Lord is a God of justice" (Isa 30:18). God's demand for justice includes both condemnation for the perpetrator and vindication of the one who has been wronged. "Oh Lord, you have seen this; be not silent. Do not be far from me, O Lord. Awake, and rise to my defense. Contend for me, my God and Lord. Vindicate me in your righteousness, O Lord my God" (Ps 35:22–24). God's justice is not satisfied with merely stopping evil. It also seeks restoration.

God's concern for the respect of human rights took its supreme expression in the frequently reiterated command to protect the rights of the weak, and in particular, those who are not automatically protected by the laws or practices of a society's economic system. "Cursed," the law said, "be the man who withholds justice from the alien, the fatherless or the widow" (Deut 27:19). The alien, the fatherless, and the widow were, in the Hebrew economy, those who lacked land and the protective care of the family. As such, they were the ones most likely to be mistreated. When Job pleads that he is righteous, he says, "Whoever heard me spoke well of me, and those who saw me commended me, because I rescued the poor who cried for help, and the fatherless who had none to assist him. . . . I was eyes to the blind and feet to the lame. I was a father to the needy, I took up the case of the stranger" (Job 29:11–16).

This is very significant because it explains the most amazing characteristic of divine justice. It is exercised especially on behalf of those who cannot secure their rights—the poor, the weak, the widows, the orphans, the strangers. In biblical times, just as in our times, there were many venal judges. "You oppress the righteous and take bribes and you deprive the poor of justice in the courts" (Amos 5:12). In a message to the king of Judah, Jeremiah said: "This is what the Lord says: Do what is just and right. Rescue from the hand of the oppressor the one who has been robbed. Do no wrong or violence to the alien, the fatherless or the widow and do not shed innocent blood in this place" (Jer 22:3–4). God is the champion of the weak and he wants his children to follow his example. It is not a case of "God is on the side of the poor," but God is on the side of all who are wronged. In our society those wronged within our economic system may indeed be poor, but they may also be of a different ethnicity, race, gender, age, or possess diminished physical capacity, as compared with the predominant population. God's call to justice, especially for those who cannot secure their rights in our courts or within our economic system, must surely be those for whom God requires of us to "do what is just and right." Discrimination against others, fueled by one's prejudice or fear or ignorance, is not just. Thus, acting in a discriminatory manner is inappropriate for the Christian.

THE CIVIL RIGHTS ACT OF 1964

While the US Constitution speaks against discrimination in various amendments (e.g., the First, Fifth, and the Fourteenth) and through various laws over the years, the most effective law against discrimination was the Civil Rights Act of 1964. This law prohibited employment discrimination on the basis of race, religion, sex, color, or national origin. Until the 1960s, members of racial minorities in some parts of the United States had to ride in different sections of a bus. They could not drink at the same water fountains or eat in the same restaurants as those of the majority race. They were not received at the same hospitals and could not buy homes wherever they wanted to in a town. As for women, discrimination in business meant a glass ceiling above which they could not rise, and they were generally treated as inferior workers. In many male minds, women were not considered to be suited for managerial positions because traditional wisdom had decreed that women could not manage or handle money. For example, banks often refused to extend credit to women until, in 1974, the US Senate passed the Equal Credit Opportunity Act, which made it illegal to discriminate against someone based on their gender, race, religion, and national origin with respect to granting credit cards. The next year the first women's bank was opened—a bank operated by women and for women.[4]

Following the passage of the Civil Rights Act of 1964, additional anti-discrimination laws were passed in 1967 (Age Discrimination in Employment Act), 1978 (Pregnancy Discrimination Act), 1990 (Americans with Disabilities Act), and 1993 (Family and Medical Leave Act).[5] These laws reflected increasing sensitivity to the labor force issues that have arisen over the last forty years, as more women entered the workforce and as the work force aged, particularly due to the aging baby boomer generation. The US Bureau of Labor Statistics predicts that for the ten-year period, 2012–2022, the US labor force will continue to age and will be more diverse in racial and ethnic composition than it is today.[6] The increased diversity within the labor force will likely put continuing pressure on business to closely monitor their actions with respect to discriminatory behaviors.

4. Eveleth, "Forty Years Ago."

5. Jones and George, *Essentials of Contemporary Management*, 392.

6. Toossi, "Labor Force Projections 2022."

DISCRIMINATION AND CULTURE

Discrimination results from the blinding power of culture and the stereotypes and attitudes it so easily fosters within us. For example, it is very difficult for many people to abandon the idea that a woman's place is in the home.[7] On that basis, women were not promoted because it was assumed that for a woman, work was a transitory stage between school and motherhood and that it was a waste of money to train women for serious responsibilities. For a long time women were excluded from many professions because it was not ladylike to do certain types of work. Many males believed that "the weaker sex" (as women were stereotypically called), could not put in a real day of work. These stereotypes began to fall in the late 1960s. For example, in 1969 in the case of *Bowe v. Colgate-Palmolive*, the court ruled that Colgate-Palmolive could not restrict women to specific jobs in order to "protect" them, but that any restrictions (in this case, a thirty-five-pound weight-lifting limit) must be applied equally to both men and women.[8]

There is no need to repeat the false generalizations that foster prejudice against members of other racial groups. This contempt of the dominant group for outsiders who are different from themselves is as old as the world itself and is often reinforced by cultural attitudes and practices. It is a characteristic of the self-centered mode of living. The Greeks looked down upon the Barbarians, the Jews upon the Samaritans and the Gentiles. Unfortunately, it is still common all over the world. For example, when a shop owner in Istanbul was recently asked by the author why all the rug weavers were women who worked in the back of the shop, but all the salespeople were men who worked in the front of the store and met the general public, the response was that women pay more attention to detail than men and thus are better suited to do the weaving. No reason was provided for why such attention to detail would not also be a valuable attribute for salespeople.

Tragically, religion has too often nurtured discrimination. It is in the name of Scripture that many chain a woman to the home and the family and refuse to let her use her talents in responsible positions. The words of the gospel have historically been used to justify pogroms and contempt for Jews.

---

7. Clark and Barry, "Business Ethics," 134–52.

8. *Bowe v. Colgate.*

Prejudice distorts our impressions. For instance, in evaluating a manager, a person who does not believe that it is a woman's place to be in management will state that a male manager is decisive; the woman who has the same quality, however, is bossy. He is enthusiastic; she is too emotional. He is good at details; she is picky. He tells you clearly what he thinks; she is too outspoken. He is confident; she is conceited.[9] Such attitudes may affect the words used, not only in evaluations but also in every day conversation. In her book *Lean In*, Sheryl Sandberg, chief operating officer of Facebook, notes:

> Men have an easier time finding the mentors and sponsors who are invaluable for career progression. Plus, women have to prove themselves to a far greater extent than men do. And this is not just in our heads. A 2011 McKinsey report noted that men are promoted based on potential, while women are promoted based on past accomplishments.[10]

Sandberg's book, which topped the *New York Times* and Amazon bestseller lists shortly after its publication in 2013, focuses more on the internal barriers to equality in the workplace that women display than the external barriers traditionally assumed. Sandberg discusses how women may sabotage themselves through their assumptions about and actions in the workplace. In her words:

> We hold ourselves back in ways both big and small, by lacking self-confidence, by not raising our hands, and by pulling back when we should be leaning in. We internalize the negative messages we get throughout our lives—the messages that say it's wrong to be outspoken, aggressive, more powerful than men. We lower our own expectations of what we can achieve.[11]

Sandberg argues that women today, in what she considers to be the third generation of working women since the Civil Rights Act of 1964, should recognize that excuses and justifications must be put aside and women must take a seat at the table if they want to succeed professionally. In her view, discrimination against women will not change until there are more women in power who will then speak up and bring the needs and concerns of all into focus. As an illustration of her point, she shares a personal experience of being asked by Facebook to seek funding for the

9. Ragins et al., "Gender Gap," 28–42.

10. Sandberg, *Lean In*, 8.

11. Sandberg, *Lean In*, 8.

company from a private equity firm in New York. After providing an overview of the company at the equity firm's Manhattan office and answering the initial questions, it was suggested that the group take a break. Sandberg turned to the senior partner of the equity firm and asked him where the women's restroom was. "He stared at me blankly. My question had completely stumped him. I asked, 'How long have you been in this office?' And he said, 'One year.' 'Am I the only woman to have pitched a deal here in an entire year?' 'I think so,' he said, adding, 'or maybe you're the only one who had to use the bathroom.'"[12] What Sandberg illustrates about the need to sensitize the majority population to women's roles in the workplace is a comment on the necessity for more inclusion of all minority groups at the power table in order to achieve more equity in business circles.

Discrimination today is not generally the result of *overt* gender bias or racism, as was true in the past, primarily because of the Civil Rights Act of 1964 and subsequent laws within the United States. It can, however, stem from what a psychologist has called "the comfort zone" complex. Often, after a meal in an Anglo-Saxon home, the men tend to gather in one corner of the living room and the women in another corner. Likewise, people who have dreamed of the end of segregation have often been chagrined that, even though segregation is officially banned, people of the same race tend to sit together in meetings and public places. They do that because they feel more at ease in their comfort zone. With members of your own gender or your ethnic or cultural group, you can interpret body language far more easily. You can empathize with concerns and reactions. Of course, the coziest zone of comfort is found among relatives and friends. If this coziness is brought into hiring decisions in the workplace, it is called nepotism—the practice of favoring friends and relatives with jobs and other workplace benefits. This is an intolerable practice when making employment decisions. The comfort zone cannot be used to justify discrimination.

A new twist on the comfort zone phenomenon is explained by Nancy DiTomaso in her book *The American Non-Dilemma: Racial Inequality Without Racism.* DiTomaso interviewed 246 white men and women to learn how they obtained their jobs. She found that they got their jobs through relatives, friends, or acquaintances—and most of those connections were with people of the same race as the person getting the job. As

12. Sandberg, *Lean In*, 6–7.

a result, individuals who were hired mirrored the ethnicity of those who presently held positions in the organization.[13] This practice of providing job opportunities and job growth because of ethnic similarity is exactly what McReynolds noted in the policies of Merrill Lynch in the opening story. One must remember that the definition of discrimination includes giving less favorable opportunities to others who differ in race or ethnicity, even if there was no overt intent to discriminate. To counteract this very real tendency, many businesses require interviews for open positions to include people of all ethnic and racial backgrounds. Other businesses carefully monitor their policies to be certain that opportunities are equally available to all.

Another almost unconscious act of discrimination may arise through the exclusion of others who are different from ourselves in social gatherings. Often this arises because we socialize most generally in our "comfort zone." In the workplace, however, social groups may form almost spontaneously to celebrate various occasions, such as birthdays, work anniversaries, and family-related announcements such as an upcoming wedding or the birth of a child. When such occasions occur, careful attention to including all appropriate parties, irrespective of their race or ethnicity or gender, should be considered. The potential for social discrimination is, in many ways, more stressful than outright discrimination, because it is unjustified. People do not want only legal admission; they also crave genuine acceptance.

UPWARD MOBILITY AND THE GLASS CEILING

Beliefs and practices that result in inequality, whether based on gender, race, or ethnicity, underuse the talent of the majority of individuals in the available labor pool. This leads to a second ethical issue: the issue of upward mobility. When all potential employees take the same paths of education and work experience to prepare themselves to be qualified candidates for upward career mobility, it is unjust to stand in their way. It is also unwise to refuse to allow a diversity of workers into one's company if one is serious about understanding the diversity of customers one wishes to woo with products and services.

A subtle form of discrimination with respect to upward mobility is known as the "glass ceiling." As noted above, since the passage of the Civil

13. DiTomaso, *American Non-Dilemma*, 30–45.

Rights Act in 1964, it has been illegal in the United States to discriminate in employment on the basis of race, ethnicity, or gender. Subsequent amendments to the original act have strengthened its antidiscrimination provisions. The Glass Ceiling Act of 1991 specifically addressed the underrepresentation of women and minorities in management and decision-making positions. Webster defines the "glass ceiling" as "an intangible barrier within a hierarchy that prevents women or minorities from obtaining upper level positions."[14] The Glass Ceiling Commission 1995 report concluded that "a glass ceiling exists and . . . operates substantially to exclude minorities and women from the top levels of management."[15]

There are several reasons why the glass ceiling is not a wise practice beyond the ethical issues of equality and upward mobility and the illegality of discrimination. First, it makes good business sense to have the largest possible pool from which to recruit employees. Women in most Western countries have similar education and skills as men, and therefore offer similar job qualifications. Recruitment from only half the pool limits the potential for getting good employees.

Second, if a company is already employing women, it has invested in their skills. It makes economic sense to meet their family needs (e.g., maternity leave, flexible hours) rather than risk losing their services. Turnover costs, including losses for training and recruiting new employees and for lost work for jobs earning less than $50,000 per year, amount to 20 percent of the person's annual salary.[16] This monetary cost should give CEOs good reason to seriously consider doing what is necessary to keep good employees. People whose careers are perceived to be blocked are often less productive; keeping the career path clear provides incentives and allows employees to reach their career goals.

Third, women bring a different perspective to an issue. Generally it has been found that women are better listeners than men and use their focus on relationship-building to get people working together. Research has also found that women are more concerned about and define themselves through relationships, as compared to men. As a result, women select actions which support relationships while men are more likely to follow absolute rules and principles. Women are more likely to delegate tasks to subordinates and give the subordinate credit for their work. They

14. *Merriam-Webster*, s.v. "glass ceiling."

15. Federal Glass Ceiling Commission, "Good for Business," 7.

16. Lucas, "How Much Does It Cost Companies?"

are also more likely to excel at teamwork than men.[17] These skills may be especially useful in today's flatter hierarchies and may be particularly appealing to today's young professionals who demand to participate in and contribute to the companies they work for.

Despite the fact that women compose 50.8 percent of the US population, in their 2013 report Catalyst found that women held only 14.6 percent of the executive officer positions (defined as executive and senior level officers as well as managers) in Fortune 500 companies. Twenty-five percent of the Fortune 500 companies had no women executive officers.[18] *Fortune* noted in 2017 that the number of female CEOs managing major corporations had reached twenty-seven, but it was expected that the number would drop to twenty-four in 2018 with the departure of HPE.N's Meg Whitman, Avon's Sheri McCoy, and Staples' Shira Goodman.[19] By comparison, in 1998 there was only one female CEO.[20] With respect to ethnic minorities, with the retirement of Dan Thompson as CEO of McDonald's in 2015, the number of African American CEOs fell to five, one of whom, Ursula Burns at Xerox, was the first African American woman to head a Fortune 500 company. In January 2017, however, Ms. Burns left Xerox, bringing the number of African American CEOs down to four. The number of African American CEOs at major corporations peaked in 2007 at seven—a small number given that in the United States, the African American population is 13.2 percent.[21] Hispanic CEOs at Fortune 500 companies number ten, with the addition of Oscar Munoz at United Airlines in 2015[22] and Geisha Williams at PG&E in 2017.[23] While one may state that the glass ceiling has been cracked, it would be difficult to argue that it has been broken.

SEXUAL HARASSMENT

Included in the Civil Rights Act of 1964, under Title VII, is the specific prohibition of sexual harassment—a matter which generates between

17. Barnett and Karson, "Managers, Values, Executive Decisions," 747–71.

18. "Fortune 500 Top Earner Positions."

19. Fortune Editors, "These Women CEOs Lead Fortune 500 Companies."

20. Fairchild, "Number of Fortune 500 Women."

21. Kell, "McDonald's CEO Exit."

22. Garcia, "Only 9 Hispanic CEOs."

23. Fortune Editors, "These Women CEOs Lead Fortune 500 Companies."

11,000 and 14,000 complaints annually to the EEOC.[24] Sexual harassment is a delicate matter because it touches on relationships between
men and women. It can involve some confusion because there is a great
difference between sexual harassment and the flirt or playful courtship
without serious intent. It is neither seduction, a nonviolent enticement
to sexual activities, nor an honest effort to start a romantic relationship.
It is, in essence, unwelcome and unavoidable sexual suggestions, contact,
or demands within the work relationship. It is an activity that creates a
"caged feeling" on the part of the object of those pressures.

Sexual harassment is not only unethical; it is illegal, as noted above.
The Equal Employment Opportunity Commission (EEOC), which was
created to enforce the provisions of Title VII of the Civil Rights Act of
1964, defines sexual harassment:

> Unwelcome [italics mine] sexual advances, requests for sexual
> favors and other verbal or physical conduct of a sexual nature
> constitute sexual harassment when submission to or rejection
> of this conduct explicitly or implicitly affects an individual's
> employment, unreasonably interferes with an individual's work
> performance, or creates an intimidating, hostile, or offensive
> work environment.[25]

Until the end of the 1980s, most companies saw a sexual harassment situation as a specific event that occurred between two or more people, as
individuals. However, the Supreme Court case of *Meritor Savings Bank v.
Vinson* made it clear that a company is responsible for making sure that
the *environment* where the employee works is not hostile. As a result of
this case, most companies now have zero tolerance sexual harassment
policies (which include grievance and punishment procedures) and educate and monitor employees' behavior with respect to this issue.

Even though sexual harassment is illegal and unethical, the recent
#MeToo movement demonstrates that it happens despite stated morals
and laws. Most often when it occurs, the recipient of the harassment is
afraid to report it, lest they be considered to be lying, or if believed, will
be branded as a trouble-maker, or lose their job. However, in the United
States in particular, since October 2017, when Ashley Judd went on record in the *New York Times* about the behavior of Harvey Weinstein,[26]

24. Ferrell et al., *Business Ethics*, 75.

25. Equal Employment Opportunity Program, "EEO Terminology."

26. Kantor and Twohey, "Harvey Weinstein Harassment."

the American film producer, sexual harassment has made headline news. What has followed are the resignations of many movie and TV personalities such as Matt Lauer, Charlie Rose, Bill O'Reilly, Mark Halperin, Leon Wieseltier, and numerous politicians, including Roy Moore. The anger at sexual harassment has grown as the complaints and the chorus of reports has exploded. *Time* magazine made "The Silence Breakers" their person of the year for 2017.[27]

The two primary types of sexual harassment are the hostile work environment where office conditions or associates interfere with an employee's work performance, and the *quid pro quo* harassment in which threats or promises are made to obtain sexual favors.

The hostile work environment can be created by insensitive or foul language about people of another sex, and the telling of dirty jokes which another member of the group finds highly unpleasant. Other examples include being subjected to sexually suggestive remarks and propositions, sexually oriented materials being circulated around the office, pornographic cartoons and pictures posted or on computer screens so that they are present in work areas, a boss rubbing an employee's back while he or she is typing, or a boss's cruelty after sexual advances are resisted.[28]

In the *quid pro quo* situation, a superior uses his or her position to extract sexual favors in exchange for advancement or a pay raise. It is the expression of the belief that power gives rights for sexual favors. For the one who makes such demands, it is evidence that he or she thinks that a person is a thing that can be bought or sold. It also suggests that wherever a company official has authority, promotions and wages are not connected with performance but with compliance. This perception will destroy any positive atmosphere in an office.

While in most of the reported cases of sexual harassment the victim is a woman and the harasser is a man, that norm is not required for harassment to take place. In the eyes of the law, the harasser may be either a woman or a man and the victim does not have to be of the opposite sex. The harasser can occupy a higher level of authority, such as a supervisor, or can be a coworker. The question to be answered in all cases is intent. If the sexual advances are intended to be mutual, then consent is created. The problem comes when it is unclear whether or not consent was given.

27. Zacharek, "Time Persons of the Year 2017."

28. Carroll and Buchholtz, *Business & Society*, 555.

In such cases, the burden of proof lies with the individual who initiated the advances.

Unfortunately, in the hands of dishonest and unethical people, sexual harassment has the potential of becoming a lethal weapon to exact revenge or seek monetary gain. From an ethical and due diligence standpoint, every workplace should appoint an individual who has both the sensitivity and the maturity to handle cases of sexual harassment. It is the moral duty of the one who feels that she or he is the victim of sexual harassment to take a firm stand, reject the harassment, and if the protest is not heeded, report the harassment to the officer responsible for such matters. Complaints should be investigated by the proper company official and counseling or dismissal recommended for the offender. It is unfair to all parties for the one in charge of harassment to delay actions, since time may allow an instance of simple misunderstanding to develop into a case that can hurt someone or that may require dismissal. Likewise, delays in handling allegations of harassment may encourage additional harassment to other employees.

THE OFFICE ROMANCE

Men and women, however, still work together, and given the long hours that are often expected in today's corporate environment, there may be little opportunity for individuals to socialize outside of work. In addition, working together on interesting, intense projects and spending many hours together, including traveling together, often generates sexual interest and heat. A likely outcome of this situation, given the high visibility and condemnation of sexual harassment, is the office romance, which can be equally tricky.

Office romance, in and of itself, is not sexual harassment because it is about *wanted advances*, not unwanted ones. The *Wall Street Journal* asked the question in February 2018: "Can You Still Date a Co-Worker? Well, It's Complicated!"[29] The article reported that over the past decade, about 40 percent of workers have stated that they have dated a colleague, with a high of 41 percent in 2016 to a low of 36 percent in 2017. It was also noted that there has been a dramatic increase in employers calling their law firms about dating rules since September 2017—no doubt a result of the #MeToo movement.

29. Koh and Feintzeig, "Can You Still Date."

Sometimes it is difficult to tell whether or not the advance was wanted, particularly in power situations where the office romance is between supervisors and subordinates. In unequal power relationships, if the romance goes sour, the subordinate may claim that the affair was not consensual. If the subordinate is subsequently discharged, he or she may claim retaliation.

Besides the danger of misunderstandings between individuals in unequal power relationships, there are other considerations which should be taken into account before an office romance is started. First, there are work and coworker issues. Coworkers may become jealous or resentful if they believe that special favors or choice assignments are being given to those in a special relationship. This may be true even in cases when the individuals are married. In addition, work critiques may be more difficult to either give or accept. Did your idea get shot down because it was not a good idea or because your lover is angry because of a quarrel the previous evening? Finally, there is office gossip to contend with. Such gossip may reduce productivity, thus bringing the relationship to the attention in a negative way to company top officials.

Second, office romances can end. When they do, it is often the woman who pays, although more recently, both parties may end up on the losing side. One famous case from the 1980s is that of the affair between William Agee and Mary Cunningham. Agee, then forty-three, was president of Bendix Corporation when he had an affair with Cunningham, then a twenty-nine-year-old who had been hired as his executive assistant, but was then promoted to Vice President for Corporate Communications after only a year on the job. Three months later Cunningham was promoted to Vice President for Strategic Planning. Questions were raised as to why Cunningham was so quickly promoted, and whether her rapid rise-to-the-top was because of her ability or because of other factors. Initially Agee attempted to deny the affair, but in the end, he acknowledged the relationship. Cunningham, not Agee, left Bendix.[30] More recently, in an affair that was listed by *Time* magazine as one of the top 10 CEO scandals for the first decade of the twenty-first century, Boeing's CEO, Harry Stonecipher, was dismissed after he admitted to an affair with Debra Peabody, a governmental affairs vice president at Boeing's Washington, DC, office. The two met at a company retreat in January 2005. By March 2005, the board asked for Stonecipher's resignation following an anonymous

30. O'Reilly, "Agee in Exile."

tip that disclosed the romantic email correspondence between the two parties. The board requested Stonecipher's resignation not only because of the affair, but also because he had violated Boeing's code of conduct by engaging in conduct that raised questions about the company's honesty, impartiality, and integrity. Eleven days after Stonecipher's resignation, Peabody voluntarily left Boeing.[31]

Despite the likelihood that workplace attractions do not generally work out well, especially when involving individuals who are at the highest company levels and have a superior/subordinate status, such attractions continue to take place. It is unrealistic to believe that men and women can work together and ignore the fact that such proximity will lead to romance and often to marriage. Leil Lowndes provides the following suggestions to those who succumb to cupid's arrow in the workplace:

1. Choose a coworker of equal status.

2. Don't ever date a married coworker.

3. Don't date anyone who has financial dealings with your firm.

4. Make sure your romance does not cause disturbances.

5. Be discreet. Keep a professional demeanor at all times.[32]

From a Christian ethical perspective, two office romances should always be avoided. First, an adulterous office romance, because it raises questions of promise-breaking, has a negative effect on families, and breaks the seventh commandment. Second, the exploitative office romance, because it raises questions of seeking favors or promotion for reasons other than merit. This violates the principles of justice and fairness.

SCRIPTURE AND OUR RELATIONSHIP WITH OTHERS

This chapter introduces issues in business that speak specifically to our relationships with our fellow human beings. In chapter 1 we noted that the first two commandments recognize the supremacy of God as the only one worthy of our worship, and that no material image can provide a substitute for God. We also noted that because God is a person, we need to respect him and his characteristics, and if we wish to honor his name, as

31. Holmes, "Affair That Grounded Stonecipher," and Rose, "Stonecipher's Partner Quits."

32. Lowndes, "Dangerous Office Liaisons," 67–68.

the third commandment requires, we need to mirror these characteristics in our lives. In chapter 2 we discussed the importance of Scripture as the ultimate authority for assisting us in knowing our obligation or duty, as compared to either conscience or choosing the loving action. The fourth commandment, which recognizes our acceptance of God's worldview through our recognition of the necessity of taking time for a relationship with him by setting aside our work and daily activities one day each week, was included in our discussion of the role of work in chapter 3.

The other commandments (five through ten) provide the principles on which a secure and happy community can be built. Of particular application to this chapter on discrimination and sexual harassment are the fifth and seventh commandments.

The seventh commandment was mentioned above in the discussion on office romances. This commandment is very clear. It plainly states: "You shall not commit adultery" (Exod 20:14). The seventh commandment protects the marriage relationship. The family is the essential core of church and society. It is the major transmitter of spiritual and moral values. For that reason, it functions as a moral fortress that must not be penetrated by strangers. The sexual union is much more than physical contact; it is the supreme expression of the one-flesh understanding of a man and a woman. While the physical act of adultery shatters all the foundations of the family and comes under the displeasure of God, who is the family's creator and protector, Jesus takes his followers beyond the sexual act to the poison of adultery in the heart. "You have heard that it was said, 'Do not commit adultery.' But I tell you that anyone who looks at a woman lustfully has already committed adultery with her in his heart" (Matt 5:27–28). Adultery grows on the ground of erotic phantasies. It feeds on pornography. It thrives on forbidden glances. The only protection is absolute purity of thought. Jesus uses the most striking language to impress his points. "If your right eye causes you to sin, gouge it out and throw it away. It is better for you to lose one part of your body than for your whole body to be thrown into hell" (Matt 5:29).

David Gill provides practical counsel for one's business and personal life when one chooses to follow God's directions with respect to the seventh commandment: "Never act, think or communicate in any way, sexual or otherwise, that violates or threatens covenanted, committed relationships. Rather, regarding such relationships as God's creation, do whatever you can to support fidelity, loyalty and commitment."[33] This counsel clearly informs the businessperson to avoid all forms of sexual harassment and any romantic thoughts or advances to married coworkers.

Equally applicable to our consideration in the context of strengthening family and avoiding actions that diminish the family's security is the fifth commandment. The fifth commandment states: "Honor your father and your mother, so that you may live long in the land the LORD your God is giving you" (Exod 20:12). This commandment speaks to the willingness to honor those who have made our existence possible.

In most societies around the world, the concept of honor is well understood, and often is specifically related to actions which diminish the sexual purity of either oneself or another member of the family.[34] It goes far beyond the commonly conveyed concept of obeying parents when one is a child, the limited interpretation of this commandment predominate in American society. Gill notes that this commandment is given to adult children, not to infants or young children (see also Exod 21:15, 17; Lev 20:9; Deut 21:18–21; Prov 1:8; 15:5; 19:26).[35]

In defining honor, Gill notes: "Honor does not imply unilateral obedience but rather treating someone with care and respect in deed and word. To honor someone is to treat that person as valuable, to grant influence, dignity, importance and authority."[36] To honor one's parents means doing nothing which would diminish either their reputation specifically, or the family's good name. It also includes providing for their needs, particularly in old age. Jesus spoke of the importance of caring for one's parents when he said to the Pharisees: "You have a fine way of setting aside the commands of God in order to observe your own traditions! For Moses said, 'Honor your father and your mother.' . . . But you say that if a man says to his father or mother: 'Whatever help you might otherwise have received from me is Corban [that is, a gift devoted to God,] then you no longer let him do anything for his father or mother. Thus you nullify the word of God by your tradition that you have handed down" (Mark 7:9–13).

33. Gill, *Doing Right*, 23.

34. Wikipedia.com, s.v. "Family Honor."

35. Gill, *Doing Right*, 161.

36. Gill, *Doing Right*, 164.

Note that the commandment states: "Honor," not "Love your father and mother." Love cannot be commanded, but honor can. Honor is the steady, rational decision to respect those who brought us into the world, even if they are far from perfect. Even if one has not experienced adequate fathering or mothering in one's life, Gill suggests that one may adopt other people, especially people within the Christian faith, for parental guidance.[37] Such people, who may provide the direction for one's decision-making and actions that normally would be filled by parents, should also be honored. Understanding the importance of honoring one's parents (or other agents God may have blessed your life with) has a deep impact on one's behavior and leads to success in all other relationships. This is the commandment to which God attached a special blessing—"so that you may live long in the land the LORD your God is giving you" (Exod 20:12).

When the Dawn Arrives

Scripture requires that in all of our relationships, whether at work or outside of work, we treat other people as human beings created in the image of God, and therefore as our brothers and sisters. We are also enjoined to keep in mind Jesus' instruction to do to others as we ourselves wish others to do to us (Matt 7:12). A Jewish rabbi once asked his pupils, "How can we determine the hour of dawn, when the night ends and the day begins?" His students gave different answers, such as when one can distinguish between a dog and a sheep, or when one can distinguish between a fig tree and a grapevine. The rabbi answered "no" to all their answers. Finally the students gave up and asked the rabbi for the answer. He responded, "It is when you have enough light to look human beings in the face and recognize them as your brothers and sisters. Until then the darkness is still with us."[38]

THINKING IT THROUGH: GEORGE MCREYNOLDS AND MERRILL LYNCH

None of the ethical theories discussed in chapter 1 would argue for discrimination or sexual harassment and all recognize the illegality of these

37. Gill, *Doing Right*, 175.

38. Nouwen, "Adam's Peace," 11.

behaviors in many countries, including the United States. To be honorable in business, the Christian worldview stands strongly against both discrimination and sexual harassment, not because human laws forbid such behaviors, but because all humans are created in the image of God and therefore must be viewed as equally valued, and treated as one would wish to personally be treated.

Chapter 5

What If My Product Becomes Dangerous?

Product Quality and Safety

No man should so act as to make a gain out of the ignorance of another.
—CICERO, CA. 63 BC

FORD MOTOR COMPANY BEGAN designing the Pinto, a small, popular automobile in 1968, and introduced it to the American market in 1970. The Pinto was Ford's answer to the competition for small, fuel-efficient cars, initially introduced to the American consumer through the popularity of the Volkswagen Bug. Other US automakers were also designing their own small cars (e.g., General Motors' Corvair and Vega), so Ford was anxious to get its product to market as quickly as possible. As a result of the rush (i.e., just over two years rather than the usual forty-three months from design to market), the prototypes were created and the necessary manufacturing molds were made before all the engineering problems were solved. The driver behind the project was Lee Iacocca, who had designed the widely-successful Ford Mustang. Iacocca insisted that the Pinto weigh no more than 2,000 pounds and sell for no more than $2,000.

During the testing of the prototypes it was discovered that with the placement of the Pinto's gas tank between the rear bumper and the rear axle (in order to allow for more trunk space), the Pinto did not pass the 1972 federal regulations requiring that the vehicle be able to successfully

withstand a twenty-mile-per-hour impact. At that speed the fuel tank of
the Pinto was driven forward and punctured, causing the fuel to spill. In
such a situation, any spark from the accident would set the car on fire. In
addition, the bumper did not provide substantial protection.

As Marianne Jennings notes, several fixes were possible.

> Among the design changes that could have been made were
> side and cross members at $2.40 and $1.80 per car, respectively;
> a shock-absorbent "flak suit" to protect the tank at $4; a tank
> within a tank and placement of the tank over the axle at $5.08 to
> $5.79; a nylon bladder within the tank at $5.25 to $8; placement
> of the tank over the axle surrounded with a protective barrier
> at $9.59 per car; imposition of a protective shield between the
> differential housing and the tank at $2.35; improvement and
> reinforcement of the bumper at $2.60; and addition of eight
> inches of crush space at a cost of $6.40. Equipping the car with
> a reinforced rear structure, smooth axle, improved bumper, and
> additional crush space at a total cost of $15.30 would have made
> the fuel tank safe when hit from the rear by a vehicle the size of
> a Ford Galaxy. If, in addition, a bladder or tank within a tank
> had been used or if the tank had been protected with a shield,
> the tank would have been safe in a rear-end collision of forty to
> forty-five miles per hour. If the tank had been located over the
> rear axle, it would have been safe in a rear impact at fifty miles
> per hour or more.[1]

Ford did not make any of these proposed changes, even though the crash
test results were known to the engineers and their superiors, and some
engineers objected to Ford's failure to make the needed adjustments. Instead, Ford's director of automotive safety, J. C. Echold, did a cost-benefit
analysis that, for decision purposes, costed a human life at $200,000 and
judged that the benefit to Ford for making the changes was just under $50
million while the associated cost was $137 million. Echold's evaluation
was accepted and production proceeded as initially designed.[2]

Accidents occurred and reports were filed. Dennis Gioia, the Ford
recall coordinator at the time, was responsible for reviewing hundreds of
accident reports, coming from numerous situations. Gioia recalled that
when he first went to work at Ford in 1973, one of the new files he handled dealt with the Pinto catching fire in rear-end accidents. However, his

1. Jennings, *Business Ethics* (7th ed.), 453–54.
2. Jennings, *Business Ethics* (7th ed.), 454.

cue for labeling a case a problem was either high frequency of occurrence or directly traceable causes. Such was not the situation with the cases in the Pinto file, and he did not flag the situation as a special case.[3] Later Gioia stated:

> When I was dealing with the first trickling-in of field reports that might have suggested a significant problem with the Pinto, the reports were essentially similar to many others that I was dealing with (and dismissing) all the time. . . . I was making this kind of decision automatically every day. I had trained myself to respond to prototypical cues, and these didn't fit the relevant prototype for crisis cases.[4]

It is of ethical interest that Gioia missed the cues that Ford had a major problem with the design of the Pinto, given his reasons for entering the business world and his assigned responsibilities. Gioia described himself as a "prototypical 'child of the '60s'" who participated in anti-war demonstrations against the Vietnam War and believed that both government and business engaged in immoral and unethical actions. His friends were surprised when he entered an MBA program, but Gioia explained his actions by telling them that he "would have a greater chance of influencing social change in business if I worked behind the scenes on the inside, rather than as a strident voice on the outside."[5] During the time that Gioia worked at Ford, he consistently voted not to recommend recall of the Pinto, drove a Pinto himself, and sold one to his sister.

Following Gioia's departure from Ford in 1975, the internal memos regarding the gas tank problem, together with the calculation of the cost of a human life as compared with the cost of fixing the Pinto design problems, came to the public's attention. In 1977 Mark Dowie wrote an exposé charging Ford with gross negligence, stonewalling, and unethical corporate conduct because they willfully sold "firetraps" to the public.[6]

On August 10, 1978, three teen-age girls stopped their Pinto on US 33 near Elkhart, Indiana, and turned on their emergency flashers. As they were getting ready to pull back onto the road, they were hit by a driver in a van (which weighed 4,000 pounds) who had been drinking and who may or may not have been smoking marijuana at the time of the

3. Gioia, "Pinto Fires," 379–89.

4. Moberg, "When Good People Do Bad Things."

5. Gioia, "Pinto Fires," 379–80.

6. Dowie, "How Ford Put Firetraps on Wheels," 46–55.

accident (there was marijuana in his vehicle). The van driver dropped his "smoke" and plowed into the Pinto. The car exploded and all three girls were killed.

This case was taken to court and Ford was charged with criminal homicide. Ford denied that the Pinto was unsafe compared with other cars of its type and era. On March 13, 1980, the jury found Ford not guilty of criminal homicide, a verdict at least partially due to the judge's absolute insistence on following the strictest rules of criminal evidence.[7] However, that action had no effect on further production of the Pinto, as it was taken off the market in 1978.

Gioia eventually became a professor of organizational behavior at Pennsylvania State University. In his classes he explored his experience at Ford. He noted that at first he continued to be convinced that he had made the right decisions when he did not recommend recalling the Pinto, given the evidence that he had available at the time. However,

> In retrospect I know that in the context of the times my actions were *legal* (they were all well within the framework of the law); they probably also were *ethical* according to most prevailing definitions (they were in accord with accepted professional standards and codes of conduct); the major concern for me is whether they were *moral* (in the sense of adhering to some higher standards of inner conscience and conviction about the 'right' actions to take). . . . It is the last criterion that remains troublesome.[8]

Gioia subsequently developed his theory of scripts, which warns us that when we are engaged in a familiar situation, our brains are often on automatic, we proceed on "auto-pilot," and therefore often do not respond appropriately. His lesson, from his own experience, is that when one is doing repetitive tasks, such as reviewing accident reports within a particular decision environment, one must be particularly vigilant to prevent an ethical lapse. As Gioia put it: "The schemas driving my perceptions and actions precluded consideration of issues in ethical terms because the scripts did not include ethical dimensions."[9]

7. Dole, "Pinto Verdict."

8. Gioia, "Pinto Fires," 384.

9. Gioia, "Pinto Fires," 385.

THE ETHICS OF SAFETY

In the above case, Ford made a decision to manufacture and sell a product known to be dangerous (at least to some people), because by their calculations the likelihood of costs for customers who would be injured was estimated to be less than the known costs of making the Pinto safer. In court, as one can imagine, Ford was severely criticized for its estimate of $200,000 for a human life. However, its calculations were based on a National Highway Traffic Safety Administration calculation of that period, which included such items as future productivity losses, medical costs, funeral costs, and property damage.[10] As Gioia noted, however, their scripts did not include consideration of ethical issues.

While their calculations were clearly an insult to the value of life, the question still remains: at what point should the manufacturer consider a product too dangerous to develop and sell? While every product can be made safer, to what extent should the manufacturer make the product safer, knowing that its cost, and therefore its price, will increase? What if the product is used improperly? Is the manufacturer responsible? What are the proper ethical considerations that should be included when products are made and sold to the public?

For most of history, such questions would have seemed both unusual and unnecessary. Prior to the Industrial Revolution, the buyer of goods knew the seller personally, as it was likely that the seller was a neighbor and/or friend. The expectations of relationship demanded that the goods be of adequate quality, and if they were not, they should be fixed. Continued acceptance within the local community demanded it. But with industrialization, the close link between the seller and the buyer vanished. Today the purchaser usually knows little about the company making the product or how the product was manufactured. Accordingly, the law recommends *caveat emptor*—buyer beware. As a result, consumers today rely on the law to make sure that products offered for sale are safe. When they do so, what do they expect?

At a minimum, they expect that the use of the product or service will not result in their death. In Scripture, the sixth commandment states clearly: "You shall not kill" (Exod 20:13). This commandment is universally accepted across all human societies.[11] Thus expecting that the law will preserve our lives from all types of threats, including threats from prod-

10. Jennings, *Business Ethics* (7th ed.), 454–55.

11. Trevino and Nelson, *Managing Business Ethics*, 413.

ucts and services, seems like common sense. However, Jesus extended the principle when he said: "You have heard that it was said to the people long ago, 'Do not murder, and anyone who murders will be subject to judgment.' But I tell you that anyone who is angry with his brother will be subject to judgment. . . . Therefore, if you are offering your gift at the altar and there remember that your brother has something against you, leave your gift there in front of the altar. First go and be reconciled to your brother; then come and offer your gift" (Matt 5:21–24). Jesus did not limit the sixth commandment only to the physical act of killing someone. He wished his followers to avoid the spirit of hatred and revenge or indulging passions that lead toward doing injury to others or even wishing them harm. But even that understanding is not sufficient. God wants his children not only to abstain from destructive behaviors, but also have different feelings. The ultimate understanding of the commandment, therefore, goes beyond finding a prohibition to adopting a positive attitude. It is not enough to refrain from killing; one must become reconciled and act toward making this goodwill happen. This commandment also covers all that makes life possible, and even dictates the application of the Golden Rule in seeking good for those around us—including good products, good services, decent living and working conditions—whatever is in our power to provide. When we speak of the sacredness of life, we see how God includes much more than mere existence.

What does this mean for a Christian in today's business world? Christians must first of all refrain from making products or offering services that destroy life. Beyond that, they must consider what promotes life and health, or as Van Duzer put it: "provide the goods and services that a community needs to flourish."[12] David Gill put it even more directly:

> Never do anything that threatens or harms the life and health of another person. Rather, regarding it as God's own creation, do whatever you can to protect that person's life and health and to promote peace and reconciliation.[13]

Often what best promotes community flourishing and the life and health of the inhabitants of the community may be determined, for any given society, by that society's view of law and culture, and their relationship to ethics. In particular, if something goes wrong with the product or service,

12. Van Duzer, *Why Business Matters*, 152.

13. Gill, *Doing Right*, 193.

should one look to the law, to culture, or to ethics for one's standard of making a dangerous product acceptable?

THE ROLE OF LAW IN AMERICA

Hiller B. Zolbel states that the law has long occupied a very unique place in America. On the frontier, the coming of the circuit court judge once or twice a year provided one of the very few live entertainments. It furnished the frontier people with the thrills and tensions of an athletic event. Even the litigants found excitement, at a low cost, in the game, because in America, the loser paid only his own expenses. In the frontier society that easily turned violent, lawsuits provided a substitute for violence.[14]

Another reason the law is so influential in the United States is the power of judicial review by the courts. This power, enunciated in 1803, gives judges the authority to declare that certain laws passed by legislative bodies are unconstitutional. The power of judicial review may provide judges the authority to go beyond the text of the Constitution of the United States to their personal understanding of the supposed intent of its writers. As an example, the prohibition of the establishment of any religion as a state-supported religion has become the principle of separation of church and state, which prohibits Christmas nativity scenes on public property. This particular outcome was probably not considered by the Founders of the country.

The law is also very close to Americans because so many of them have served on jury duty and thus have had a very direct contact with the judicial system. In spite of its weaknesses, which at times may be glaring in highly publicized trials, the jury system is perhaps the greatest contribution of the English-speaking world to justice. In this system the destiny of one person is not determined by a few legal specialists, but by his or her peers.

For products manufactured and sold in the United States, the law is the source of both the rights of the consumer and the responsibilities of the manufacturer with respect to products created for sale to the general public.

14. Zobel, "In Love with Lawsuits," 58–66.

Tort Law

With respect to product liability, three theories are traditionally used to determine the responsibility of the manufacturer.[15] The first theory is the *due care theory*. This theory means that manufacturers "should take all reasonable precautions to ensure that products they put on the market are free of defects likely to cause harm."[16] The buyer is liable for acts of negligence, as defined by the *Second Restatement of Torts* (Section 282). The usual standard for negligence is for the buyer to act in a manner not in agreement with the actions of a "reasonable person." For example, if a driver was reckless, he or she would be responsible for an accident, not the manufacturer.

The theory of due care extends to foreseeable misuse of the product, but it is difficult to apply in situations where standards evolve due to increasing knowledge and technology. Courts often ask the question: What was the negligent behavior on the part of the manufacturer, given the knowledge they had *at the time* of manufacture? The answer to this question is not always clear, as what someone knew (or could have known) in the past is difficult to apply to a product that causes harm today. Finally, this theory provides for two defenses for the manufacturer: contributory negligence on the part of the buyer (i.e., failing to act prudently), and assumption of risk, where the consumer knowingly accepts risk by using the product in a potentially dangerous situation.

The second theory is the *contractual theory*. Under this theory the buyer and seller are considered to be in a contractual relationship which can be either implied or explicit.[17] It is expected that the product will be of acceptable quality, that manufacturers cannot take unfair advantage of the customer, and that the customer understands that many products involve some danger or risk. Questions often arise because sales agreements may be vague or may even limit the rights of the consumer. In addition, it may not be clear as to whether or not the consumer understood the risk he/she was taking.

The third theory is the *strict liability theory*. This theory "holds that manufacturers are responsible for all harm resulting from a dangerously defective product even when due care has been exercised and all contracts observed. . . . The mere fact that a product is put into the hands

---

15. Boatright, *Ethics and the Conduct of Business*, 295–304.

16. Boatright, *Ethics and the Conduct of Business*, 295.

17. Boatright, *Ethics and the Conduct of Business*, 297–98.

of consumers in a defective condition that poses an unreasonable risk is sufficient for holding the manufacturer liable."[18] Under this theory the consumer can obtain compensation from a manufacturer for injury from a product without having to prove that the manufacturer was negligent. A defective product is defined as one that is unsuitable for use as intended or for any misuse that could have been reasonably foreseen. We see the results of this legal perspective in the warning labels on manufactured goods—some of which make sense, and some of which seem ridiculous, such as warnings not to use a hair dryer in the shower or not to use the wrong end of a chain saw. The usual criticism of strict liability theory is that it ignores the element of fault—a concept with which we may be familiar because of the common acceptance of no-fault auto insurance. Regarding fault, Boatright notes:

> Under a system of strict liability, consumers give up a right they have in the due care theory—namely, the right not to be forced to contribute to the compensation of accident victims when they (the consumers) are not at fault. Prices are also higher under a strict liability system in order to cover the cost of paying compensation. But consumers gain more than they lose by not being required to spend money protecting themselves and making up their own losses. They also acquire a new right: the right to be compensated for injuries from defective products without regard to fault. Thus, everyone is better off under a strict liability system than under a negligence system.[19]

Because of the legal concept of strict liability, Americans tend to look to the law for protection not only from injustice but also from all the risks of life. Foreign observers are amazed at the number and nature of liability suits in the United States. Among the countries of the world, the United States is considered to be the most litigious society.[20] Kevin Drum suggests this is true because America's common law culture gives lawyers more power than is the case in other countries. First, because the law in most European countries states that if you sue and lose, you have to pay your own costs and the other side's costs as well. Second, in the United States, trials by a jury are likely to result in higher award damages than a

---

18. Boatright, *Ethics and the Conduct of Business*, 300.

19. Boatright, *Ethics and the Conduct of Business*, 303.

20. Rubin, "More Money into Bad Suits."

trial by a judge. In most other countries, a judge decides the case rather than a jury.[21]

THE LAW AND ETHICS

There is no question that the law has a deep influence upon our conduct. Our choices are constantly affected by our laws. Laws tell us to drive on the right hand side of the road, but in many British countries, the law requires that people drive on the left hand side of the highway. Laws also determine the way we build our houses, the place where we locate the building on the lot, building materials that must be used, how plumbing and electricity must be installed, and the number of electrical outlets that must be provided in a room. Laws regulate the way our food is manufactured and the ingredients that may be used. The arm of the law is long, and at times, seems to be lengthening.

Sometimes legal principles are the ideals of justice and fairness that should be the ground of all laws. These principles are then closely related to basic ethical principles. For example, the principles of justice and honesty are the same in law as in ethics. It is best when there is a close bond between ethics and law as the authority of a law depends to a great degree on its expressing an ethical ideal. People tend not to recognize the authority of a law which they believe is immoral. The Founders of the United States believed that it was immoral to set taxes without any input from those who paid the taxes, and they rebelled. The Abolitionists felt that the laws protecting slavery were immoral and they challenged them. Eventually they went to war against them. Today those who believe that abortion is immoral are becoming bolder and bolder in defying laws that protect what they believe is "murder of the unborn." Thus, when a discrepancy between a law and an ethical principle is felt, we can expect a strong reaction.

However, many laws are positive laws, rather than legal principles. Positive laws state the conduct that is required in specific situations. For instance, public safety is a legal principle that is translated into positive laws that set the speed limit on the highway, regulations for sanitary conditions in restaurants, size and location of exits in public buildings, etc. There is a dimension of arbitrariness in some of these regulations. Why should sixty-five or seventy miles per hour be the speed limit on a given

21. Drum, "Why We Sue."

highway? In other countries the maximum speed is set much higher. Thus positive laws come under constant scrutiny and review. While there is much agreement between legal and ethical principles, there are often strong discrepancies between positive laws and ethical principles. For instance, until the 1960s, discrimination was not only commanded by culture in the United States, but was also protected by law.

Even when laws do not contradict ethics, there are essential differences between laws and ethics. The spirit of legality is not the same as the spirit of ethics. In the first place, laws are usually the expression of a political compromise rather than the statement of an ideal. Politics has been defined as the art of the possible, and laws are crafted by men and women who are well aware of the limits of the possible. To pass a law, you must appeal to a multitude of potentially conflicting interests that too often deny in the small print what is perceived to be the intent of the law. For instance, in the major revision of the US tax code in 1986, it was ruled that sport enthusiasts could not deduct gifts to their colleges if they received a seating preference at home games in exchange for their support. The law somehow exempted graduates of Louisiana State University and the University of Texas. The simple reason for the difference of treatment was the presence of powerful congressmen who were alumni of those institutions on the committee that drafted that law.[22]

The law is often the expression of a pragmatic spirit. For instance, the legalization of prostitution in many countries is more pragmatic than idealistic. Legalization cuts down the burden of police; it assigns limits to areas where prostitution can be practiced; it seeks to protect the health of those who engage in it. Unfortunately, it does not go to the core of the problem—the frightful depersonalization of young women and men who become things that can be sold and thrown away at will. It does not protect the innocents who come to large cities and are caught in the dragnets of pimps.

A legalistic attitude is totally different from an ethical attitude. Legalism fosters minimum compliance—just what the letter of the law demands. For instance, when driving, many drivers are only concerned about how fast they can go above the speed limit without risking a ticket. For most people, laws exist outside of themselves in legal manuals. They keep the law out of fear rather than out of agreement with the ideal, and

22. Eichelberger and Babcock, "Football-Ticket Tax Break."

they devote much effort to respecting the letter of the law while circum-
venting its spirit.

Finally, laws too often reflect the power of money. Legions of lobbyists harass our representatives and shower them with gifts to obtain legislation that is favorable to their clients, or to block laws that would hurt
their financial interests. We have, for instance, the total inconsistency of
requiring tobacco manufacturers to state that their products are harmful
to health, and yet we use tax money to subsidize the growing of tobacco.
This illustrates the power of the huge quantities of money involved in the
tobacco industry. Another evidence of the power of money and lobbyists
on legislation is the continuing lack of laws to curb the sales of powerful guns despite the recent and continuing rash of mass shootings in the
United States over the past few years, including Newtown, Connecticut;
Charlestown, South Carolina; San Bernardino, California; Orlando,
Florida; Las Vegas, Nevada; and Parkland, Florida.[23] In the case of the
Pinto, mentioned above, for eight years Ford lobbyists battled the National Highway Safety Administration's attempts to insist that the cars be
able to withstand a fixed barrier impact of twenty miles per hour without
losing fuel (until 1977). If the proposed regulations had been made into
law earlier, the Pinto fuel tank would have been corrected.[24] The automotive industry argued that such guidelines should not be put into place
because small cars, while more fuel efficient, were also inherently unsafe,
as compared with the larger American-made automobiles, because of
their size and weight.[25] Thus, technically, Ford was not in violation of the
law when it manufactured the Pinto as the letter of the law had been met.
But as Gioia asked: Does obeying the law equate to being ethical?

THE ROLE OF ORGANIZATIONAL CULTURE: JOHNSON
AND JOHNSON AND TYLENOL

Occasionally we see companies that choose to act on behalf of the consumer without resorting to any legal requirements. Probably the most
famous case of a company going beyond what the law required is the case
of Johnson and Johnson and the Tylenol scare.

23. *Economist*, "Why the Gun Lobby Is Winning."
24. Dowie, "Pinto Madness."
25. Gioia, "Pinto Fires," 381.

In September 1982, someone or several persons (who were never identified) replaced Tylenol Extra-Strength capsules with cyanide-laced capsules, resealed the packages, and deposited them on the shelves of at least a half-dozen or so pharmacies and food stores in the Chicago area. The poisoned capsules were purchased and seven people died. These deaths occurred over a period of five days. Fear and confusion swept across the nation as first the uncertainty of what had happened, then the extent to which it had happened, and ultimately who/what was responsible for the poisonings unfolded. There was concern that there might be copy-cat poisonings. There was no clear reason for why Tylenol or Johnson and Johnson had been targeted. What was clear was that someone had selected the capsules for their deadly deed. Initially the company did not know whether the tainting of the capsules occurred at the factory or at the point of sale or somewhere in-between, and whether the tainting had occurred only in the Chicago area or was widespread across the United States. While the capsule form of Tylenol represented 30 percent of Tylenol sales and was increasingly popular, it was possible to take the capsule apart, insert the poison, and return the capsule to the package without providing any evidence that the package had been opened.

If Johnson and Johnson and their subsidiary, McNeil Consumer Products, abandoned the Tylenol capsule, they would give their competitors a major advantage. However, not to recall the Tylenol capsules could result in additional deaths. Jim Burke, the CEO of Johnson & Johnson, decided to abandon the capsule at a cost of $150 million (just 1982 lost sales, expressed in 1982 dollars). Johnson and Johnson offered caplets (tablets in the shape of a capsule) to consumers in place of the capsules and withdrew all Tylenol capsules from across the United States (not just in Chicago) on October 5, five days after the first reported poisoning. Why did he act so promptly, even at a high financial cost? Fink notes:

> There are many in the company who say with sincere conviction that when they were faced with stressful, crisis-induced decisions during the Tylenol crisis they looked to the Credo for guidance and, specifically, to see if the decision they were about to make (such as whether or not to withdraw the product) was in keeping with the first line of the Credo.[26]

26. Fink, *Crisis Management*, 217.

The Johnson and Johnson Credo, written by General Robert Wood Johnson, the son of the company's founder and himself its CEO from 1932–1963, lists the company's four responsibilities *in order*:

1. We believe our first responsibility is to the doctors, nurses, and patients, to mothers and fathers and all others who use our products and services.

2. We are responsible to our employees, the men and women who work with us throughout the world.

3. We are responsible to the communities in which we live and work and to the world community as well.

4. Our final responsibility is to our stockholders.[27]

Johnson and his successors believed that if the first three responsibilities of the Credo were met, the stockholders would be well served.[28] Subsequently Johnson & Johnson created the packaging we are familiar with today—the tamper-proof bottles, and Tylenol in capsule form was returned to the market. Within a year of the poisonings, Johnson & Johnson regained its 40 percent market share for Tylenol, a favorable outcome that could not have been envisioned at the time the recall decision was made.[29]

In a business organization there is a collective atmosphere that influences behavior. Gioia spoke of the culture he was surrounded with at Ford during the time he worked there. While aware that his job involved life-and-death matters, he also recognized that from a practical perspective, people accept risks when they drive a car. He also noted that in the early 1970s the United States was experiencing its first oil crisis, which had a deadening effect on the entire auto industry, as most of the US cars were not fuel efficient. Due to higher gas prices, if the Pinto (and other small cars) did not succeed, layoffs in the auto factories were imminent. When the crash test data became known within the Ford Company, the Pinto was compared with other small cars in the industry—a comparison that only confirmed the suspicion that all small cars were unsafe as

27. Murphy, *Eighty Exemplary Ethics Statements*, 123–24.

28. Murphy, *Eighty Exemplary Ethics Statements*, 124.

29. Jennings, *Business Ethics* (7th ed.), 444–45.

compared to larger cars. The culture at Ford at that time did not encourage a recall decision.[30]

The culture at Johnson and Johnson in 1982 reflected the company's Credo which dealt with how the organization would treat its customers, its suppliers, and its employees. Often what is believed to be moral consensus within an organization is really cultural consensus, usually driven by the "tone at the top." While at times such moral consensus can lead to company standards for honesty and treatment of customers in positive ways, this same pattern of consensus has historically allowed racial and sexual discrimination. Thus one cannot say that the culture of a company or a country is necessarily Christian, even if most of the individuals of a particular culture call themselves Christian. Regulators of actions have often hoped to use clearly spelled-out regulations (the law) to force desired behavior, rather than to depend on what was seen as abstract ethical principles or moral consensus of the culture. However, culture, whether organizational, ethnic or tribal, or country-specific, deeply affects human conduct. The question arises: what is the relationship between culture and ethics? Can one depend on culture, especially if deeply embedded, to provide the foundation for ethical decisions?

THE DEVELOPMENT OF CULTURE

While societal culture will be discussed more extensively in chapter 10, it is important to note at this time that culture not only exists in a particular society, but it also exists within organizations and other subgroups within a particular society. Culture itself is a great simplifier of life because it provides us with an automatic answer to diverse social situations and saves us from embarrassment. When in one's home culture, the culture informs us regarding our expected behavior, but once we take our initial steps into a culture that is totally foreign to us, whether geographically near or far, we quickly feel clumsy, odd, and often misunderstood. Knowing the culture in which we find ourselves simplifies life in so many ways.

Culture aids communication. It tells us how to address a superior, how to make a request, how to provide a word of sympathy. Culture supplies us not only with words but also with body language, which we trust even more than words. We also depend upon culture to judge people, correctly or incorrectly. The way they dress, the cars they drive, are

30. Gioia, "Pinto Fires," 382.

interpreted as telling us something about their character and their stand-
ing in life. In business, the way offices are furnished and laid out will be
interpreted as success, progressiveness, or lagging behind the times.

Unfortunately, it is also from culture that we inherit our stereotypes
about other people. Unconsciously the negative images created by our
stereotypes shape our reactions when we meet people. In such situations
we may feel superior or distrustful and thus find it difficult to establish
genuine friendships. Many ethical problems that arise in the business
organization are due to stereotypes.

Culture, whether within an organization or within society, has a
dictatorial power. It continually attempts to force its values upon us. It
punishes its despisers with ridicule or with rejection. Children are particularly sensitive to what the youth culture demands and feel it keenly
when their own house, the furniture, or the car do not meet the standards
of the neighbors. For older adults, changes in culture are often bitterly
resisted. They disturb well-established relationships and bring elements
of misunderstanding and division. Demands to change the culture of a
social group are seen as a threat to its very existence. In the business
organization, the insertion of people of different ethnic backgrounds or
of the minority gender into a workforce has often been bitterly opposed
because it did not fit the reigning culture. Thus we watch struggles in the
United States to give equal access to organizational administrative positions to women and minorities.

The most damaging power of culture, however, is its power to make
one blind to unethical actions. We saw this in the questions raised by
Dennis Gioia in his reflections on his time at Ford. We see it again in the
writings of Philip Yancey, a well-known Christian writer who grew up in
Atlanta, Georgia, in the 1960s. Yancey recalls how as a youth he was totally swayed by his cultural environment. For him, the Ku Klux Klan was
"a last line of defense to preserve the Christian purity of the South." He
remembers the "adolescent thrill" with which he greeted violence against
African Americans, never asking how that harmonized with the Christian faith he believed. He never questioned how people could be church
deacons and leaders of Bible study groups and at the same time don a
KKK uniform and wreak violence upon members of another race. He
could not imagine that his culture could be wrong. It was only as an adult,
while reading biographies of Martin Luther King Jr. following his death,

that Yancey began to realize the truth of what Martin Luther King Jr. lived and preached and how blinded he was by the culture of his youth.[31]

Culture cannot be trusted to tell us the ethical actions that we should take. It is helpful in decision making when it agrees with Christian principles, as was exhibited by Johnson and Johnson in 1982. But even an admired culture can change. The actions taken by Johnson and Johnson, which were so widely admired in 1982, did not result in equally admirable choices roughly twenty-five years later.

Beginning in mid-2009, McNeil, the subsidiary of Johnson and Johnson that makes children's Tylenol, began receiving complaints about the presence of "black specks in the liquid on the bottom of the bottle" of Infants' Tylenol. As a result,

> In April, 2010, McNeil recalled 136 million bottles of liquid pediatric Tylenol, Motrin, Benadryl, and Zyrtec because the medicines contained too much metal debris or too much of the necessary active ingredient in these over-the-counter-drugs. Because of the presence of metal debris, the medicine batches failed FDA testing. However, prior to the FDA testing and the recall, there was evidence that McNeil was aware of the developing problem but took no public action.[32]

Investigations identified the Fort Washington, Pennsylvania, plant as the location where the children's liquid medicines were adulterated "because they were not manufactured, processed, packed or held in conformance with current Good Manufacturing Practices (cGMP), in violation of the Federal Food, Drug and Cosmetic Act (FDCA)."[33] On March 10, 2015, McNeil pleaded guilty in Federal District Court in Philadelphia in connection with adulterated infants' and children's over-the-counter liquid drugs. The company agreed to pay a criminal fine of $20 million and forfeit $5 million. "In addition to McNeil's guilty plea, McNeil remains subject to a permanent injunction entered by the US District Court in 2011, requiring the company, among other things, to make remedial measures before reopening its manufacturing facility in Fort Washington, Pennsylvania."[34]

---

31. Yancey, "Confessions of a Racist."

32. Jennings, *Business Ethics* (7th ed.), 446.

33. Department of Justice, "McNeil Pleads Guilty."

34. Department of Justice, "McNeil Pleads Guilty."

NECESSITY OF DISTINGUISHING BETWEEN LAW, CULTURE AND ETHICS

When business people talk about difficult decisions, one quickly discovers that law, culture, and ethics are often placed on the same level. Some managers proclaim, "As far as I am concerned, if it is legal, it is all right!" Those men and women seem to take for granted that a businessperson does not need to raise questions concerning the ethics of some laws. Some attempt, as did Ford in the early 1970s, to use legal means, such as lobbying legislatures to delay safety regulations on small cars, to keep laws from being made which would be detrimental to their business.

As other business people discuss the tensions of attempting to be successful in business in the ultra-competitive climate of today when so many use moral shortcuts to profitability, they say, "In the world of business it is, "In Rome do as the Romans do!"" As a result, for these people the right solution is to do what most people do. Culture for them is a satisfactory norm.

But can the law, culture and ethics be regarded as equivalent? Or as Gioia put it: Is legal equal to ethical (as defined by professional standards)? The answer must be NO! Culture, while very useful, must be constantly questioned and evaluated. It cannot be obeyed blindly. Saying that "in Rome, do as the Romans do" is not an ethical truth. One cannot make ethical decisions by observing how large the percentage of the population is which supports a certain conduct. Ethics by statistics has no validity. Culture does not automatically produce sensitivity to right and wrong, even in a highly educated and sophisticated culture. There may be times when either society's culture or organizational culture may lead to actions which are subsequently praised as the "right thing" to do. Such was the case with Johnson and Johnson when it made the decision to pull Tylenol capsules off the shelves of all American stores. But it is dangerous to trust blindly in the humanizing effects of sophistication and education. The brutal Nazi guards often were lovers of the arts and music. From the outset we can posit that to be ethical one must have the heart and the courage to defy public opinion. Rosa Parks dared to brave cultural codes when she refused to sit in the back of a bus.

To break down the cultural blindness of America it took people like Martin Luther King Jr. who strove to "awaken a sense of shame within the oppressor." To accomplish that, King told Mayor Daley of Chicago, the blacks had "only their bodies." As Yancey stated:

> By forcing evil out into the open, he [Martin Luther King Jr.] was attempting to tap into a national reservoir of moral outrage—a concept my friends and I [Yancey] were not equipped to understand. Many historians point to one event as the single moment in which the movement attained at last a critical mass of support for the cause of civil rights. It occurred on a bridge outside Selma, Alabama, when Sheriff Jim Clark turned his policemen loose on unarmed black demonstrators. . . . Most Americans got their first glimpse of the scene when ABC interrupted its Sunday movie, *Judgment at Nuremberg*, to show footage. What the viewers saw broadcast from Alabama bore a horrifying resemblance to what they were watching from Nazi Germany. Eight days later President Lyndon Johnson submitted the Voting Rights Act of 1965 to the US Congress.[35]

It took bleeding bodies to make the cultural scales fall from many Americans' eyes. In later referring to his article in *Christianity Today*, and the responses he received to its publication, Yancey asked the question: "Only one thing haunts me more than the sins of my past: What sins am I blind to today?"[36] This question mirrors the questions Gioia asked about his time at Ford: "The major concern for me is whether they [my decisions] were moral (in the sense of adhering to some higher standards of inner conscience and conviction about the "right" actions to take)."[37] It is a question that all Christians must ask themselves about their relationships to their own cultures when facing difficult decisions.

A Christian cannot allow culture to rule him or her, nor can a Christian assume that by following the law one has done their ethical duty. Christians must remain on moral alert. They must question their culture; they must not equate minimalistic legal requirements as sufficient for ethical behavior. To be salt and light Christians are required to demonstrate the willingness and the courage to confront received ideas and ways. They must remember that Christianity is not a subculture; most of the time it is counterculture. Many times culture reflects a way of thinking which expresses pride and selfishness, not the Christian's desired perspective. Many times the law reflects only the minimum actions one should take, and at times it may even support non-Christian practices. At other times the law may not have caught up with the changes

---

35. Yancey, "Confessions of a Racist."

36. Yancey, *Soul Survivor*, 39.

37. Gioia, "Pinto Fires," 384.

in technology or society, so that possible actions, whether in the marketplace or in the factory, may not yet be covered by a specific ruling. At such times, Christian ethics requires consistent Christian responses, irrespective of what counsel may be available from a legal perspective.

Jesus continually challenged the culture of his time. The Son of God disregarded the mores of his contemporaries when he engaged a Samaritan woman in conversation. He did it again when he accepted dinner invitations from tax collectors or when he allowed children to come near him. By being born with blood considered racially stained, by working with his hands and talking with the accent of the place of his birth, by being crucified between two criminals, Jesus set aside the barriers that culture had erected in his land between human beings and the values it tried to impose upon all.

In a culture that is drifting more and more away from Judeo-Christian ideals and becoming more and more secular, Christians cannot allow themselves to be ruled by peer pressure. As Kinnaman and Lyons note in their book *Good Faith: Being a Christian When Society Thinks You're Irrelevant and Extreme*, American culture today advocates the morality of self-fulfillment where "enjoying yourself is the highest goal of life."[38] This is exactly the opposite of the centuries-old response to the Westminster Catechism's first question: "What is the chief end of man?" Christians have responded: "To glorify God and enjoy him forever"—not to seek fulfillment of one's own desires. Our contemporary cultural environment gives more urgency to the Apostle Paul's advice: "Do not conform any longer to the pattern of this world but be transformed by the renewing of your mind" (Rom 12:2).

THINKING IT THROUGH:
FORD MOTOR COMPANY AND THE PINTO

The case of the Pinto is considered a classic case, included in most business ethics textbooks. Its longevity can be attributed to the fact that similar situations occur year after year with many products and in many industries. The difficulty of determining when a product has become unsafe *and* taking responsibility for the unsafe product, removing it from the market, and repairing the damage continues to plague all businesses.

38. Kinnaman and Lyons, *Good Faith*, 57.

The ethical decisions that must be made along the way are never easy at the time, but often seem clear in hindsight.

The Pinto case illustrates utilitarian thinking on the part of Ford's management team in the early 1970s. From their perspective, when the decision to launch the Pinto was made, the possibility of accidents which could result in injury or death to the car's occupants was recognized, but considered to be small enough that the benefit of getting the car to market ahead of the competition, thus saving the company and the jobs of its workers, won the day. While the use of figures to "cost" the value of a human life may seem unbelievable, the thinking it represented is often done, with or without actual monetary calculations.

Kant would argue that risking the life of even one individual who rode in the Pinto was a price too high to pay for the financial benefits to the employees and the stockholders of getting the car to market ahead of the competition. He would have insisted that production be stopped and the car be made as safe as possible, given the knowledge available at the time it was manufactured. Kant would argue that every person is as valued as every other person and therefore must be equally considered. The consumer, for Kant, is as valuable as the employee of Ford. No person is to be used for the benefit of another.

To be honorable in business, the Christian worldview would stress the importance of human life, and accordingly would not consider any action that endangers human life to be ethical. Further, the Christian worldview would take a broad view of "life" and insist that to be ethical, the businessperson must not only preserve physical life, but seek to enhance and enrich the lives of those with whom he or she comes into contact, whether they are employees, customers, suppliers, or stockholders.

Chapter 6

If It's Easily Available,
Isn't It Smart to Make It Mine?

Privacy, Property, and Technology

Watch out! Be on your guard against all kinds of greed; a man's life does not consist in the abundance of his possessions.

—Luke 12:15

Between September 1999 and February 2000, Jonathan Lebed used AOL and E-trade accounts to trade on Wall Street and, according to the SEC, triggered chaos in the market to the tune of $800,000 in profits.[1] According to Lebed, who was a fifteen-year-old high-school student when he discussed his actions, he was merely bored and wanted something to do. Since he was a fan of CNBC, he traded stocks.

When Lebed was eleven he opened an account with America Online. To have something to say to his father, who was interested in stocks, Lebed began watching the stock-market ticker on CNBC every day when he came home from school. He watched for stocks that his father was interested in and reported their numbers to his dad. When he was twelve, he acquired his own stock with $8,000 from a matured savings bond that his parents had purchased for him when he was born. His first stock

1. Lewis, *Next*, 27–28.

purchase was America Online—a stock not recommended by his father. However, the stock price rose and Jonathan sold. From this experience Jonathan learned "(a) you could make money quickly in the stock market, (b) his dad didn't know what he was talking about, and (c) it paid him to exercise his own judgment on these matters."[2]

CNBC announced a stock-picking contest for student teams, so Jonathan and two of his friends formed a team called "Triple Threat" and entered the contest. They came in fourth, which provided a great deal of publicity for the team, both in the local paper and on CNBC. Now Jonathan had a following, as a number of people, including grown-ups, sought his advice on stocks. When he was thirteen, Jonathan opened an account with Ameritrade and turned his $8,000 into $28,000. He also created his own website devoted to penny stocks, named Stock-Dogs.com, where he touted stocks he liked.[3] This site attracted the attention of a man named Ira Monas, who fed Jonathan information about some of the companies he followed. Unfortunately for Jonathan, the SEC was watching Monas, as some of the information Monas fed to Jonathan was false. The SEC thought Jonathan had received money from Monas to post false information in order to inflate the stock prices of companies Monas worked for. Jonathan had not received any funds; he posted the information because he thought it was good information.

Jonathan continued trading, picking stocks in the morning before he went to school and posting messages about them in as many places as possible on Yahoo Finance. He used several AOL screen names in order to circumvent the AOL rules regarding the number of postings that could be sent from any one email address. Over time he learned that messages with caps and exclamation points had a better effect on the stock price. For example, one of his postings read:

> FTEC (Firetector) is starting to break out! Next week, this thing will EXPLODE. . . . Currently FTEC is trading for just $2½ . I am expecting to see FTEC at $20 VERY SOON. . . . Let me explain why. . . . I see little risk when purchasing FTEC at these DIRT-CHEAP PRICES. FTEC is making TREMENDOUS PROFITS and is trading UNDER BOOK VALUE!!! This is the #1 INDUS-TRY you can POSSIBLY be in RIGHT NOW.[4]

2. Lewis, *Next*, 39.

3. Lewis, *Next*, 41–42.

4. Lewis, *Next*, 35–36.

After the stock price went up, Jonathan sold the stock. On these trades Jonathan's daily profits ranged from more the $12,000 to nearly $74,000.[5] Jonathan's friends were impressed, as were his teachers. But the SEC was not. On September 20, 2000, the SEC settled civil fraud charges against Jonathan Lebed for using the Internet to conduct a stock manipulation scheme that made total profits of $272,826 (SEC figures) on eleven counts of identified stock trades. Jonathan was the first minor to be charged with stock market fraud.[6] Jonathan maintained that he had made $800,000 from his six months of trading, and argued that what he did was exactly what the adult stock market analysts were doing. As Michael Lewis described it:

> When he wasn't either asleep or in some dreary classroom, he lived on the Internet, which he scoured for small cap stocks that he thought might appeal to other Internet investors. He sifted the small cap stocks with three things in mind: (a) "It has to be in the area of the stock market that is likely to become a popular play"; (b) "it had to be under-valued compared to similar companies"; and (c) "It had to be undiscovered—not that many people talking about it on the message boards."[7]

Perhaps Jonathan was right about his activities. What he did in pumping his favorite stocks is what he perceived adult market analysts do every day. The difference, however, was that Jonathan was not who he pretended to be on the Internet. He was not an adult market analyst who had carefully researched the company's financial fundamentals and on the basis of that information, recommended a particular stock to a client. Jonathan was a student who chose stocks that sounded interesting to him and pretended to be a market analyst expert. The anonymous nature of the Internet allowed him to be perceived as someone he was not. Others have tried the same scam. For example, Marcus Arnold, a fifteen-year-old high school student, pretended to be a lawyer and handed out legal advice over the Internet based on what he learned about the law from TV crime shows.[8]

Today Jonathan maintains a newsletter, Lebed.biz Alert, and promotes various penny stocks. Over the years since he initially began

5. Lewis, *Next*, 28.

6. Lewis, *Next*, 27.

7. Lewis, *Next*, 77.

8. Lewis, "Faking It."

promoting stocks, he has been sued by various organizations for using their projections as if they were his own.[9]

THE RISE OF THE INTERNET

What Jonathan Lebed did would not have been possible prior to the invention of the Internet because who would have purchased a high-school student's choice of stocks for one's own investment portfolio? Prior to the Internet, the stock purchaser would have known the market analyst from whom they obtained counsel. The stock purchaser would not have accepted advice from someone they could not see or whose identity, since it was anonymous, could be faked. An anonymous expert would not have been trusted.

The Internet was not initially created to sell products or services. It was created as a research-sharing tool. The Internet's birth resides in a series of memos written by J. C. R. Licklider of MIT in August 1962, in which he "envisioned a globally interconnected set of computers through which everyone could quickly access data and programs from any site."[10] Lawrence G. Roberts and Thomas Merrill connected the first computers between California and Massachusetts in 1965, using a low speed dial-up telephone line.[11] These early creators of the Internet were academics, looking for a way to share research information and computer time. They presumed they could trust the other users, and that the other users were, like themselves, technically competent and interested in sharing their research—not their personal lives. Thus the Internet was, from the beginning, built for resiliency, not privacy or security.[12]

By the early 1980s, vendors were interested in the commercialization of the Internet, initially to provide basic networking products and connectivity. The official "birthday" of the Internet is considered to be January 1, 1983, when the ARPANET host network changed to the TCP/IP standard (Transfer Control Protocol / Internetwork Protocol), the universal language still used today.[13] With the coming of the World Wide Web in the mid-1990s, users were interested in easy access to in-

9. Sykes, "Exposing Convicted Penny Stock Manipulator."
10. Leiner et al., *Brief History of the Internet.*
11. Leiner et al., *Brief History of the Internet.*
12. Lucas, *Cyberphobia*, 34–35.
13. Leiner et al., *Brief History of the Internet.*

formation, and products were developed to meet that interest.[14] Today we expect all our devices to be connected to the Internet so that we can search the web, receive email, post on Facebook, take and send pictures, text, talk, and watch our favorite movies with the touch of a finger.

The Internet, however, has been more than a technological advance. Now it reaches into every business and home through e-commerce, information acquisition, and basic communication. Its influence on society, particularly with the World Wide Web, is far greater than any of its original inventors would have guessed possible. Some, however, were ahead of their time. In 1992, the Computer Ethics Institute developed "The Ten Commandments of Computer Ethics." Perhaps, because of the cautions they raised, they foresaw more of the future than most did. Their ten commandments are:

1. Thou shalt not use a computer to harm other people.

2. Thou shalt not interfere with other people's computer work.

3. Thou shalt not snoop around in other people's computer files.

4. Thou shalt not use a computer to steal.

5. Thou shalt not use a computer to bear false witness.

6. Thou shalt not copy or use proprietary software for which you have not paid.

7. Thou shalt not use other people's computer resources without authorization or proper compensation.

8. Thou shalt not appropriate other people's intellectual output.

9. Thou shalt think about the social consequences of the program you are writing or the system you are designing.

10. Thou shalt always use a computer in ways that ensure consideration and respect for your fellow humans.[15]

Another person who was ahead of her time was Virginia Shea, who wrote ten rules for Internet etiquette (or ethics) in 1994. These rules are helpful as we seek to both provide and use information with integrity and courtesy in the virtual world of today. Shea's rules are as follows:[16]

---

14. Leiner et al., *Brief History of the Internet*.

15. Computer Ethics Institute, "Ten Commandments of Computer Ethics."

16. Shea, *Netiquette*, 32–45.

Rule 1: Remember the human. In your electronic communication, remember you are dealing with real people. The Golden Rule is a good test: Do unto others as you would have others do unto you.

Rule 2: Adhere to the same standards of behavior online that you follow in real life. You would not be rude in a face-to-face conversation. Accordingly, do not be rude in a virtual world conversation.

Rule 3: Know where you are in cyberspace. Are you communicating with a friend, with a work colleague, or with your boss? Communicate with the audience in mind.

Rule 4: Respect other people's time and bandwidth. Make your written communication meaningful and to the point, without unnecessary graphics that take a long time to download. Don't use "reply all" unless the message is intended and needed by all members of the group.

Rule 5: Make yourself look good online. If you are posting pictures, they will speak for themselves. If, however, you are sending a written message, check the message for spelling and grammar errors, state your message as clearly as possible, and be polite.

Rule 6: Share expert knowledge. Offer information you have to assist others and help people who have questions.

Rule 7: Help keep flame wars under control. Refrain from participating in angry posts between two or three people. Don't feed the flames.

Rule 8: Respect other people's privacy. You may read private information, especially if it is posted on Facebook. Err on the side of caution when deciding whether or not to discuss this information with others, especially with work colleagues.

Rule 9: Don't abuse your power. In face-to-face situations, some people have more power than others. The same is true in cyberspace. Use your power wisely and well.

Rule 10: Be forgiving of other people's mistakes. If you see mistakes being practiced, be kind. If you choose to correct someone, do so privately, not in a public forum.

TECHNOLOGY AND THE VALUES
OF OWNERSHIP AND EXPERTISE

Thomas Donaldson argues that technology in itself can change values.[17] For example, the printing press undermined the authority of the Catholic Church in the Renaissance by printing Bibles in local languages so that all had access to the scriptures. Thus people developed their own relationship with God and were no longer forced to rely on priests for their understanding, knowledge, and interpretation of the Bible. Today the Internet, which touches every aspect of our lives, is more than just a fast delivery service for information. It has, as Donaldson notes, changed society's values in several ways, including where and from whom one obtains knowledge and expertise, and who owns the information which is so easily accessible and so cheaply reproduced and/or altered.

Previously society sought knowledge from those who were supposed to possess it and in those places where it was traditionally found, such as schools, libraries, and through consultation with professionally-licensed experts. But on the Internet, the traditional sources of power have been tossed aside. As Lewis puts it: "Power and prestige and profit were up for grabs. The Internet undermined all the old sources of insider power: control of distribution channels, control of intellectual property, control of information."[18] The Internet made it possible for people to thwart what in the past have been rules and conventions and authorities by which society operated. Lewis states: "The Internet [is] rock 'n' roll all over again. Not rock 'n' roll now, but rock 'n' roll in the 1950s and 1960s, when it actually terrified grown-ups. The Internet [is] enabling a great status upheaval and a subversion of all manner of social norms. And the people quickest to seize on its powers [are] the young."[19] In the opening story, Jonathan Lebed undermined the authority of the Wall Street analysts because financial information was available to him over the Internet. Even though he was an amateur, he promoted certain stocks as if he were

17. Donaldson, "Ethics in Cyberspace," 273–91.

18. Lewis, *Next*, 158.

19. Lewis, "Faking It."

an equal authority with other analysts on the marketplace. With anonymity, no one knows for sure who is providing the information available on the Internet—it could be an expert or not. As the *New Yorker* cartoon showing two dogs sitting by a computer, talking to each other, portrayed so vividly: "On the Internet, nobody knows you're a dog."[20]

The Internet can hide the source of the information and thus its integrity and reliability. We expect information that has integrity to be as accurate as possible. We expect that information which is reliable to be unaltered in form and in content. We further expect that information which is both reliable and has integrity cannot be read by those who do not have access to it, and if it is proprietary or sensitive information, it is kept confidential and secure.[21] Users of the Internet must learn to distinguish credible information from junk. Traditional sources of information, such as articles in journals or books, have been subjected to peer review and editorial examination. Authors of works on the printed page must take responsibility for what is printed. Newspaper tabloids have been sued if they defame public figures, even though it is common knowledge that such sources may fall into the gossip category. But on the Internet there is not even minimum control. Anyone can place anything on a website. While this is not necessarily a bad thing, it does mean that the user of the information must be more discerning when accepting such information as reliable.

Beyond the issue of where the information comes from is the matter of replication. The Internet's power of replication allows access to libraries and art galleries for everyone, irrespective of where they live. Children in rural or inaccessible areas no longer are disadvantaged because they cannot "see" the same sights as those who live in the cities or have access to historical or cultural heritage sites.

But information available on the Internet disappears. Websites can be available today and gone tomorrow. When they are gone, the material they contained also disappears. Electronically-stored material requires elaborate equipment to read. Thus not only must the file be preserved, but also the equipment to read the file. This is not the same as preserving a book.

Electronic text can also be altered without detection. One can use a trusted website, but not all websites are trustworthy. One can see an

20. Steiner, *New Yorker*, July 5, 1993.

21. Spinello, "Information Integrity," 158–80.

image—even an image supposedly in a famous gallery—but the image may have been altered. We are familiar with this phenomena through computer-enhanced special effects in movies. We may not be as sure of identifying when image-altering has occurred when viewing a published picture of a famous figure in a compromising situation on the Internet.

While we all recognize that information is expensive, with the Internet it is only expensive to produce the first copy. The Internet allows for copying a vast quantity of material and copying it so well that it is impossible to distinguish the copy from the original. Thus it is nearly costless to produce succeeding copies of information and to distribute these copies over a network with the greatest of ease. As a result, software and music piracy abound. This ease of reproducibility has changed long-standing values regarding ownership rights, particularly in the music and other creative industries where the authors of songs, books, and other artistic works formerly enjoyed copyright protection. The long-held value that artistic work belonged to the author/creator and that he or she had an exclusive right to publish, sell, or distribute the material for their own benefit for their lifetime and seventy years after their death, has been replaced by common practices of copyright infringement. Technology has made reproducibility so easy. The Recording Industry Association of America (RIAA) notes that "many different actions qualify as piracy (or music theft) from downloading unauthorized versions of copyrighted music from a file-sharing service to illegally copying music using streamripping software or mobile apps." They also note that "technology has made digital copying easier than ever. But just because advances in technology make it possible to copy music doesn't mean it's legal to do so."[22] While technological advances have challenged long-standing values regarding ownership, does the lack of law enforcement or legal specificity that lags behind technology's advances make the violation of ownership rights ethically correct? Are the rights of composers, inventors, and authors of no importance in a world where duplication is so easy and so cheap?

Universities are particularly concerned about file sharing because much of it is done by students using the university's Internet service. For example, Washington State University's published policies state:

> Presently, the most flagrant copyright-infringing activity on the Internet is sharing music, movies, or software. . . . Students who use the University's Internet service to download

22. RIAA, "About Piracy."

or upload music, movies, or other unauthorized materials face consequences including being sued by the RIAA or the MPAA and losing a lawsuit that costs you thousands of dollars, being charged with criminal violations, or serving prison time. When copyright infringement, through file sharing or otherwise, occurs on the University Internet services, WSU is also vicariously liable for copyright infringement. It is in violation of the *Electronic Publishing and Appropriate Use Policy* to download or upload materials from the Internet without permission. Any one on campus who is discovered engaging in this activity is required to take a class in copyright law and may lose their Internet service.[23]

Perhaps of equal concern is the widespread use of another's work as if it were one's own. Today students freely download research papers which others have prepared, and submit them as if they had done the work. While plagiarism has always occurred, today it has risen to new heights. It is no longer confined to copying large sections of another's publication into one's own research paper; now the entire paper can easily be submitted as one's own and the difference between the original and the copy can hardly be distinguished. Websites exist which advertise availability of "models" of research papers, but which actually provide downloadable papers on thousands of topics which can either be purchased with a credit card, or in some cases, are available for no charge. By claiming that they market to students for research purposes and only provide "model" documents, these term paper mills attempt to avoid state laws which prohibit the sale of term papers to students for class submission.[24] Does the easy availability of model papers make plagiarism acceptable? Does offering another's work as if it were one's own constitute stealing, because one takes from others what was theirs and acts as if it is now one's own creation?

SCRIPTURE'S PERSPECTIVE

The Internet forces one to seriously reconsider God's words when he spoke the eighth commandment: "You shall not steal" (Exod 20:15). Traditionally the commandment has been applied to physical items such as property and goods, which were seen as the material expression of a

23. Washington State University, "Internet & Copyright."
24. Roach, "High-Tech Cheating," 26–28.

family's hard work and perseverance and as the result of God's blessing. Such material items had much to do with the family's self-esteem. In the past, when property was carefully transmitted from father to son, it established a link between generations. Because property was so closely bound with the family name, its care required family members to be honorable in their material dealings. Property was not to be acquired by exploiting and defrauding others or by theft and robbery. The commandment, however, also condemns attempts to advantage oneself by the ignorance, weakness, or misfortune of another. It demands strict integrity in every detail of business and personal life. It forbids overreaching in business and requires the payment of just debts and wages. In previous generations, bankruptcy as a "way out" of debt stained the reputation not only of the individual but also of the entire family.

But stealing does not only involve physical items. For example, we may present someone else's ideas or creations as our own, whether in the workplace or in personal life, or fail to give credit to the actual author or inventor. We can overcharge customers or provide them with poor products or services. We can fail to work during the time we are being paid. We may choose to be silent when we are not charged enough on an invoice due to an error on the vendor's part, or when we receive incorrect change from a cashier.[25]

With the Internet, taking what is not one's own is even easier. It can be done within one's own house, without requiring one to physically go to another location. Stealing another's ideas or creative work is particularly easy over the Internet, as noted above. But this does not make it less of a violation of the eighth commandment.

David Gill challenges us to interpret this commandment broadly: "We must not live in a manner that, however indirectly, deprives other people of the necessities of life, for that would be theft."[26] Instead, we should "think biblically, critically, creatively and redemptively about the economic policies, practices and institutions of our time. The Christian economic 'theory' is stewardship. The guiding principle is to avoid taking anything or any profit that rightfully (i.e., in the eyes of God) should belong to someone else and, rather than focusing on personal gain, to seek to give to those in need."[27]

25. Gill, *Doing Right*, 267.
26. Gill, *Doing Right*, 278.
27. Gill, *Doing Right*, 270.

THE INTERNET AND PRIVACY AND ANONYMITY

The Internet provides wonderful opportunities to communicate around the world, to search for information and provide others with information, to shop, advertise, and pay for goods without the usual access barriers, to express political or artistic thoughts, and to play games and chat with friends. But the Internet can also be a medium for the darker side of life—violence, crime, deception, greed, rudeness, cyber-terrorism, identity theft, child pornography. To some extent, the ethical issues introduced by the Internet are merely extensions of ethical issues which have always been with us. For example, privacy has been an ethical issue for as long as time has existed. What people say in a public place and what they say privately has long been held to different standards. Private letters have legal protection; it is against the law to open private mail. But today people use email in a manner similar to how personal letters were used in the past. Email, however, does not currently have privacy protection; the courts are treating email as if it were a postcard rather than a private letter.

Internet technology changes both the face of the ethical issue and the extent to which it affects society. The Internet has forced us to look at many traditional norms and conventions with new glasses. Old issues such as privacy and anonymity, which we will discuss next, must be viewed through new lenses. New issues, which we discussed above, include ownership, expertise, and replication.

Privacy

Not long ago violations of personal privacy consisted of being followed around the mall by a person tracking your purchases, or by having someone listen in on a telephone conversation you had while using the old "party line." Today on the Internet, cyberspace marketers track customer's purchases through cookie tracking, and employers "listen in" to email conversations which take place during working hours. One can argue that there is nothing new with respect to the privacy issues presently associated with the Internet but rather these are earlier issues have been intensified by the use of technology.

But in fact the Internet has done more than merely intensify privacy issues. With the Internet, privacy threats can occur on a scale which would not have been possible with pre-Internet technologies. Today computerized and Internet connected "watchdogs" invade one's home and private space. Some, such as Amazon's Alexa, are invited on the pretext of helping manage our lives. These enhance old privacy concerns. In addition, there are specific privacy issues that relate to the Internet which did not exist before. For example, today the quantity of personal information that is available and retrievable on the Internet would be mind-boggling to our grandparents. Facts which in the past were held to be deeply private are now readily available—if not for free, at least for a very small fee. Of recent concern is Google's tracking of K-12 students' activities on its laptops (Chromebooks) and word processing and related software which are used in the US public schools. Google has overtaken Apple and Microsoft in sales to schools, primarily because of the low cost of their products. But in their privacy agreements with the schools, Google only covered their education suite services—Gmail, Calendar, and Google Docs—but did not cover other Google services such as Google News, Search, Maps, and Youtube. If students use these services while on Chromebooks, Google acknowledged that it collects the data, which they indicate will be used to improve their products. Some parents have expressed concern that the collected information may be used for targeted advertisements and other unidentified purposes.[28]

In mid-summer, 2016, Nintendo released "Pokemon Go"—a smartphone game that used augmented reality (AR) to let players hunt for Pokemon characters in real world locations. The game literally took off and quickly exceeded all records for downloads. Accompanying the game were all types of other goods which Pokemon fans could also purchase, such as stuffed animals and Pokemon cards. Businesses near a "Poke-Stop" took advantage of the influx of potential customers to increase their own business profits. Taxi-cab business in major cities also expanded, especially as some cab drivers offered to take customers on game-specific tours.

Some concerns were expressed about the safety of available locations where Pokemon could be found, including subway platforms and city streets in New York City. However, of apparently little concern to the players of "Pokemon Go" were the privacy concerns. When downloading the app on one's iPhone, players gave Niantic (a spinout from Google's parent company, Alphabet Inc., which shares ownership of Pokemon Company with Nintendo) access to all their data associated with the

28. Peterson, "Google Tracking Students."

Google account, "including email, calendar and contact information."[29] The *Wall Street Journal* noted that "Nintendo, Pokemon Company, and Niantic declined to comment on the privacy issue. Google didn't respond to requests for comment."[30]

Privacy issues in 2016 with Pokemon were only a precursor of what was to come. In 2017 and 2018, Internet privacy concerns became a matter of daily conversation. Questions arose in the media about the impact of Cambridge Analytica and the Facebook information they used for campaign targeting during the 2016 presidential election in the United States. Did the data this British company harvested from Facebook actually sway the voting public or did the Facebook platform and information it already possessed allow the spread of disinformation and phony news reports? Congress asked those questions and others of Mark Zuckerberg, Facebook's chief executive, when he testified in April 2018 regarding how personal information on up to eighty-seven million Facebook users ended up in Cambridge Analytica's hands. He was also asked how Facebook intended to protect user privacy in the future.[31]

The European Union's General Data Protection Regulation (GDPR), passed in 2016 to replace their older Data Protection Directive of 1995, went into effect on May 25, 2018. It requires companies to tell individuals what information they have about the person and get the person's permission before the company can use the information.[32] The immediate impact of this law for Facebook was a decline of three million users in Europe,[33] but whether this is a signal that the general public is becoming more aware and concerned about privacy on the Internet remains to be seen. As Andy Kroll stated in his article in *Mother Jones*: "Cambridge's controversial foray into US politics spawned larger questions about how our social-media habits can be turned against us, and how companies such as Facebook hold more power over our lives—the ability to shape public conversation, even political outcomes—than many people are comfortable with."[34]

29. Mochizuki and Needleman, "Pokemon Game Jolts Nintendo."

30. Mochizuki and Needleman, "Pokemon Game Jolts Nintendo."

31. Singer, "What You Don't Know about Facebook."

32. Satariano, "What the G.D.P.R. Means for You."

33. Timberg and Dwoskin, "Privacy Controversies with Facebook."

34. Kroll, "Cloak and Data."

Thus, the use of the Internet as a surveillance medium is not business as usual, but is in fact a unique privacy concern. When the Internet was first developed there was fear that the primary surveillance usage would be by the government. In fact, businesses are by far the greatest users of this Internet capability. Businesses monitor the activities of persons who visit their websites, including how often the website is visited and what preferences the customer demonstrates during the visit. This information is then mined to combine and recombine it in ways that construct profiles of individuals. The usual purpose of this activity is to create consumer categories. Customers experience this phenomenon when, after ordering books from Amazon.com, they receive specialized messages from the company about books which other individuals in the defined customer category have ordered. The purpose of such messages is to encourage more purchases by using peer pressure to inform the prospective customer that "individuals just like you prefer these other products which are now available." It is interesting to note that when discussing the tracking of buying preferences with the millennial generation, they generally see the specialized messages and targeted advertisements as time-savers because they are informed about goods they are interested in, rather than violations of privacy. Michael Lewis warned us of this reaction seventeen years ago when he wrote:

> Privacy is no longer a right but a wasteful luxury. The Internet has not merely created terrifying economic incentives for people to abandon their charming old attachment to their privacy. Privacy is newly inefficient if the larger social goal is to get the most stuff to the most people at the cheapest prices. And who would deny that the consumer demands for ever more stuff at ever cheaper prices is one of the great deterministic forces in history? Any technology that gives the consumer what he wants, when he wants it, at a better price, is likely to succeed, in spite of a lot of objections from hoary old privacy nuts.[35]

Anonymity

Unfortunately, the loss of privacy has led to a lack of integrity with respect to our identity and reputation. Because individuals share so much about themselves, especially on Facebook and LinkedIn, people can

35. Lewis, *Next*, 185.

impersonate others as a joke or for more malicious purposes. Lucas notes that while we freely give up information about ourselves, "we are not getting things that would make us safer, particularly the ability to identify ourselves, and make binding decisions, smoothly and securely. Nor do we have the ability to identify other people and authenticate their decisions. Not only are we liable to impersonation, we do not know if the people we are dealing with are real."[36] He likens our situation to being "visitors to a masked ball, but without the ability to take our masks off, or to see if others are doing so. This undermines the concept of identity which underpins our political, legal and economic systems."[37] To have a well-functioning society, there must also be a high level of trust, which cannot be developed with an anonymous person.

Like privacy, anonymity is not a new ethical issue. We are aware of anonymous letters, telephone calls, authors of books and articles in other venues besides the Internet. But on the Internet, an anonymous person can reach many more people and anonymity can provide privacy. The question is: For what purpose?

Weckert identifies three major Internet purposes for anonymity: communication in a chat room; email for the purposes of spamming and flaming; and to protect privacy (i.e., to visit a website anonymously).[38]

If one has nothing to hide, there is no purpose in being anonymous. But individuals may prefer anonymity because they feel freer to express opinions (as in a chat room), or because they wish to annoy or insult others, or because they wish to appear to be someone other than who they actually are. Sometimes individuals use anonymity to establish expertise, as was the case of Jonathan Lebed, who correctly assumed that if others knew he was in his early teens, they might not have seen him as a reliable expert on the stock market. Others have used anonymity to facilitate spreading harmful rumors which defame people, or to visit pornography sites while hoping that their actions cannot be traced.

On the other hand, the purpose for anonymity may actually be much darker. An individual may seek intentional deception or commercial manipulation. Or one may seek to perpetrate a crime, such as laundering money, organizing terrorist activities, acting as a sex or child

---

36. Lucas, *Cyberphobia*, 64.

37. Lucas, *Cyberphobia*, 65–66.

38. Weckert, "What Is New or Unique," 47–64.

predator, or obtaining confidential information. People know that they cannot be held accountable for their actions while they are anonymous.

The legal environment in which the Internet operates, which was initially established to support its growth, now supports the use of the Internet for darker purposes. The July 12, 2016, issue of the *Wall Street Journal* ran a front page article entitled: "Web Freedom's Role in Sex Trafficking." The article noted that the Communications Decency Act of 1996 absolved websites of most responsibility for user posts—a decision made in the early stages of the Internet which probably encouraged the rise of web sites such as YouTube and Yelp. Under this law, hosting or republishing third-party speech is not charged against the host, in the same way that telephone companies are not charged for illegal activities that use phone lines. But today, websites such as Backpage and similar websites that encourage adult sexual encounters, are charged with fostering non-adult listings which encourage trafficking of underage victims. In 2013, forty-nine state attorney generals requested that Congress reverse the 1996 legislation and require that firms hosting adult ads provide the ages of the people in the ads. The tech firms fought back, indicating that the legal immunity granted in 1996 was essential for Internet business.[39]

SCRIPTURE'S PERSPECTIVE

The dark side of anonymity is in direct contrast to the Scripture's portrayal of God. In 1 John 1:5, John writes: "God is light, in him there is no darkness at all." Paul states in 1 Thess 5:4–5: "But you, brothers, are not in darkness. . . . You are all sons of light and sons of the day." Jesus describes his followers as the light of the world, a city on a hill that cannot be hidden (Matt 5:14). Further, God states that we are known by him, engraved on the palms of his hands (Isa 49:15–16). Jesus further asserts that even the hairs of our heads are numbered (Matt 10:30). We are not anonymous to God.

Humans were created with freedom of choice, but with that freedom came responsibility for one's choices and actions. Adam and Eve realized this after they unsuccessfully attempted to hide from God in the garden after eating from the Tree of the Knowledge of Good and Evil. God confronted them with their actions and reminded them of the consequences of their choices. They could not bypass their responsibilities,

39. McKinnon, "Web Freedom's Role in Sex Trafficking."

and neither can we. We are counseled to avoid deception (Lev 19:11) and to remember our accountability to God (Matt 12:36; Rom 14:12; Heb 4:13). Thus, for Christians to operate in an anonymous manner in any venue (including on the Internet) does not mirror God's openness and light, and reflects a belief that somehow we can be anonymous. In fact, all we do is always open to the eye of God (Ps 38:15–16; Prov 15:3).

LIFE@INTERNET SPEED

The book of Genesis describes how God created the world and human-kind. Humans were created in the image of God, were placed in a garden, and were invited to dress and keep the garden. Gardens do not grow quickly; they require care and time which, based on Scripture, seems to be God's preferred way to work. Humans were also invited into relation-ships with God and with each other through the establishment of the Sabbath—a specific time set aside for contemplation and rest.

The Internet has created a very different world. We speak of Life@ Internet speed, and, by this term, we mean moving faster and faster. This can be very good when we wish to send information to far-off places or accomplish mathematical calculations which previously were impossible due to the amount of time required. However, living at this speed may alter our perception of who we are and who we wish to become.

Jeffrey Rosen[40] discusses this issue by first referring to the work of Erving Goffman,[41] who identified the need for people to be able to circulate between "on stage" and "off stage" personalities. Rosen then maintains that having every aspect of our lives revealed over the Internet, from personal financial information to email conversations to electronic surveillance to reading habits and shopping preferences, to what we ate for breakfast and where we are headed in the next few minutes, will affect others' views of who we are, as well as our view of self. The small bits of information which Internet surveillance absorbs and transmits through on-line profiling cannot accurately describe or understand the entire per-son. Because such vast amounts of information overwhelm those who wish to understand and analyze us, individually or collectively, the solu-tion will be to mine the data through word searches. This greatly increases the risk that such information will be taken out of context and individu-

40. Rosen, "Eroded Self."

41. Goffman, *Presentation of Self in Everyday Life.*

als will be reduced to bits of information which have been collected. This information may indicate demographic data, personal tastes in reading or food or movies, but this information is not a complete picture.

As Rosen explains, bits of information are no substitute for how we actually learn about each other—through conversation, slowly, over time.

> Friendship and romantic love can't be achieved without intimacy, and intimacy, in turn, depends upon the selective and voluntary disclosure of personal information that we don't share with everyone else. . . . Privacy is necessary for the development of human individuality. Any writer will understand the importance of reflective solitude in refining arguments and making unexpected connections. In an odd but widely shared experience, many of us seem to have our best ideas when we are in the shower. Indeed, studies of creativity show that it's during periods of daydreaming and seclusion that the most creative thought takes place, as individuals allow ideas and impressions to run freely through their minds without fear that their untested thoughts will be exposed and taken out of context.[42]

Without the opportunity to be "off-stage" and keep some information about ourselves private, we may believe that we are in fact merely a collection of bits of information rather than complete persons. We may allow ourselves to be defined by market research pronouncements or statements made on Facebook, rather than defining who we are through intimate interaction with other humans. We may forget that God did not create humans as bits of data, but as complete persons in his image.

In "New Ethics . . . or No Ethics?" Jerry Useem, quoting Dennis Moberg of Santa Clara University, notes that "ethics implies contemplation and deliberation and working through a moral calculus."[43] God invites us to "be still and know that I am God" (Ps 46:10). He invites us to contemplate our actions in light of their consequences. Life@Internet speed does not allow for time to deliberate or contemplate. If one does not move faster and faster, someone else will win the money game. This may lead to a coarsening of ethical standards.

In her book *The Sabbath World*, Judith Shulevitz discusses the 1973 John Darley and Daniel Batson study of whether students at Princeton Theological Seminary would stop to help someone in distress. In this study, the seminary students, on their way to give an assigned lecture on

42. Rosen, "Eroded Self."
43. Useem, "New Ethics . . . or No Ethics?," 86.

the Good Samaritan, were forced to confront a person who sat slumped motionless in a doorway, coughing and groaning. (This slumped person was actually an accomplice of the experimenter.) Some of the students were told they had to rush to get to the lecture on time. Some were told they had enough time to get to the lecture if they moved along at a good speed. The final group was told they had plenty of time to get to the lecture. In the experiment, the researchers unfortunately found that few of the students stopped to help the person in the doorway.

> After the data was weighed and the variables analyzed, only one variable could be used to predict who would stop to help and who wouldn't. The important factor was not personality type or whether a student's career or the parable of the Good Samaritan was foremost in his mind. It was whether or not he was in a hurry. . . . The study made it hard not to conclude, said Darley and Batson, that ethics becomes a luxury as the speed of our daily lives increases.[44]

ARE HUMANS STILL NECESSARY?

Bill Joy, cofounder and chief scientist of Sun Microsystems, in his article "Why the Future Doesn't Need Us," goes a step further to contemplate a world where people would no longer be necessary at all—where robots do things better than humans, including making decisions, and where humans might gain immortality by becoming one with robotic technology. Interestingly, his concern is not that such technology will be driven by the government for military purposes, but by business for commercial purposes. He finds such a world frightening.

> A technological approach to Eternity—near immortality through robotics—may not be the most desirable utopia, and its pursuit brings clear dangers. Maybe we should rethink our utopian choices. . . . Clearly, we need to find meaningful challenges and sufficient scope in our lives if we are to be happy in whatever is to come. But I believe we must find alternative outlets for our creative forces, beyond the culture of perpetual economic growth; this growth has largely been a blessing for several hundred years, but it has not brought us unalloyed happiness, and we must now choose between the pursuit of unrestricted

44. Shulevitz, *Sabbath World*, 25–26.

and undirected growth through science and technology and the
clear accompanying dangers.[45]

God offers us a better option. He invites us to use our talents to
create and to use what we create, not to be used by it. He urges us not to
replace ourselves with machines, and he promises us a future with him
forever—not oblivion where our lives are less useful than the robots we
create.

THINKING IT THROUGH:
THE CASE OF JONATHAN LEBED

Was Jonathan Lebed really doing anything wrong, or was he merely taking advantage of the Internet in the same way that many others have done
and continue to do every day?

While a utilitarian would not openly condone the actions of a deceitful person, those who subscribe to a utilitarian philosophy might
raise questions regarding how much harm was really done by Jonathan
Lebed's actions. They might argue that many people, in following his
advice, actually made money, as did he. Thus while he pretended to be
someone he was not (i.e., a licensed stock analyst), and perhaps people
were fooled to some extent, the end result did not apparently mean these
people suffered financial loss by following his counsel.

Kant would respond: "Tell the truth!" He would argue that a world
where anonymity permits a person to pretend to be someone he or she
is not, and, thereby to deceive others (like Jonathan Lebed), is a world
where one actually lives and supports a lie. Since one does not wish to
live in a world where one cannot trust others, one should not act in an
untrustworthy manner.

To be honorable in business, the Christian worldview would consider the ninth commandment applicable to the Lebed situation. Christians
are urged not to bear false witness (Exod 20:16), which may be restated
in the positive to require that Christians speak and live the truth. Psalm
15:2 states that it is the one who "speaks the truth from his heart" who
will dwell in the Lord's sanctuary and live on his holy hill, and Prov 12:19
states that "truthful lips endure forever, but a lying tongue lasts only a
moment." Finally, the Christian will recall that Scripture states that it is
the devil who is the father of lies (John 8:44), while "the Lord detests lying

45. Joy, "Why the Future Doesn't Need Us," 258.

lips, but he delights in men who are truthful" (Prov 12:22). To pretend to be someone one is not, or to pretend to have knowledge one has not honestly gained, is to live a lie. The Christian should avoid such deceit, even if it is done anonymously so that others are fooled. The Christian knows that God is not fooled, but he sees what is done in secret (Matt 6:18).

Chapter 7

How Can I Sell More Goods and Services?

Marketing and Advertising

Advertisements are now so numerous that they are very negligently perused, and it is therefore become necessary to gain attention by magnificence of promises, and by eloquences sometimes sublime and sometimes pathetic.

—SAMUEL JOHNSON, 1758

IN 1860, HENRY NESTLE, a Frenchman, developed a formula that substituted for breast milk to save the life of an infant who could not be breast-fed. Since that time, Nestle, a Swiss-based corporation, has continued the development of infant formula for the purpose of providing nourishment for babies who, for various reasons, are in the same situation. In the 1950s, Nestle and other infant-formula makers (e.g., Abbott Laboratories, American Home Products, Borden's, Bristol-Myers, and other Japanese and European companies) began marketing infant formula in Africa, Asia, and Latin America. Two factors drove the expansion of the infant formula market to these areas. First, the birth rate increase in Western nations was declining. Second, the developing world expressed concern about infant malnutrition associated with milk allergies and mothers who were unable to nurse adequately. However, by 1968, this market expansion was fraught with controversy.

At issue were the marketing and advertising techniques used. The major infant formula companies used "milk nurses" who dressed in nurses' uniforms and worked the halls of the maternity wards, encouraging mothers of newborns to allow their babies to be fed with formula. These women were employed by the companies on a sales commission basis. Understaffed hospitals welcomed these "nurses" who not only provided formula, but also instructed new mothers on all aspects of child care and feeding. Nestle not only promoted its products through these "nurses" but also used mass-media advertising, including sound trucks, newspapers, television, radio, popular magazines, and billboards. Some advertisements suggested that formula-fed babies were healthier than those who were breast-fed, and that formula feeding was more socially appropriate, or "modern," than breastfeeding.

Despite the promises made through advertising, the use of infant formula posed a health-risk to infants in these countries for three important reasons. First, the formula had to be mixed with water, which was contaminated in many of the countries where the formula was sold. Using contaminated water resulted in diarrhea or other diseases in the babies. In addition, written instructions for mixing the formula were impossible for many mothers to read, due to insufficient education.

Second, the cost of the formula was higher than the mothers could easily afford, so the formula was often diluted, which contributed to malnourishment and other health problems for the babies. Once the formula was mixed and/or diluted, lack of refrigeration meant it could not be stored safely.

Finally, women who chose not to breast feed, even if that choice was made in the hospital and in response to pressure from the "nurses," found they could not easily return to breast feeding after they were home because their own milk production diminished. They were thus forced to rely on the formula.

In 1974, the journalist Mike Muller wrote a pamphlet entitled "The Baby Killer," which was published by War on Want, a London-based nonprofit activist group concerned with hunger, poverty, and other problems of the Third World. The pamphlet singled out Nestle, and in particular its practices in India, because it held the largest (50 percent) share of the Third World infant formula market, even though Nestle's advertising actions were not unique to the market. The pamphlet galvanized public opinion in both Europe and North America against Nestle and its advertising and marketing practices.

In November 1975, several infant formula manufacturers, including Nestle, formed the International Council of Infant Food Industries (ICIFI) and adopted a code of marketing ethics for the advertising and selling of infant formula products. Unsatisfied with this code because it lacked enforcement methods, the Infant Formula Actions Coalition (INFACT) was formed in 1977. INFACT announced a consumer boycott of all Nestle products in protest of its Third World marketing practices, and asked for hearings in the US Senate's Subcommittee on Health and Human Resources, chaired by Senator Edward Kennedy. Ultimately the World Health Organization (WHO) entered the picture, and through its efforts, the United Nations adopted a "Code of Marketing of Breast-Milk Substitutes," which Nestle agreed to conform to. The Nestle boycott was formally terminated in early 1984, although the distribution of free samples of infant formula was not stopped by the International Association of Infant Food Manufacturers until the end of 1992.[1]

MARKETING: INFORMATION OR DECEPTION?

Broadly speaking, marketing includes promoting, selling, and distributing products and services. However, it also involves making decisions about what products to create, determining who the customers might be and how to persuade them to buy the products and services, as well as how to price the products and services so that the exchange process is mutually beneficial to all parties. In marketing classes, students cover this broad spectrum of marketing responsibilities through considering the four Ps of marketing: product, price, promotion, and placement.[2]

Each of these Ps involves ethical responsibilities on the part of a business. We considered the ethical issues relating to products in chapter 5 on product safety. With respect to pricing, ethics requires a transparent market so that consumers can make valid comparisons. The price of any good should reflect all available information about its value and thus enable market participants to make rational economic choices. Without this openly available information, the market cannot be efficient. This is the theory behind the stock market and how it sets stock prices, and the reason why insider trading is considered unethical. The same principle holds true for the pricing of products and services. Therefore

---

1. Adapted from Jennings, *Business Ethics* (7th ed.), 335–37.
2. Boatright, *Ethics and the Conduct of Business*, 272.

a transparent market precludes actions such as price fixing, collusion, and price discrimination so that some customers are charged more than others. It also precludes predatory pricing where one company reduces prices with the intent (and that is the *key* factor) of driving competitors out of business so that once there is no competition, the company becomes a monopoly and can recoup its losses by charging above-market rates.

Ethical placement requires open channels of distribution available to all so that the customer has access to the desired product or service. The availability of goods and services through the Internet has expanded the channels of distribution to the extent that many of the formerly questionable marketing practices, such as controlling distribution channels and slotting allowances to stores, are no longer practiced.

The most visible ethical responsibilities for the marketing professional, at least in the eyes of the public, relate to the promotion of the products or services. Consumers understand that companies must provide information about their products and services, both for the purpose of informing the public about what is available, as well as selling their products in order to sustain their business. Questions, however, often arise regarding the methods companies choose to use. Sometimes consumers react to advertising by ignoring it or discounting the statements made in the advertisements as hyperbole. Sometimes, as in the case with Nestle as described above, consumers react negatively against the company as a whole if they believe the company stepped over the lines of fairness, truthfulness, and good ethical practices in their advertising. The usual criticisms of advertising focus on the possibility of deception and manipulation of the consumer through the advertising process.

ADVERTISING

Businesses have an obligation to provide clear, accurate, and adequate product and service information because the economy is too large and too complex for consumers to become self-made experts on all the products and services that they might need. The way business communicates with consumers is through advertising. Advertising is *big* business! In 2017, $205 billion was spent on all forms of advertising in the United

States. Of that, $83 billion was in digital advertising, an amount that included social network advertising of $21.1 billion.[3]

Advertising comes under ethical scrutiny because there is a conflict between the informative nature of advertising and its persuasive functions. Two specific criticisms are often levied. The first relates to the general effect advertising has on society by constantly urging the conspicuous consumption of many unnecessary goods. The critics argue that by constantly seeing and hearing advertising, people are led into an endless cycle of consumerism that keeps them economically and spiritually impoverished.[4] These critics argue that advertising is an engine that drives greed, waste, and materialism.

The second criticism relates to the persuasive form of advertising which often seeks to mislead and manipulate consumers into purchasing products. In seeking to persuade, businesses may use or create advertising that is ambiguous to the point of deception, conceal facts, exaggerate, or employ psychological appeals. An advertisement may be deceptive if it takes advantage of the customer's ignorance or lack of full understanding. It can also mislead by concealing the facts with the message. For example, a person selling a medical insurance policy might list a number of illnesses covered by the policy, but fail to inform the potential purchaser that the policy does not cover some common illnesses. At stake is the ethical responsibility to provide full information to the consumer so they can make a rational choice.

Companies are regularly challenged by consumer groups and/or by the Federal Trade Commission (FTC) for engaging in "false and misleading" advertising. For example, General Mills was challenged in 2005 regarding its claim that Cheerios reduced bad cholesterol by 4 percent in six weeks. The FTC found that one would need to eat three cups of Cheerios and one and one-half cups of fat-free milk a day to get a seven point drop (from 160 to 153) in LDL ("bad") cholesterol. That amounts to 450 calories. It was thought that Cheerios was an unlikely choice for that proportion of caloric intake for the day, given the recommended 2,000–2,200 calorie American diet. In another cereal example, Kellogg's was challenged for its statement that Frosted Mini-Wheats would "increase your child's attentiveness by 20 percent." Upon challenge, that

---

3. Griner, "18 Bullish Stats about Advertising."
4. Pierard, "Where America Missed the Way," 19.

claim was removed.[5] In the early 1970s, the Continental Baking Company, maker of Profile Bread, advertised that eating Profile Bread would lead to weight loss. In fact, Profile Bread had the same number of calories per ounce as any other bread, but it was sliced thinner, so each slice had fewer calories. The implication to the consumer was clear, however; eating the bread would lead to weight loss. The consumer did not know that Profile's bread was sliced thinner than the competitor's bread. The FTC required Continental Baking to issue a corrective statement.[6]

The Scriptural Requirement: Truth-Telling

From an ethical point of view, advertising that conceals facts and is ambiguous to the point of deception undermines truth telling. Generally the reason for concealing facts or using ambiguity is that "if the truth were told," the product would be less desirable. Scripture is very clear regarding the importance of truth-telling. "Better to be poor than a liar" (Prov 19:22). Liars are listed among those who will not be in heaven (Rev 21:8), and Jesus ascribed lying to the devil, calling him the "father of lies" (John 8:44). As Gill points out, truthfulness is a core attribute of God's character and presence (Num 23:19; 1 Sam 15:29; John 14:6; Titus 1:2).[7] The Decalogue proclaims the sacredness of truth in the ninth commandment. "You shall not give false testimony against your neighbor" (Exod 20:16). Truth provides the foundation on which a society can exist. There must be honesty in material dealings and there must be honesty in speech.

In his condemnation of false witness in the ninth commandment, God includes all attempts and intents to deceive or mislead. It forbids defaming a person's good name, misrepresenting facts, conscious misquoting, half-truths, gossip and tale bearing, stereotyping, and creating arguments with the intent to suppress truth or create an erroneous or exaggerated impression which might bring injury to others. Jesus referred to the use of language in an ambiguous manner when, in speaking of making an oath, he said: "Do not swear at all: either by heaven, for it is God's throne; or by the earth, for it is His footstool; or by Jerusalem, for it is the city of the Great King. . . . Simply let your 'Yes' be 'Yes,' and your 'No,' 'No'; anything beyond this comes from the evil one" (Matt 5:33–37).

5. Jennings, *Business Ethics* (7th ed.), 432–33.

6. *Newsweek*, "Mea Culpa, Sort Of," 98.

7. Gill, *Doing Right*, 287.

But truth-telling is particularly at risk today. As David Gill rightly points out, "Our cultural and communications context is false-witness friendly. The ease of anonymous, unaccountable and inexpensive smearing of people's names, spreading rumors and half-truths, is ominous. Of course our new technologies can also be used to spread true witness, but are people today prepared to recognize the difference?"[8] Thus one must be particularly on guard to "never communicate false or irrelevant information in a way that could harm someone's life or reputation."[9] In the case of advertising, it seems very clear that Scripture, at a minimum, requires disclosure of any negative features or costs of a product, and avoidance of making promises that are false, unrealistic, or unable to be fulfilled.

What about Puffery?

The consumer, however, has come to expect a certain amount of exaggeration in advertising. Commonly used words in advertisements include "best," "finest," "most," "original," and other synonymous superlatives. Such usage is known as "puffery." Most puffery is harmless, as people generally anticipate such claims and therefore discount for them. In fact, Theodore Levitt argues in his classic article "The Morality (?) of Advertising" that consumers actually feel good about a certain level of puffery.

> Advertisements are the symbols of man's aspirations. They are not the real things, nor are they intended to be, nor are they accepted as such by the public. . . . Thus, the issue is not the prevention of distortion. It is, in the end, to know what kinds of distortions we actually want so that each of our lives is, without apology, duplicity, or rancor, made bearable. . . . The consumer suffers from an old dilemma. He wants "truth," but he also wants and needs the alleviating imagery and tantalizing promises of the advertiser and designer. Business is caught in the middle. There is hardly a company that would not go down in ruin if it refused to provide fluff, because nobody will buy pure functionality. Yet, if it uses too much fluff and little else, business invites possibly ruinous legislation.[10]

8. Gill, *Doing Right*, 291.

9. Gill, *Doing Right*, 287.

10. Levitt, "Morality (?) of Advertising," 91–92.

But problems arise when the consumer draws conclusions from the advertisement which are unwarranted and may thus be deceived, at a minimum, or injured at a maximum. Greater problems arise if the advertisement seeks to appeal to a human emotion and/or emotional needs rather than reason. At this point the advertisement has moved out of fulfilling a legitimate need by providing information sufficient for rational choice, and may have instead moved into the area of "creating the need" where previously none existed. Ethical issues of truthfulness arise when what is promised is psychological satisfaction, when in fact, it is unlikely that the product will deliver what is promised.

Psychological Appeals in Advertising

The most common psychological appeals are made through ads which use sex to sell products and in the process, promise that the product will enhance masculinity, femininity, acceptance, approval, or relationships. Other ads may appeal psychologically by the use of fear or pity (e.g., certain insurance ads). These psychological appeals are based on the recognition that much advertising is subliminal in that *what* is communicated cannot be separated from *how* it is communicated. Thus advertisements which use amateur or professional sports figures, celebrities, rock stars, race car drivers, or other famous people have particular appeal to minors. Using such individuals, for example, in connection with advertisements for liquor products adds a great deal of psychological appeal for the product because there is the suggestion that if one uses the product, one can be like, or look like, the person who is associated with the product.

John Waide calls such advertising "associative advertising." He uses the example of Nestle, described at the beginning of the chapter, to illustrate the concept. In order to induce poor women to buy the formula rather than to breast feed their babies, Nestle used non-market appeals as the basis for its advertising—specifically the love for one's child and a desire to be a "modern" mother. Waide argues that in these cases, the advertisers wish to influence people without regard to their well-being, just as Nestle wished to influence mothers to use infant formula without regard to the well-being of the baby or the mother. When this occurs, Waide states that it is likely that one's sensitivity to the well-being of others is reduced. Then, in his opinion, associative advertising becomes "prima facie morally objectionable."[11]

Because the advertisement promises psychological benefits which cannot be fulfilled, the acquisition of more and more of the advertised goods results in less and less enjoyment. This is true whether or not the product lived up to the specific claims made about its service or usefulness. Because more was promised than any item purchased with money could give, the consumer is always disappointed. Waide notes:

> We buy all the right stuff and yet have no more friends, lovers, excitement or respect than before. Instead, we have full closets and empty pocketbooks. Within the advertising which washes over us daily we can see a number of common themes, but the most important may be "You are what you own." The quibbles over which beer, soft drink, or auto to buy are less important than the overall-message. Each product contributes its few minutes each day, but we are bombarded for hours with the message that friends, lovers, acceptance, excitement, and power are to be gained by purchases in the market, not by developing personal relationships, virtues, and skills.[12]

The greatest criticism of advertising is that it teaches us that "to live is to consume"—a life that leaves us both economically and spiritually impoverished. Many see this result as not only shallow but also grossly immoral in view of the standard-of-living inequities in wealthy nations in contrast to other parts of the globe. Viewed in this light, advertising can be attacked as the engine of a system of greed, waste, and materialism.

The Advertiser's Responsibility

Given this criticism, advertisers have a great responsibility to provide information to consumers which is both informative and helpful. Without this information, consumers cannot make responsible and reasonable choices in the marketplace. Advertisers must choose between the high road and the low road when it comes to persuading consumers. While business may argue that the advertiser is only giving the consumer what he or she wants, one cannot deny that advertising does not always reflect reality. It is well-known that both print and media ads "create" beautiful,

11. Waide, "Making of Self and World," 75.
12. Waide, "Making of Self and World," 76.

but unreal, people through airbrushing and computer graphics, and then use these people to supposedly demonstrate the effects of the advertised product. While adults may argue that they are not deceived, we are aware that children can be deceived. Even those who are most supportive of all advertising seek legislation to protect young children from targeted ads for cereals, toys, and liquor. They recognize that while we want to believe that consumers are rational, such is not always true, or even possible.

In their book *Scriptural Foundations for Marketing*, Wrenn et al. argue that Christians must consider four constructs when integrating Christian ethics with marketing and advertising: *needs, exchange, value*, and *society*. When meeting *needs*, the Christian must consider not only one's own needs, but also the needs of others (Deut 15:8; Rom 12:13; Titus 3:14; Jas 2:16).[13] The product or service *exchange* must be transparent and must focus "upon authentic service, genuinely seeking to serve real needs and solve consumer problems rather than agitating consumers in order to place them on the hedonic treadmill."[14]

When considering *value*, Christian marketers must promote something that has real value to their exchange partners. Wrenn et al. use Psalm 15 as a guide to creating value for people engaged in marketing.

> Lord, Who may dwell in your sanctuary? Who may live on your holy hill? He whose walk is blameless and who does what is righteous, who speaks the truth from his heart and has no slander on his tongue, who does his neighbor no wrong and casts no slur on his fellow man, who despises a vile man but honors those who fear the Lord, who keeps his oath even when it hurts, who lends his money without usury and does not accept a bribe against the innocent. He who does these things will never be shaken.

Commenting on these verses, Wrenn et al. state:

> Is the message free from deception and guile, ("speaks the truth")? Is the message constructed in a way that demonstrates concern for the feeling of the other party, (i.e., is it "from the heart")? Not "slandering, wronging, or casting slurs" suggests that marketing should be positive in tone, avoiding any insult to the message receiver and not promoting your product by denigrating the offering of another organization. Despising a "vile person" and honoring those who "fear the Lord" could be

13. Wrenn et al., *Scriptural Foundations for Marketing*, 6–7.

14. Wrenn et al., *Scriptural Foundations for Marketing*, 14.

interpreted as choosing spokespersons to represent your organization who share your desire to order their lives in ways that reflect honor on God.

"Keeping an oath even when it hurts" requires marketers to be willing to sometimes go beyond the terms of the contract out of concern for their exchange partners' welfare, even when it might mean taking a loss on the exchange. Recalls, product liability, unforeseen damages from product usage, and many other consequences arising from good-faith exchange might cause an organization to need to "keep their oath, (i.e., their explicit and implicit promises to a consumer) even when it hurts." "Not changing their mind" means that once you have given your word to do business with someone, you don't go back on that agreement, even if a better offer comes your way. "Not charging interest" or "accepting a bribe" are general statements referring to the maintenance of integrity in exchange transactions. Christian marketers should never take advantage of a superior position to coerce another party to accept terms against their will or long-term interest. Neither should you accept bribes or favors that violate honest business practice. The fact that you can get away with such practice never justifies your agreement to do it. Psalm 15 ends with the assurance that your integrity is seen by God and rewarded with God's favor.[15]

Finally, Christian marketers must consider the welfare of *society* as part of the picture. As Phil 2:4 states: "Let each of you look not only to his own interests, but also to the interests of others." Wrenn et al. suggest that considering the good of the wider society will shift the focus from the immediate moment of the exchange transaction to a larger mission which takes into account how the company might ultimately assist in addressing major societal problems and providing solutions to these issues.[16]

THE NECESSITY OF INTEGRITY

The above discussion about truthfulness, framed in the specific challenges that come to businesspeople working in the field of marketing and advertising, is actually an important matter for all Christians in business. The issue at hand, as identified in the ninth commandment, is the matter

---

15. Wrenn et al., *Scriptural Foundations for Marketing*, 15–16.
16. Wrenn et al., *Scriptural Foundations for Marketing*, 17–19.

of integrity, a matter of utmost importance in advertising, in business, and in personal life.

The word "integrity" is derived from the Latin *integer*, which describes something that does not have a crack. We use the word "integration," which comes from the same root, to indicate the effort to make a whole out of pieces. It can mean forging the unity of diverse elements of a society, or the coordination of different aspects of an intellectual concept. In art, integrity means clinging to one's artistic ideals when much money could be earned if one chose to provide popular paintings that betrayed one's commitment to excellence. Scientific integrity demands that no claim for the solution of a problem be made before the research is truly completed. Scholastic integrity forbids claiming authorship for something that has been borrowed from another author. In ethics, integrity describes the behavior of someone in whom we find no gap between profession and practice. In the Bible, the most shining example of integrity is Daniel in Babylon. His political enemies knew that it would be impossible to find a murky spot in his record, except for his consistent allegiance to God as demonstrated through his daily worship practices. No other questionable practices could be attributed to the man who was one of the three top administrators in the kingdom (Dan 6:4–5).

Integrity for a Christian is a virtue derived from the divine *qadosh* (holy) and *emeth* (faithfulness). It reflects the absolute consistency of God's actions and his moral transparency. Just as God is true to himself, so humans must be true to themselves and never allow circumstances or the environment to shape their decisions. Just as God is morally transparent, so the children of God must act in such a way that they are never ashamed to have their record open to the view of everyone. To have integrity is to recognize and imitate the character of God.

In the book of Proverbs, there are frequent references to the difference between the straight course of the righteous and the crooked path of the wicked. "A man of understanding keeps a straight course" (Prov 15:21). "Wisdom will save you from the way of wicked men, from men whose words are perverse, who leave the straight paths to walk in dark ways, who delight in doing wrong and rejoice in the perverseness of evil" (Prov 2:12–14). "The righteousness of the blameless makes a straight way for them" (Prov 11:5).

The straight course describes the actions of people whose lives are determined by a moral north from which they do not deviate. They do not rely on flattery or bribery to obtain what they want. Their word is as good as cash. They look at promises as sacred. On the other hand, the wicked follow a crooked path that is chartered according to circumstances and opportunities. Thus they do not hesitate to break their promises. They are skillful at manipulating others, flattering to the powerful, exploiting the poor and the ignorant. Their conduct is totally inconsistent and it is not wise to bank on any agreement with them. One minute they can be arrogant, the next one they can crawl on the ground. They are deft at self-justification, but the constant strain of covering their tracks takes away the joy of living.

To have integrity often requires suffering loss and misunderstanding. Most people think that a person who refuses to make money if it means breaking a promise is a fool. They deem that one who does not try to create a network of relationships by any means, honest or not, in the effort to climb to the top is stupid. One cannot have integrity if he or she is not willing to withstand great pressures. A man or a woman who wants to have integrity must refuse to be a moral coward.

In the Old Testament we find different facets of integrity. For example, Prov 20:10 states: "Different weights and different measures—the Lord hates them both." In terms of today's marketplace, this may refer to treating people differently when they are powerful or when they are weak. It means not exploiting the ignorant. Exod 23:8 says: "Do not accept a bribe, for a bribe binds those who see and twists the words of the righteous." Proverbs adds: "Whoever flatters his neighbor is spreading a net for his feet" (Prov 29:5). While open bribes are not as much a part of business life in the United States as in some other countries, we can see applications to other contemporary practices. For example, does not the businessperson who gives large election campaign donations hope for easy access and assistance if he or she is in need of such for a special project? Do not salespeople who provide unlimited food and drinks to press representatives at trade shows try to insure favorable reviews of new products? While we may not call these actions "bribes," they have much the same purpose.

Another characteristic of integrity according to Proverbs is the refusal to exploit others. "He who increases his wealth by exorbitant interest amasses it for another, who will be kind to the poor" (Prov 20:17). "Exorbitant interest" may well cover the issuing of credit to those who may not be able to repay. It may also apply to low wages. It certainly covers situations like sweat shops in any country where immigrants, particularly those who for various reasons such as facility with the local language, cannot obtain other employment and work long hours under very unhealthful conditions for a pittance. It may even relate to corporations closing their manufacturing operations in highly developed nations where the wages are high and moving them to countries where the wages are pitifully low in the name of "increased profits." While one may argue that any job at any wage is better than no job at all, a person of integrity will not seek to exploit those who are economically or personally disadvantaged for their own personal or business-related gain.

THE POWER OF GREED

The underlying issue, the greatest threat to integrity, is the power of greed. Greed, unfortunately in some cases, drives the engine of advertising, particularly when it encourages a life-style that exemplifies the thought that "to live is to consume." In the case of Nestle and other pharmaceutical companies, greed led them to exploit the ignorance of the consumers with respect to the ultimate health of their babies when they switched to using formula rather than breastfeeding. Greed also drives the advertising world to promise desirable outcomes (e.g., health, popularity, beauty, success, "good times," and friendships) through the unstated but underlying assumption that purchasing the product will bring fulfillment to one's deepest desires.

Greed can go much further, of course. In the 1980s investors acquired companies and sold assets, plundering the retirement funds and leaving companies picked as clean as a carcass by vultures. In the late 1990s and early 2000s, lies were told to investors in an effort to encourage purchases of stocks, thus increasing the stock prices to the benefit of the personal wealth of the corporate officers and the investment bankers. When the stock prices fell, it was the workers and the retirees who lost jobs and pension funds. In 2008 the United States' financial markets imploded through activities that while not technically illegal, were certainly unethical. Because of low interest rates, many prospective home buyers entered the market, irrespective of their ability to repay the money borrowed. Mortgage lenders, anxious to do business, abandoned traditional lending standards, with the result that many mortgages issued were actually fraudulent. These mortgages were "securitized" and resold to other investors who presumed that the underlying mortgages were trustworthy. Traders were compensated on their activity and thus took enormous risks with other people's money. New complex investment vehicles were created to market these new arrangements, and the excitement of the possibility of quickly getting rich precluded consideration of the more sane counsel to not invest in anything you do not understand. In the end, huge insurance companies, investment houses, and banks were caught up in the investment "opportunities" and when the bubble burst, many went bankrupt, like Lehman Brothers. Others were merged to "save" themselves, such as Merrill Lynch's merger with the Bank of America, while those considered "too big to fail," like AIG, were bailed out with US taxpayer monies.

The power of greed is enormous. It feeds on lies, misrepresentations and exploitation of others in order to achieve its goal of "more for me." It is the essential characteristic of self-centered living, the temptation that underlies all other temptations. It leads one to desire to possess goods and money for the sake of impressing others, and it denies the damage done to others through whatever actions are undertaken to obtain whatever it desires. Marketing and advertising are not alone in encouraging greed and lack of integrity within society, of course. But they are often used by business as vehicles to encourage the acquisition of things under the promise that things will define or ensure a meaningful life, while at the same time providing great profit to the seller. Jesus reminds us, however, to seek first God's kingdom and his righteousness (Matt 6:33), and he promised that as we do so, God is well aware and able to provide all that will make our lives not only possible, but fulfilling, both today and eternally (Luke 12:22–31).

THINKING IT THROUGH: THE NESTLE CASE

The Nestle case, like the Pinto case in chapter 5, illustrates the difficulty of balancing the push for profits against the necessary and timely recognition that when things go wrong with a product or a service, the company must decide what steps to take next and when to take them. Does it take a lawsuit, as was the case with Ford, or international public pressure, as was the case with Nestle, for the "next steps" to be taken?

The utilitarian would support the expansion of Nestle into the developing world marketplace because of the advantages of increased profits and job security that accrue to the stakeholders with increased product sales growth. Once the results of the initial decision were known, it would be impossible for anyone to argue that the death of babies was ethical. At that point, the utilitarian's primary focus would be on establishing the direct cause of the babies' deaths. Was it because of Nestle's formula and marketing methods? Or was it for other reasons over which the company did not have control, such as poor water or illiterate customers? Were more babies better fed with the formula than died? Answers to these questions might take time to determine, much to the frustration of those who immediately blamed the company for the babies' deaths.

Kant would appeal to the universal rule of protecting life, including one's own, and for the importance of living in a society that protects life. Because the steps necessary to protect life may be difficult to determine when involved in situations outside of one's own culture, Kant would have argued for clarity and understanding of the entire situation before encouraging mothers to choose not to breastfeed. He would oppose using human beings in any way for one's own benefit (including for the benefit of increased corporate profit), rather than for human well-being.

To be honorable in business, the Christian worldview would agree with Kant. However, the Christian's primary reason for insisting on protecting human life would be based on the fact that human life comes from God and therefore cannot be something humans have a right to destroy (Exod 20:13). Should a decision to advertise through the use of "nurses" and mass media have been initially undertaken, and then later discovered to have detrimental effects on babies, the Christian would be quick to change the company's marketing approach, rather than choosing to wait until public opinion and international organizations demanded change.

Chapter 8

What If I See Something Wrong?

Whistle-blowing

Real integrity is doing the right thing, knowing that nobody's going to know whether you did it nor not.

—OPRAH WINFREY

AFTER JIM ALDERSON GRADUATED from Montana State University, he began his accounting career in Whitefish, Montana—a town well-known for great skiing and other outdoor activities. Several years later he accepted a position as chief financial officer at North Valley Hospital in Whitefish. In 1990, six years after Alderson took the CFO position, the top administrator retired and the hospital board voted to ask the management company, Quorum, to run North Valley. Quorum promised they would bring increased purchasing power and strong financial procedures, including an enhanced cost-reporting system, to North Valley. The result would be improvement of the hospital's bottom line through cost savings and increased reimbursement from the government.

About two months after Quorum took over North Valley, Quorum's administrator, Clyde Eder, asked Alderson to prepare two cost reports—one which would be an aggressive reimbursement cost report to be sent to the government, and a more conservative report which would be used internally. If the government paid the full amount reported on the aggressive cost report and the two-year audit period passed, the "extra" reimbursement received would be used to enhance the hospital's reserves. Alderson responded that he had never done two tax returns when he was in private tax practice and he was not going to prepare two cost reports for North Valley now.

Five days later Alderson was fired, with the only explanation given that the arrangement was not working out. Because he could not find another job in Whitefish that paid enough for him to support his family, Alderson took a job in Dillon, Montana, while his family stayed in Whitefish. Being frustrated about losing his job because he had refused to perform the unethical act of keeping two sets of books, he decided to file a wrongful termination lawsuit. For that lawsuit he asked for and received copies of the reserve reports and related records from North Valley. Once he had this information in hand, he realized that the problem was larger than Quorum and North Valley, and that in fact Quorum was following procedures established by its former parent, Hospital Corporation of America (HCA). This meant that what Alderson was seeing in Whitefish was happening nationwide.

From a colleague, Alderson learned about the False Claims Act which allows an individual to file a fraud suit on behalf of the government—known as a *qui tam* case. But to file such a suit, he would have to notify the government before filing, *hope* the government would find merit in the case and thus be willing to join in the filing, and in the meantime, say nothing to anyone about what he was doing. This meant that essentially he had two jobs—his regular day job and an evening job of examining cost reports in an attempt to document the fraud. During this time the neighbors noted that Alderson was receiving many boxes at his house and wondered what the boxes contained. Were the Aldersons involved in something illegal? Alderson and his wife could not explain. Neither could he explain the many trips he took at personal expense to Washington, DC, to meet with the Justice Department. When asked, his wife stated that he was visiting family.

It wasn't until October 1998, eight years later, that the government decided to officially join the case, finally allowing the family to explain the double life they had been leading. In 2004, the government thanked Alderson for helping them save $1.7 billion in Medicare fraud and paid him and his colleague, John Schilling, a former reimbursement specialist for HCA who had joined Alderson in his fight, $100 million. Mr. Alderson also received an additional $20 million in another settlement. Because of the kind of person he is, Alderson used major portions of these funds to make charitable contributions to the Montana State University College of Business for an Entrepreneurship Center, and for a new aquatics center in Whitefish.

It looks like Alderson "won" by being a whistle-blower. But remember, it took thirteen years (1990–2003) for Alderson and his family to get their life back. When asked if he would do things differently, Alderson said that he would not, although he regretted missing his son's football games. He noted: "You risk everything when you do it [blow the whistle]."[1] He also stated: "It feels good to have been a big part of this change. At the end of the day, this just seemed so wrong."[2] Clearly, money was not Alderson's motivation to whistle blow. Changing what he saw as a fraudulent system was his goal.[3]

WHISTLE-BLOWING DEFINED

The term "whistle-blowing" may have originated from the practice of the police, blowing their whistles to stop an illegal activity, or from a referee's use of the whistle during a sporting event.[4] In either case, the point of blowing the whistle is to stop an observed activity. From a business-related perspective, whistle-blowing is defined as "the release of information by a member or former member of an organization that is evidence of illegal and/or immoral conduct in the organization or conduct in the organization that is not in the public interest."[5] However, the point of blowing the whistle is to bring the matter to the attention of those who can stop the unsportsmanlike, illegal, or immoral conduct.

Unfortunately, such conduct does occur in business. Examples of wrongdoing include Enron and WorldCom, who engaged in accounting fraud; Bernie Madoff and Goldman Sachs, known for defrauding investors, and HCA, described above, who sought to defraud the government through additional Medicare charges. The Association of Certified Fraud Examiners (ACFE), in their *2018 Report to the Nations*, noted that fraud losses from asset misappropriation, financial statement fraud, and

1. Associated Press, "For Some Whistle-Blowers, Big Risk Pays Off."
2. Pettinger, "Jim Alderson."
3. Eichenwald, "He Blew the Whistle."
4. Miceli and Near, *Blowing the Whistle*, 15.
5. Boatright, *Ethics and the Conduct of Business*, 90.

corruption, amount to approximately 5 percent of the organization's revenues in any typical year. Their 2018 study of 2,690 fraud cases worldwide identified total losses of US$7.1 billion, with the average loss per case of US$2.75 million.[6] Of particular interest in our consideration of whistle-blowing is that the most common fraud detection method was "tips" (40 percent of cases), followed by internal audit (15 percent) and management review (13 percent).[7] Employees provided 53 percent of the "tips" while customers (32 percent) and anonymous (14 percent) were the other major sources of information about fraudulent activity.[8] The whistle-blowers used a variety of methods to convey their messages to those who could stop the wrongdoing, including telephone hot lines (42 percent), email (26 percent), web-based/online options (23 percent), and mailed letters (16 percent).[9] When reporting hotlines or similar options were not available, whistle-blowers reported the matter to a variety of people, including direct supervisors (32 percent), executives (15 percent), fraud investigator teams (13 percent), coworkers (12 percent), and internal audit (10 percent).[10]

In Alderson's case, because top management was the party engaged in misconduct, he contacted an external body—the government—and used the False Claims Act to engage the government in a lawsuit against HCA for their practices of bilking the government through falsified Medicare claims. The intent of Alderson's disclosures was to both correct past wrongdoing and prevent these false claims from happening in the future. Whistle-blowing cannot be gossip; it must be carefully documented. It also must be in the public interest, not done for reasons of personal retaliation. Both of these requirements were met by Jim Alderson.

Initially whistle-blowers were government employees who went public with complaints of corruption or mismanagement in the government organization where they worked.[11] Today the term is applied to individuals in all organizations who reveal concerns about any misconduct they observe. Whistle-blowing is ethically problematic because it involves a conflict between an employee's obligation to his or her company and a

6. ACFE, "Report to the Nations: 2018," 9.

7. ACFE, "Report to the Nations: 2018," 17.

8. ACFE, "Report to the Nations: 2018," 17.

9. ACFE, "Report to the Nations: 2018," 19.

10. ACFE, "Report to the Nations: 2018," 19.

11. Boatright, *Ethics and the Conduct of Business*, 89.

general obligation to the public. Deciding whether or not whistle-blow-ing is morally justified requires a balancing of many different obligations.

When employees take a job, they are required not only to do the work they are assigned but also to be loyal to their employer, preserve the confidentiality of company information, and work in the best interest of the company. An employee is an agent of his or her employer, and through this relationship is legally required to act in the interest of the other party, known as the principal. As an agent, however, the employee is only required to obey *reasonable directives* of the principal. For ex-ample, a principal cannot require an agent to do an act which is illegal or immoral. Thus, if an employee sees something which will cause harm to other people and can do something to stop the harm, then the employee has a moral obligation to act in the public interest and an employment agreement cannot require that the employee remain silent.[12] Robert Larmer argues that in fact the employee who engages in whistle-blowing is practicing utmost loyalty to the company, its mission, and its values by reporting a harmful or illegal act, even if the act is done by the top management of the organization.[13]

CHARACTERISTICS OF WHISTLE-BLOWERS

Deciding to blow the whistle is not an easy decision. It can have enormous costs. Jim Alderson spent thirteen years of his life gathering evidence and convincing the government that it was being cheated by HCA. Because of the personal costs, such as great stress, career loss, financial ruin, some-times ill health, and the loss of friends and family, many individuals who see something wrong choose not to report it. The 2013 Ethics Resource Center report noted that 41 percent of US workers observed misconduct. While over half (63 percent) of those who saw misconduct reported it, 21 percent of those who reported experienced some kind of retaliation be-cause of their report. Retaliation can take many forms, including physical harm, online harassment, harassment at home, a demotion, a pay cut, and/or a job transfer.[14] The organization's administration and/or one's co-workers may see the whistle-blower as a troublemaker and not a member of the team. The whistle-blower may be accused of being disloyal to the

12. Boatright, *Ethics and the Conduct of Business*, 93–94.

13. Larmer, "Whistleblowing and Employee Loyalty," 184–89.

14. "National Business Ethics Survey (NBES) 2013."

company, the department, or his or her colleagues. If the whistle-blower has incorrect or incomplete facts or lacks the entire picture of what actually happened, he or she will be further alienated from his/her fellow workers. The decision to blow the whistle should be carried out only after careful thought and as far as possible, complete assurance that one has the correct information and understands the entire situation at hand.

So what type of person would choose to report misconduct when it is observed? Often the individual who engages in whistle-blowing is intensely loyal to their company, holds a high-level or supervisory position, and believes that they will be thanked for bringing the wrongdoing to the attention of general management. Seldom do they consider the possibility of retaliation because they assume that those with the authority to fix the situation will be happy to do so. These individuals also exhibit a strong belief in individual responsibility, are very ethical, often have high religious values, and high allegiance to a community.[15]

One such person was Cynthia Cooper, who was featured as one of *Time* magazine's "Persons of the Year" in 2002, along with Sherron Watkins (Enron) and Coleen Rowley (FBI). Cooper, WorldCom's vice president of internal audit, uncovered accounting practices that inflated the company's profit by $3.8 billion. After performing late-night investigations (working at night because she had been told by the CFO to not follow up on the fraudulent accounting practices that had been reported to her) and documenting her findings, she reported the results to the audit committee of the Board of Directors of WorldCom. The board subsequently fired the CFO and the controller, and ultimately the company went bankrupt. In her interview for *Time*, when asked why she didn't go along with the fraud like others in top management, Cooper spoke of the values her mother instilled in her to not be intimidated or to think of the consequences of her actions. She stated that she felt that she was just doing her job, but the further she got into the scandal, the more certain she was that she would lose her job. She said: "I told my husband that I am going to report to the [WorldCom board's] audit committee what I need to report. I even cleared some things out of my office. But the fear of losing my job was very secondary to the obligation I felt."[16] While Cooper was featured on the cover of *Time*, not everyone was happy with her decision to report the wrongdoing. *Time* noted that "some employees think the

---

15. Boatright, *Ethics and the Conduct of Business*, 95–97.

16. Lacayo and Ripley, "Time Persons of the Year 2002: The Whistleblowers," 59.

company could have borrowed its way out of its problems and avoided bankruptcy if she [Cooper] had stayed quiet."[17] There is little likelihood that whistle-blowers will be thanked for their actions. They will, however, often mirror Jim Alderson's and Cynthia Cooper's satisfaction with the decision they made. As Cooper said: "I feel like I did my job."[18]

The qualities exhibited by many whistle-blowers (strong belief in individual responsibility, highly ethical, strong religious values, high allegiance to a community) are often the qualities exhibited by Christians in the workplace. It is therefore likely that many Christians may seriously consider whistle-blowing as an action plan when wrongdoing is observed.

RECOMMENDED ACTION STEPS

Richard De George was one of the first to consider whistle-blowing obligations, stemming from his involvement in the Ford Pinto case, which was discussed in chapter 5. De George, in his essay entitled "Whistle-Blowing,"[19] outlined three options for consideration: first, that whistle-blowing should be *morally prohibited* because it is disloyal to one's employer; second, when whistle-blowing is *morally permissible*, and finally, when whistle-blowing is *morally required*. He refuted the first position regarding the prohibition of whistle-blowing using many of the arguments outlined above, and then developed criteria for when whistle-blowing is *morally permissible* and *morally required*. De George's criteria were initially developed for the external whistle-blower who works in the private sector for an organization that produces a product or provides a service to the public.[20]

De George argued that whistle-blowing is *morally permissible* when (*italics mine*):

1. The harm that will be done by the product or policy to the public is *serious and considerable*, and

2. The employee makes his/her concerns *known to their superiors*, and

17. "The Whistleblowers," 50.
18. "The Whistleblowers," 59.
19. De George, *Business Ethics*, 2nd, 221–38.
20. De George, *Business Ethics* (6th ed.), 301.

3. The immediate superiors do not act on the identified concerns, the employee then *exhausts the channels available within the corporation*, including even going to the board of directors.

For there to be a *moral obligation* to whistle-blow, De George added two additional criteria that must be met:

4. The employee must have *documented evidence* that would convince a reasonable, impartial observer that his or her view of the situation is correct and the company is in the wrong, and

5. There must be strong evidence that making the information public will *prevent the threatened harm*. As De George puts it: "The chance of being successful must be worth the risk one takes and the danger to which one is exposed."[21]

In their discussion of De George's points, Hoffman and Schwartz[22] modify the criteria in the following ways. First, with respect to *serious and considerable harm*, Hoffman and Schwartz suggest that this notion should include more than physical harm and encompass financial harm, psychological harm, serious breach of the law, and actions "that infringe basic moral rights or involve serious injustice," such as sexual harassment, violations of privacy, industrial espionage, insider trading, and falsification of previous serious misconduct.[23]

When making the situation known to one's superior (points 2 and 3), Hoffman and Schwartz include the option of reporting anonymously, such as through a company's "hotline." They also recommend that, when possible, the whistle-blower inform the perpetrator that the action will be reported (whereas De George focuses on reporting to the superior). With this recommendation, however, Hoffman and Schwartz insist that the firm have a written anti-retaliation policy in place and enforce it— thus providing protection to the whistle-blower. If such is not the case they do not recommend confronting the perpetrator and believe that there is no obligation to blow the whistle internally.

Hoffman and Schwartz note an exception for professionals (e.g., lawyers, engineers, and accountants) who face additional responsibilities because their professional codes of ethics require they fulfill their duty to prevent harm to the public. Therefore these individuals have an

21. De George, *Business Ethics* (6th ed.), 308–13.
22. Hoffman and Schwartz, "Morality of Whistleblowing," 771–81.
23. Hoffman and Schwartz, "Morality of Whistleblowing," 773–74.

obligation to report wrongdoing, even in situations where personal risk might be great. They point out that these additional obligations to society were known and accepted by the professionals when they received their professional designations.

Regarding the requirement of documented evidence (point 4), Hoffman and Schwartz opt for the Dodd-Frank Act's legal test "of 'reasonable belief,' i.e., one should hold a reasonable belief that the misconduct is taking place based on first-hand knowledge."[24] They place the requirement of documentation on the media or a government regulator who will follow-up on the whistle-blower's report. They disagree with De George's fifth point as well. They argue that if indeed the whistle-blower has gone through the internal steps up to the board level (points 1, 2, and 3,) and nothing has changed, it is too high an expectation for the whistle-blower to be convinced that external whistle-blowing will actually lead to a different outcome. Their concern is that if a whistle-blower were to take point 5 seriously and therefore fail to report the illegal or immoral action because they don't think reporting will make a difference, such silence could encourage continuing or increasing the inappropriate actions by the organization in the future.

Hoffman and Schwartz's primary concern is the safety of the whistle-blower. As they put it: "Unless one is a professional working within the firm, legal protections for employees that blow the whistle externally must exist and be effective (i.e., enforced) in order for external whistle-blowing to ever be morally required."[25] In their opinion, if an employee were to blow the whistle without legal protection, that individual would be morally praiseworthy, but one who did not report would not be criticized or condemned. They take issue with corporate codes of conduct that require an employee to blow the whistle internally but do not provide for the protection of the whistle-blower against any reprisals. Instead, they argue that blowing the whistle internally is always morally permissible if points 1, 2, and 3 are met, but morally obligatory only when a firm has an effective anti-retaliation policy in place.

---

24. Hoffman and Schwartz, "Morality of Whistleblowing," 775.
25. Hoffman and Schwartz, "Morality of Whistleblowing," 776.

APPLYING THE DE GEORGE AND HOFFMAN/ SCHWARTZ MODELS

Hoffman and Schwartz compare their model with De George's criteria by applying it to three well-known whistle-blowing situations.[26] The first is the Ford Pinto case (see ch. 5). In this situation, points 1 through 3 are met (potential for serious harm to the public, and employees, supervisors, and top administration are aware of the defect). In the 1970s no anti-retaliation policy existed, so according to Hoffman and Schwartz, there was no moral obligation to blow the whistle externally. De George agreed, probably because of his concern that even reporting the matter externally would be unlikely to have made any difference in terms of making the Pinto safer for the public's use.

The second whistle-blowing case is that of Sherron Watkins of Enron (an accounting fraud situation which will be discussed in chapter 9). Sherron Watkins was Vice President of Corporate Development and a professional accountant. She would then have been morally obligated to blow the whistle both internally and externally under the Hoffman/ Schwartz criteria. In this situation, the harm was financial rather than physical, and Watkins reported her concerns to her supervisor Ken Lay, who was the CEO and chairman of the board of directors, so the first three criteria were met. De George, however, would not hold Watkins morally obligated to whistle-blow because of lack of evidence that reporting the situation externally would have resulted in any change in the situation.

The third fairly well-known whistle-blowing case is that of Dr. Jeffrey Wigand, former Vice President of Research and Development at the Brown & Williamson Tobacco Company. Dr. Wigand's whistle-blowing saga is portrayed in the Academy Award-nominated film *The Insider*. This film identifies not only the problem of the firm's manipulation of nicotine quantities which enhanced cigarette addiction and public health concerns, but also the particulars of Wigand's personal situation, including his need for continued salary and medical benefits and his signed confidentiality agreement with Brown & Williamson. In this case, Wigand had firsthand evidence of the harm being done to the public and reported his concerns to his superiors, who ignored them. Thus the first three points were met. However, Wigand was not a professional and therefore under no moral obligation to whistle-blow under Hoffman and Schwartz's

26. Hoffman and Schwartz, "Morality of Whistleblowing," 778–79.

criteria because there was no effective anti-retaliation policy in place. De George would agree, but for the reason that Wigand had no evidence that his external whistle-blowing report would change the tobacco company's actions. The fact that Wigand chose to blow the whistle to *60 Minutes* was a morally praiseworthy act, but not obligatory by either De George's or Hoffman and Schwartz's criteria.

SCRIPTURE'S PERSPECTIVE

Scripture agrees with the process outlined in the initial three points as discussed above: when there is harm, first speak to the individual involved as recommended by Hoffman and Schwartz, then to one's supervisor and if they do not heed the message, continue up the organization's ladder, reporting ultimately to the board of directors or the board's audit committee. While Jesus' counsel is directed specifically to matters in the church, the procedures are applicable to any situation where wrongdoing is observed. Our work colleagues are our brothers and sisters because we are all children of God. Matthew 18:15–17 states:

> If your brother sins against you, go and show him his fault, just between the two of you. If he listens to you, you have won your brother over. But if he will not listen, take one or two others along, so that every matter may be established by the testimony of two or three witnesses. If he refuses to listen to them, tell it to the church, and if he refuses to listen even to the church, treat him as you would a pagan or a tax collector.

The point of Jesus' counsel is that if an individual will listen to the warning and choose to cease from wrongdoing, it is best for all that the matter not become a publicly known event, but rather be kept private.

However, Scripture insists that the whistle-blower not be judgmental, because as humans we are unable to read motives. As Matt 7:1 warns: "Do not judge, or you too will be judged." The context of this warning particularly cautions against hypocrisy by adding a further warning just a few verses later: "You hypocrite, first take the plank out of your own eye, and then you will see clearly to remove the speck from your brother's eye" (Matt 7:5).

Scripture also cautions that one be certain of the circumstances before making an accusation. Several verses (Deut 17:6; 19:15; 1 Tim 5:19) note the necessity of two or three witnesses before accusations are to be substantiated and punishment administered. De George's insistence on documented evidence affirms this counsel. Even Hoffman and Schwartz's lesser test of "reasonable belief" requires first-hand knowledge.

However, Scripture would not give a "pass" for either uncertainty as to whether or not the external reporting would make any difference or whether or not there were legal protections for the whistle-blowers— two points that De George and Hoffman/Schwartz consider qualifiers. Scripture does not permit the Christian to consider his or her own safety or security when confronting a situation where wrong has been done or harm is likely to come to others. For example, after David's affair with Bathsheba and Uriah's death following David's orders that he be placed "where the fighting is fiercest," Nathan was sent to confront David, the king, about his wrongdoing. Nathan exhibited the utmost tact in his confrontation by telling David a story about a rich man and a poor man and the unjust actions of the rich man in killing the only sheep the poor man owned in order to satisfy the needs of his own guest. However, he was still confronting the king who had power to put him to death (see 2 Sam 12:1–14). Fortunately for both Nathan and David, David's response was a confession of his sin and a prayer that God would help him change his ways (see Ps 51).

But not all confrontations in Scripture have such happy results. Saul was pursing David with three thousand men, because he knew that David had been anointed to replace him as king. David was hiding in the cave that Saul entered and with Saul at his mercy, chose to cut off a corner of his robe rather than harm him. As Saul was leaving the cave, David confronted Saul, showed him the proof that Saul had been in his power, and asked him why he was so bent on killing him. Saul immediately confessed his wrongdoing and declared that David was "more righteous than I [because he] had treated him well but I have treated you badly" (1 Sam 24:17–21). But Saul's decision to quit pursuing David was short-lived. In 1 Samuel 26 we again find Saul pursing David—demonstrating that his decision to turn from his wrongdoing was only temporary, not a permanent change of actions. In a final example, when Jeremiah was instructed to inform King Zedekiah that the Babylonians would return, attack the city, and Jerusalem would be destroyed because of the evil works of the king and his counselors, they refused to listen and put Jeremiah in prison. His calling out wrongdoing exacted a heavy price on Jeremiah (see Jeremiah 36 and 37). These scriptural examples illustrate that there are no guarantees that when confronted, the wrongdoer will listen. He may listen and change his ways. She may appear to change her actions for the moment, but at a later time return to the same unwise behaviors. He may find that the wrongdoer refuses to listen and instead turns on the whistle-blower.

No matter the results, Christians are called to "act justly" (Mic 6:8), and justice requires first confronting the wrongdoer and then proceeding with the appropriately outlined steps to alert others who may be able to persuade the wrongdoer to change his or her course of action, or to administer the appropriate punishment. Jesus calls us to a higher commitment to "do to others what you would have them do to you, for this sums up the Law and the Prophets" (Matt 7:12). Private warnings give a chance for changing behaviors without public embarrassment. Acting irrespective of the outcome may lead the Christian to act in ways that others would not consider to be obligatory, but would call "morally praiseworthy," because the Christian chooses to do what they believe is right, even when the outcome is unknown.

CORPORATE POLICIES

Most large companies, following the corporate scandals of the early 2000s and the enactment of Sarbanes-Oxley in 2002, developed their own internal whistle-blowing policies as part of their response to both government and public pressure to improve the corporate ethical climate. These companies were also instructed through published research on how to develop an ethical corporate culture. Mark Schwartz outlined three key elements of such a culture in his 2013 article in *Business Horizons*. He urged that in order to minimize illegal or unethical activity, an organization should establish the following:

1. A set of *core ethical values* (*italics mine*) that permeate its policies, processes, and practices, with the suggested values being trustworthiness, respect, responsibility, fairness, caring, and citizenship. Many corporations reflect these values in their mission statements, codes of ethics and other public documents.

2. *A formal ethics program* (*italics mine*) which includes a code of ethics, ethics training, an ethics hotline (or similar whistle-blowing channels), and an ethics officer or other designated official who monitors ethics complaints and reports directly to the board of directors, not to the CEO.

3. *Foster ethical leadership, (italics mine)* often identified as the "tone at the top," which is reflected by the board of directors, senior executives, and managers. Schwartz notes that if ethical leadership is to occur, the leader must be both a moral manager and a moral person.[27]

From a cynical perspective, the recently established corporate codes of ethics and ethics hotlines could be seen as primarily created to address misconduct internally and thus avoid embarrassing public disclosure. Hopefully, however, corporations are seeking to create an ethical organizational climate where policies ensure that reports of unethical activity are properly investigated, appropriate action is taken, and retaliation against the whistle-blower will not occur.

When developing whistle-blowing policies, Boatright recommends that the following be included:

1. An effectively communicated statement of responsibility.

2. A clearly-defined procedure for reporting.

3. Trained personnel to receive and investigate reports.

4. A stated commitment to take appropriate action.

5. A guarantee against retaliation.[28]

An example of such a policy is that of the Whirlpool Corporation. In their corporate code of ethics, the final section, entitled "Support for Our Code of Ethics," reads as follows (*italics mine*):[29]

> Whirlpool is committed to supporting its people in meeting their obligations under this code. In a similar fashion, all Whirlpool employees must comply with this code in their work conduct.
>
> If you observe or know of violations of this code, or a violation of the law, or have questions about the meaning, intent, and/or application of the underlying policies, it is your responsibility to report such situations or pose any questions promptly. *Whirlpool will not tolerate any reprisal or retaliation against any person who, in good faith, reports a known or suspected violation of this code or law. Whirlpool will take disciplinary action, up to*

27. Schwartz, "Developing and Sustaining an Ethical Corporate Culture," 39–50.

28. Boatright, *Ethics and Conduct of Business,* 103–4.

29. Whirlpool Corporation homepage.

and including termination of employment, against any employee involved in any reprisal or retaliation.

Instructions are then provided in the code on how and to whom an employee should make a report or pose a question, including information on how to access the hotline both within and outside of the United States, and how to report in a language other than English, if needed.

Unfortunately, even when corporate policies officially promise no retaliation, such promises may not always be kept either by corporate officials or by coworkers who may see the whistle-blower as disloyal or not acting as a member of the team. The 2013 National Business Ethics Survey found that many supervisors or coworkers make the working environment so impossible that the whistle-blower effectively experiences retaliation and may choose either to not report misconduct in the future or quit because of the work situation.[30]

Following are two examples of such illegal retaliations. First, Matthew Lee, the head of global balance-sheet and legal-entity accounting at Lehman Brothers, informed the CFO and chief risk officer that he was observing conduct on the part of senior management that was in violation of the investment code, and that Lehman Brothers' balance sheet contained billions of dollars of unsubstantiated figures. His warnings were ignored by the auditors, Ernst & Young, and Mr. Lee was fired. Four months later Lehman Brothers declared bankruptcy. In the subsequent court proceedings, Mr. Lee's allegations were not only found to be correct, but it was established that top executives at Lehman Brothers knew about both the risk exposure and the accounting practices used to cover up that exposure.[31]

Second, in violation of the Dodd-Frank Act, Health Net, Inc., an insurance provider, agreed to pay a $340,000 penalty in settlement of SEC allegations that they amended severance agreements to require former employees to waive their right to any monetary recovery available to them for whistle-blowing to state and federal officials about actions of the company. The SEC charged that hundreds of former employees had signed the amended severance agreements between August 12, 2011 and October 22, 2015.[32]

30. "National Business Ethics Survey (NBES) 2013."

31. Jennings, *Business Ethics* (8th ed.), 269.

32. Petersen, "Health Net Tried to Block Employee Whistleblowers."

LEGAL PROTECTION

Thus the question remains: what legal protection can a whistle-blower expect to enjoy? In the United States there are several laws that make retaliation against whistle-blowers illegal. First, there is the Whistleblower Protection Act (1989) which protects federal employees who report waste and corruption in government. Second is the Sarbanes-Oxley Act of 2002 which created protection for private-sector employees. This act was passed in response to the accounting frauds at Enron, WorldCom, and other companies in the early 2000s. The Act also mandates that all publicly traded companies have internal procedures that provide for employee confidential reporting of suspected fraudulent activity (i.e., a confidential "hot line"). Third, the Dodd-Frank Wall Street Reform and Consumer Protection Act (2010) requires the Securities and Exchange Commission (SEC) to create a whistle-blower program for rewarding individuals who report wrongdoing which ultimately results in SEC sanctions of $1 million or more against the organization.

Internationally a large number of countries have passed legislation to protect whistle-blowers, including Australia, New Zealand, the United Kingdom, South Africa, Japan, the Netherlands, Ireland, Canada, India, Germany, Switzerland, and Belgium.[33] However, it is important to note, as already discussed, that an unethical organization will not only fail to keep its own promises regarding non-retaliatory behaviors, but also will not honor what the law requires.

QUESTIONS TO CONSIDER

Given that the decision to blow the whistle is one fraught with serious consequences and uncertain legal protections, John Boatright developed the following list of questions the prospective whistle-blower should ask himself or herself before acting:[34]

1. *Is the situation of sufficient moral importance to justify whistle-blowing? To what extent is the harm a predictable and direct result of the activity? How imminent is the harm?* In the Alderson case, once Alderson reviewed the materials provided for his own lawsuit regarding wrongful termination, he came to the conclusion that the

33. McMillan, "Retaliation against Whistle-Blowers."
34. Boatright, *Ethics and Conduct of Business*, 97–99.

situation of two sets of books was not localized, but was an activity that was occurring in other hospitals across the nation. This increased his concern and drove him to bring his case to the attention of the Department of Justice.

2. *Do you have all the facts and have you properly understood their significance? Be careful about situations which may be beyond your expertise.* As CFO of North Valley Hospital, Alderson understood the significance of the numbers. He also understood the purpose of the request that he create two cost reports and he understood that to do as he was asked would result in cheating the government.

3. *Have all internal channels and steps available for reporting the situation been exhausted?* In Alderson's case, because the wrongdoing was "at the top" of the hospital management company which had been hired by North Valley Hospital's board, he had no choice except to go to external parties (i.e., the government) with his information. In his situation it was the government that was being wronged. But in most situations, the wrongdoing is at a lower level. It is appropriate to use the provided internal channels in keeping with the command of Jesus. To do so gives the organization the opportunity to correct the problem internally if they wish.

4. *How should the whistle-blowing be done? Who should receive the information? How much information should be revealed?* Alderson had both the law—the False Claims Act—and legal counsel to guide him through the process of informing the government of the fraud. However, the law required that until the government joined the case, total silence regarding the situation had to be maintained. In Alderson's case, the government took eight years to join the case. Until that happened, Alderson was collecting evidence on his own without any guarantee that the information would ultimately be accepted as authentic and credible.

5. *What is my responsibility in view of my role within the organization?* Alderson was the CFO; he was the one who was fired because he refused to create two cost reports. He was the one who was directly affected by the wrongdoing. These factors made it more obligatory for him to act, as other employees at the hospital would not have been in the same responsible position because of their job, nor would they have had the same knowledge of the misconduct.

6. *What are the chances for success? Will whistle-blowing achieve some public good?* This is probably the most difficult question of all to answer prior to the act of whistle-blowing. When Alderson initially filed his case with the Department of Justice, he had no guarantee that the government would listen. Likewise, when Cynthia Cooper worked nights to unravel the accounting fraud at WorldCom, she had no guarantee that what she would find would lead to the firing of the CFO and the controller, and ultimately to the conviction of the CEO as part of the fraud. In answer to this question the motivation, the perseverance, and the wisdom of the whistle-blower are often the keys to the achievement of success.

When one sees something wrong, good business ethics and scriptural guidance concur that one should first point out the wrongdoing to the appropriate party in private, on a one-to-one basis. As Scripture states: "If he listens to you, you have won your brother over." It is only when the one-to-one conversation is not successful that additional steps should be taken to counsel with others, thereby involving more people in the situation. By following these steps one may avoid the embarrassment of having incomplete information or being incorrect about what they thought they observed. We are all human and we can all benefit by being careful in our accusations. While we want wrongs corrected, we want to do it in a way that the wrong-doer will hear us. Following the given counsel can help to ensure that wrongs are corrected in the most effective way.

THINKING IT THROUGH: JIM ALDERSON AND NORTH VALLEY HOSPITAL

Since whistle-blowing is a protected act by United States' law for governmental and publicly-traded company employees, no ethical theory would oppose the actions taken by Jim Alderson. However, the above discussion regarding De George's criteria for when to engage in whistle-blowing is informative. As noted, the Christian would first approach the wrongdoer in hopes that the situation might be resolved privately. In Alderson's case, top management had already made its decision regarding Alderson's refusal to prepare two reports, and therefore the only recourse available to Alderson in terms of repairing the damage done was to work with outside authorities. It appears, based on Alderson's subsequent actions, that he was not motivated by any promised reward when he decided to notify the government of the fraud. A person desiring to be honorable in business would likewise be motivated by the desire to correct the wrong action(s) rather than by a personal opportunity to receive financial rewards or public recognition.

Chapter 9

What If I Can Make More Money?

Accounting Fraud, Insider Trading, and Conflicts of Interest

Although gold dust is precious, when it gets in your eyes it obstructs your vision.
—HSI-TANG CHI 735–814

THE POSTER CHILD FOR unethical business activities undertaken for the purpose of making more money for top management is Enron, at one time the world's largest energy company. Enron was created in 1985 by Ken Lay through a merger of two gas pipelines—Houston Natural Gas and Internorth. It grew rapidly as the general economy in the United States at that time favored deregulation of electricity and other energy sources. Enron initially made its money by providing power to utility companies through locking in supply contracts at fixed prices and then hedging those contracts in other markets. Before the company filed for bankruptcy in December 2001, it had been listed as the "most innovative company in America" by *Fortune* for six consecutive years, and in 2001 was ranked among the top five companies in terms of quality of management, quality of products and services, and employee talent by the same magazine.[1]

1. Joint Committee on Taxation, "Report of Investigation of Enron," 57.

While initially involved in energy trading, Enron ultimately branched out into water and fiber optics, and built power plants in Brazil and India. In total, Enron was operating in over twenty countries.[2] This diversification proved to be disastrous, especially in the case of the overseas plants, as Enron over-anticipated the market and thus overbuilt, going into debt in the process.

Enron used mark-to-market accounting, permitted by generally accepted accounting principles (GAAP), so that expected future profits on energy contracts could be included in current earnings. The intent of GAAP was to match contracts to market price in the commodities market and allow for price fluctuations. However, mark-to-market accounting is based on assumptions about future market factors, and especially in companies where bonuses and performance ratings were based on financial profitability, the bias toward overstating revenues was strong. The company's assumptions behind the numbers in the financial statements were very subjective. Unfortunately these assumptions were not made available to investors and shareholders so they could review and understand the calculations.

Some financial analysts, like Jim Chanos of Kynikos Associates, became skeptical when Enron's margins and cash flow did not match up with its trumpeted earnings record.[3] However, many analysts chose not to ask questions, especially since Ken Lay, president, and Jeffrey Skilling, CEO, pushed back against those who doubted their financial reports. One reporter from *Fortune*, Bethany McClean, asked the now famous question: "How exactly does Enron make its money?" Skilling responded: "Enron is *not* a black box. It is very simple to model." He continued to explain that Enron was a "logistics company," not a trading company . . . and then noted: "People who raise questions are people who have not gone through our business in detail . . . people who don't understand want to throw rocks at us . . . anyone who is successful, people would like to take them down based on ignorance." With that, he closed the interview. The next day Andrew Fastow, Enron's CFO, tried to explain Enron's model to McClean. He said: "We create optionality. Enron is so much more valuable—hence our stock price—because we have so much more optionality embedded in our network than anyone else."[4] McLean's story

2. Joint Committee on Taxation, "Report of Investigation of Enron," 66.

3. McLean and Elkind, *Smartest Guys in the Room*, 319–21.

4. McLean and Elkind, *Smartest Guys in the Room*, 322.

was published in the February 2001 issue of *Fortune* under the title "Is Enron Overpriced?" In answer to the question: "How does Enron make its money?" Todd Shipman at S&P responded: "If you figure it out, let me know."[5]

Enron created "off the books" transactions relating to their debt and obligations and placed these in special purpose entities (SPEs), thereby keeping these negative items off their balance sheets. Ultimately Enron had $60 billion in assets, of which $27 billion were in the SPEs. Because the SPEs were unconsolidated with Enron's financial statements, Enron was able to book revenue from these "affiliates" without showing the debt.[6] Officers of Enron, and in particular, Andrew Fastow, the CFO, served as principal partners for the SPEs, thus creating related-party transactions. When McLean asked Fastow about the related-party transactions, he said: "One of our senior executives runs that fund. It's confidential who it is." In fact, it was Fastow himself.[7]

Marianne Jennings describes Enron as "a company with a swagger."[8] It was not only aggressive in its business dealings, but also with its employees. Enron's employee rating system required that annually 20 percent of all employees were to be rated at below-level performance, thus requiring that they leave the company. As a result, employees generally chose not to bring bad news to their superiors. One employee who dared to question what was happening was Sherron Watkins, at the time Vice President for Corporate Development. She informed Ken Lay in a written memo in August 2001 that unless matters were clarified and corrected, "we will implode in a wave of accounting scandals." She specifically stated that she was concerned about the SPE transactions, the related party-transactions, and the equity derivative transactions. Her recommendation was that Lay bring in auditors and legal counsel other than those presently used by Enron, but Lay declined. He turned the matter over to Enron's usual legal counsel who recommended that there be no changes to current procedures.[9]

Enron paid its top employees well—the top 200 (out of a total of 7,500) were paid $1.4 billion in 2001—the same year that Enron reported

5. McLean and Elkind, *Smartest Guys in the Room*, 323.

6. Joint Committee on Taxation, "Report of Investigation of Enron," 70–71.

7. McLean and Elkind, *Smartest Guys in the Room*, 322.

8. Jennings, *Business Ethics* (7th ed.), 239.

9. Joint Committee on Taxation, "Report of Investigation of Enron," 79.

$975 million as their net earnings on their financial statements.[10] The top executives received $433.6 million.[11] These top executives "essentially wrote their own compensation packages,"[12] which were then rubber-stamped by the compensation committee of the board of directors. "As a result, Enron's top executives earned enormous amounts of money and even used the company as an unsecured lender. . . . From 1997 through 2001, Mr. Lay borrowed over $106 million from Enron through a special unsecured line of credit with the company."[13]

Enron had a 401k plan for its employees, but the majority of the plan's investments were in Enron stock. In August 2000, Enron stock was selling a $90.75 per share; by September 28, 2001, just over a year later, it was selling at $27.33.[14] After Jeffrey Skilling resigned in August 2001, and news of Enron's financial difficulties began to surface, Enron put a lockdown on the retirement plan so that employees could not sell their shares (although by that time most of the executives had sold off large blocks of *their* Enron stock).[15]

On October 16, 2001, Enron reported its first quarterly loss, due to write-offs on asset impairments.[16] By the end of October the share price had dropped to $13.90.[17] On November 8, Lay announced the restatement of Enron's revenues from 1997–2000, in the amount of $1.7 billion.[18] The stock price closed at $0.26 on November 30.[19] Enron filed for bankruptcy on December 2, 2001.[20] The creditors received 18.3 cents on the dollar.[21] Thirty-two Enron executives were indicted, with guilty pleas or convictions for all.[22] Ken Lay and Jeff Skilling were convicted in 2006. Ken Lay died of a heart attack prior to appealing his verdict. Jeff Skilling was sentenced to twenty-four years in prison, but his sentence was reduced to

---

10. Joint Committee on Taxation, "Report of Investigation of Enron," 36.

11. Joint Committee on Taxation, "Report of Investigation of Enron," 42.

12. Joint Committee on Taxation, "Report of Investigation of Enron," 36.

13. Joint Committee on Taxation, "Report of Investigation of Enron," 36.

14. Joint Committee on Taxation, "Report of Investigation of Enron," 77.

15. Jennings, *Business Ethics* (7th ed.), 241.

16. Joint Committee on Taxation, "Report of Investigation of Enron," 79.

17. Joint Committee on Taxation, "Report of Investigation of Enron," 72.

18. Joint Committee on Taxation, "Report of Investigation of Enron," 82.

19. Joint Committee on Taxation, "Report of Investigation of Enron," 84.

20. Joint Committee on Taxation, "Report of Investigation of Enron," 84.

21. Pacelle, "Enron's Creditors to Get Peanuts."

22. Jennings, *Business Ethics* (7th ed.), 243.

fourteen years in 2013 in a settlement whereby, for the reduction in the length of the sentence, Skilling gave up all future opportunities for appeal.[23] Finally, the Enron accounting scandal also brought down its audit firm, Arthur Andersen. The firm was indicted in 2002 for obstruction of justice, based on its shredding of Enron audit documents after the SEC opened its formal investigation of Enron. With this conviction, the firm could no longer conduct audits, and thus had to close its doors, eighty-nine years after its founding.[24] While the conviction was overturned in 2005, with the public's confidence in Arthur Andersen destroyed, the audit firm could not recover.

FINANCIAL FRAUD

In chapter 7 we noted that greed is the enemy of integrity. It was never better demonstrated than in the case of Enron and other similar financial scandals of the early 2000s. Among the many unethical practices Enron employed were: aggressive earnings targets and management bonus compensation based on those targets; the use of aggressive accounting practices in order to maintain stock price or to meet earnings projections; and aggressive financial targets and expectations for operating personnel.[25] In addition, Enron developed an internal culture where problems were not acknowledged and where its employee ranking system was extremely harsh. While the company's stated values were respect, integrity, communication, and excellence (RICE), its operational value was profit, and employees who did not produce profits were quickly replaced. In Jeffrey Skilling's division (Enron Finance Corporation), the annual turnover was 15 percent. As a result, the internal environment was extremely competitive as employees sought to make a quick buck in order to keep their jobs and survive the employment reviews, to the exclusion of focus on long-range goals and strategy.[26] Fraudulent financial numbers were not far behind the rising pressure, especially as questions arose from the press and investors and stock prices began to tumble.

The Association of Certified Fraud Examiners (ACFE) defines occupational fraud as "the use of one's occupation for personal enrichment

23. Wilbanks, "Ex-Enron CEO."
24. Jennings, *Business Ethics* (7th ed.), 251.
25. Thomas, "Rise and Fall of Enron," 41–48.
26. Thomas, "Rise and Fall of Enron," 41–48.

through the deliberate misuse or misapplication of the employing organization's resources or assets."[27] The ACFE's biennial report issued
in 2018 covered 2,690 cases of occupational fraud in 125 countries.[28]
It categorized occupational fraud, to which a typical organization loses
approximately 5 percent of its revenues each year, into three categories:
asset misappropriation, corruption (e.g., conflicts of interest; bribery), and
financial statement fraud. Asset misappropriation accounted for the largest number of cases (89 percent) but was the least costly, with a median
loss of US$114,000. Financial statement fraud was the least frequent
(10 percent) but the most costly (US$800,000 median loss).[29] Over 77
percent of the occupational fraud occurred in the areas of accounting,
operations, sales, executive/upper management, customer service, administrative support, finance, and purchasing.[30] Owners/executives were
responsible for only 19 percent of the cases, but the median losses were
the highest among this group (US$850,000). Employees were responsible
for 44 percent of the cases, with the median loss of US$50,000, and man-
agement was responsible for 34 percent of the cases, with the median loss
of US$150,000.[31] The report noted that the higher the level of authority
of the perpetrator, the greater the fraud loss.[32]

Traditionally one thinks of occupational fraud and insider trading
as an individualized activity. An individual chooses to embezzle funds,
create fraudulent financial statements, take office supplies or other assets that belong to the organization, or use insider knowledge to trade
on the company's stocks and make extra money for himself or herself.
However, today what has traditionally been identified as unethical actions occurring in the physical workplace have moved online. Among the
major Internet crimes reported are overpayment fraud, non-delivery of
merchandise, advance fee fraud, and identity theft.[33]

27. ACFE, "Report to the Nations, 2018," 6.

28. ACFE, "Report to the Nations, 2018," 6–7.

29. ACFE, "Report to the Nations, 2018," 8, 10.

30. ACFE, "Report to the Nations, 2018," 38.

31. ACFE, "Report to the Nations, 2018," 33.

32. ACFE, "Report to the Nations, 2018," 33.

33. Ferrell et al., *Business Ethics*, 172.

THE FRAUD TRIANGLE

Donald Cressey was the initial identifier of three conditions which, when they coexist, are likely to encourage a financially-related fraudulent act. His concept is known as the fraud triangle and it is made up of three parts: pressure, opportunity, and rationalization.[34] First, the perpetrator has a non-sharable personal or professional financial problem (the pressure). This is usually something that cannot be solved through legitimate means, so an illegal act is considered. Examples may include unpaid but immediately due family bills, living beyond one's means, or wishing to do so by purchasing a status symbol, such as a new car, or the need to meet earnings expectations to keep up the company's stock price. In the case of Enron, the driver was the need to meet earnings expectations and the pressure to maintain a high stock price, at least until top management could cash in a large proportion of their stock options.

The second piece of the triangle relates to the method by which the crime will be committed (opportunity). The perpetrator seeks resolution of the problem through the abuse of his or her trusted financial position. It is essential, to the perpetrator's mind, that the solution (the chosen unethical act) be kept secret. To be exposed or detected would reduce the individual's current social status. It was therefore essential that Andrew Fastow not disclose *to the reporter* that he was in charge of the related-party SPEs, even though others within Enron knew of his SPE administrative positions.

Finally, most individuals engaging in fraud do not have a previous criminal record.[35] They do not see themselves as criminals—just as ordinary people caught in a tough situation (rationalization). The criminal act is justifiable in their minds. Examples of common rationalizations include: "I was only borrowing the money." Or "my wages are too low." Or "any fraud is covered by insurance anyway, so my employer really isn't out any money." Or "my employer is dishonest anyway, and deserves whatever he gets back in dishonesty."[36] In the case of Enron, when Jeff Skilling was asked about Enron's accounting practices, he responded: "We are doing God's work. We are on the side of angels."[37]

34. Cressey, *Other People's Money*, 30.

35. ACFE, "Report to the Nations, 2018," 66.

36. ACFE, "Fraud Triangle."

37. Jennings, *Business Ethics* (7th ed.), 244.

Nick Leeson and Barings Bank

Sometimes the individuals involved in fraudulent actions are in fact the "stars" of the company. Such was certainly the case with Nick Leeson, the twenty-eight-year-old derivatives trader in Barings Bank's Singapore office, who is credited with the collapse of Barings, Britain's oldest merchant bank, in late February 1995. In their discussion of his case, Lemon and Wallace note that "Leeson was perceived as a star who had produced unusual profits for the bank" and that it was possible that "management and, in turn, the internal auditors overestimated the trader's competency."[38]

But Leeson turned out to be a star who chose, over a period of time, to engage in accounting fraud. All three of the fraud triangle conditions were present in Nick Leeson's situation—a non-shareable problem, opportunity to commit and conceal the fraud, and a belief, at least initially, that he was still a good person.

Leeson's non-shareable financial problem occurred when a newly hired, inexperienced trader sold, rather than bought, twenty futures contracts—an error of 20,000 British pounds—in mid-1992. When Leeson told his immediate superior in Singapore of the error, he was counseled to contact the next higher superior. But Leeson was angry because he believed that inferior salary levels prohibited him from hiring competent staff. Instead of reporting the error, Leeson booked a fictitious trade to a customer in a dormant bona fide error account (88888) to cover the situation over the weekend. The following week the market dropped, and by failing to care for the matter immediately, the loss grew too large for Leeson, in his opinion, to confess to any of his superiors. Covering was possible and convenient because Leeson was both a floor trader and in charge of settlement operations. Soon Leeson began booking other errors in the 88888 account. He banked on the error losses being small and the income through subsequent trading large enough so he could clear the error account before the auditors arrived. That didn't happen. Due to personal problems, one of his traders began drinking heavily, and the mistakes he made became more frequent and larger. Once established, the pattern of covering the errors by using the 88888 account became routine.

Once, in mid-1993, Leeson was able to clear the 88888 account through successful trading. While he intended to stop using the 88888 account, he didn't, because, as Leeson expressed it, "I was probably the

38. Lemon and Wallace, "Ethical Issues Facing Internal Auditors," 197.

only person in the world to be able to operate on both sides of the balance sheet. It became an addiction."[39] The absence of the basic internal control practice of separation of duties gave Leeson the opportunity to prepare fraudulent entries in the accounting records. The motive evolved from covering errors for his traders to ultimately booking losses and thus creating mammoth profits for Barings and large bonuses for himself. Barings in London did not question the large daily transfers of cash which Leeson demanded to cover the margin requirements of the Singapore stock exchange. Ego pressure was created by Leeson's acquisition of a large trader as his client, who brought a great deal of business to Barings and prestige to Leeson among his fellow Singapore traders. When the internal auditors came they noted the lack of internal controls, but they failed to do even the most simple of reconciliations which would have brought to the surface the existence of the 88888 account and its loss balance.

Ultimately, as one might predict, the market collapsed. The final blow was the Kobe earthquake on January 18, 1995. The arrival of Coopers & Lybrand to do the 1994 year-end audit at the same time brought pressure to Leeson to "tell a good story" and in the process, to create through forgery the necessary documentation to support the fictitious figures which he had booked. His personal awakening to the situation is eye-opening.

> Throughout the grotesque build-up in the 88888 account I'd taken some comfort in the fact that I was trying to trade out of a loss which had been forced upon me. I could have admitted to the early loss but I tried to trade out of it. I could have come clean and Barings would have sacked us all and written off the loss and that would have been the end of the matter. But all along I'd traded and traded and dug myself deeper and deeper into trouble. Then I'd covered up the loss at month-end, but that had been a rolling forward operation. . . . Under such prolonged pressure to make profits, I had allowed my sense of criminality to become warped, and the loss had become hidden. . . . But once I'd forged these two documents, I knew that I was damned. These were forgeries. Up until now I had prevaricated, been economical with the truth, refused to separate the numbers which others could have easily found, and made outrageous claims for funding from London. If I had to stand in front of a jury, I'd have confessed to false accounting and probably obtaining property by deception. But now I'd added a new crime to this catalogue

39. Leeson, *Rogue Trader*, 64.

. . . I had physically cut out somebody's signature, glued it to a piece of paper, taken it to my flat, faxed it back to myself, and now I was going to hand it to Rachel Yong to pass on to the auditors. . . . I'd become a criminal and I couldn't stop it. I'd been caught up in my own web of deceit, and I was drowning in the tangle—a tangle of 8s. I needed something, anything, to get me out, and morals no longer mattered.[40]

By the end of the month, Coopers & Lybrand had given an unmodified audit report on the consolidation schedules of Baring Futures Singapore. Leeson went back into the market, betting that the Nikkei futures would move higher so that he could cover the fraudulent 7.78 billion yen trade he had made at the end of December to cover his losses. But in fact, the Nikkei slumped. On February 27 the headline in the Singapore paper read: "British Merchant Bank Collapse." Barings suffered losses of more than $1.3 billion. Leeson and his wife, who until that moment was unaware of the fraud, fled Singapore. Leeson was arrested in Germany where his plane stopped on its way back to London. Barings was forced to declare bankruptcy. Nick Leeson served his six-and-a-half-year sentence in Tanah Merah prison, Changi, Singapore.

CONFLICTS OF INTEREST

Nick Leeson's case not only illustrates financial fraud, but also conflicts of interest and insider trading. Boatright defines a conflict of interest as "a conflict that occurs when a personal interest interferes with a person's acting so as to promote the interests of another *when the person has an obligation to act in that other person's interest.* This obligation is stronger than the obligation merely to avoid harming a person and can arise only when the two persons are in a special relationship, such as employer and employee."[41] Because of his employee relationship with Barings Bank, Leeson had an obligation to protect the bank from loss of assets through improper and reckless trading. Instead, in an effort to cover, initially, the mistakes of others, but over time, his own mistakes as well, he acted in his own self-interest, thereby earning huge bonuses and a reputation for excellent trading. Leeson exhibited one of the most common types of conflict of interest—biased judgment. In their work, most employees en-

40. Leeson, *Rogue Trader*, 176–77.
41. Boatright, *Ethics and the Conduct of Business*, 123–24.

counter situations where they must use their judgment. Most often this occurs in the purchasing area, where the purchasing agent is faced with a choice of vendor. If the vendor has offered a kickback or a bribe to do business with their company and the purchasing agent accepts the kickback or bribe, the agent's judgment is biased in favor of that company to the exclusion of other viable vendors. Other common types of conflicts of interest are direct business competition between employer and employee, misuse of position, and the violation of confidentiality through disclosure of privileged information.[42]

The actions of Enron's auditor, Arthur Andersen, illustrate another classic example of conflict of interest. Professional standards require auditors to maintain an attitude of professional skepticism when dealing with their clients. Therefore the profession's ethical standards have a number of rules and examples designed to identify the necessary parameters required to maintain appropriate distance from the clients and to avoid conflicts of interest. The purpose of these rules is to assist the auditors in fulfilling their professional obligations to the public when they give an opinion, as an outside party, on the fairness of the financial statements. Among these rules are prohibitions against close personal relationships with clients and working for the client during either the period under audit or during the audit itself.

The Andersen audit partner in Houston was David Duncan. He was a close personal friend of Richard Causey, Enron's chief accounting officer, and often joined Causey on fishing and golf outings. Many of Andersen's employees, including Mr. Duncan, had offices at Enron, and auditors working for Andersen often switched employment to work for Enron. For example, in 2000, seven Andersen auditors joined Enron. Finally, the two firms were so entwined that employees at Enron often did not know which individual worked for which firm and therefore invited everyone, including the auditors, to Enron office parties.[43] The end result, as noted above, was that when Enron used the SPEs to hide liabilities and mark-to-market accounting to book nonexistent revenues, Arthur Andersen continued to grant the company unmodified opinions on their financial statements. Duncan expressed concerns over the conflict of interest that existed with Andrew Fastow controlling the SPEs, but in the end, failed to follow his profession's ethical standards (or the counsel

42. Boatright, *Ethics and the Conduct of Business*, 126–29.
43. Jennings, *Business Ethics* (7th ed.), 247.

from Arthur Andersen's head office in Chicago). Duncan succumbed to the pressure Enron exerted on him and his audit team to permit what they had already persuaded their board to approve.

The ethical issue with respect to conflicts of interest is the matter of trust. Trust is developed with individuals and organizations when they believe they are treated fairly, openly, and equally. Conflicts of interest break down trust through the appearance (or the fact) of providing special favors to some, but not all, participants in the transaction.[44]

The best way to handle a conflict of interest is to avoid it whenever possible. Unfortunately, avoidance may sometimes be impossible, especially in situations where the appearance of a conflict of interest, which can be as damaging as the real thing, may be beyond the control of the employee. To protect against conflicts of interest, most organizations create rules and policies that prohibit certain actions (e.g., accepting gifts from suppliers) and require disclosure of potential conflicts. Requiring disclosure encourages transparency, and ideally will cause the individual with a potential conflict of interest to think carefully before putting themselves into a conflict situation.[45]

INSIDER TRADING

Insider trading happens when a corporate insider trades the stock of a publicly-held corporation on the basis of information which is nonpublic. Two ethical principles are violated when insider trading occurs. First, the insider who traded on nonpublic information essentially stole that information from the corporation to use it for his or her own financial advantage. Second, the insider trader has an unfair advantage over other traders because he or she is trading on information no one else knows. As a result, the expected level playing field for market trades is no longer maintained.[46]

Martha Stewart, best known for her magazine *Martha Stewart Living*, her television shows, and her line of household goods, practiced insider trading when she approved the sale of 3,928 shares of ImClone based on "inside" information from a friend, Mr. Faneuil. Faneuil informed Stewart that others were trying to dump their ImClone stock prior to the

44. Trevino and Nelson, *Managing Business Ethics*, 125.

45. Boatright, *Ethics and the Conduct of Business*, 130–32.

46. Boatright, *Ethics and the Conduct of Business*, 324.

announcement that the FDA had refused to approve ImClone's anti-cancer drug, Erbitux, and that she might wish to do the same. Stewart's trade occurred on December 27, 2001. ImClone made the announcement of the FDA's decision on December 28, 2001. As anticipated, the price of Im-Clone stock declined with the announcement. The price advantage that Stewart acquired by selling prior to the announcement was $39,507—an insignificant amount of money given her financial situation. On March 5, 2004, she was found guilty of conspiracy and obstruction of an investigation and was sentenced to five months in federal prison and five months of house arrest.[47] In this case, given the known outcome, Stewart's choice to dump the stock prior to the public announcement of corporate bad news was not only illegal and unethical, but also unwise. Others have learned the same lesson the hard way, including Galleon Group founder Raj Rajaratnam and former Goldman Sachs director Rajat Gupta, as well as former hedge-fund manager Doug Whitman.[48] Insider trading is a particular temptation for those dealing with investments who are under constant pressure to make quick gains in the market.

THE ROOT CAUSE: COVETOUSNESS

While the initial drivers of financial fraud are almost as numerous as the examples one could provide, the underlying commonality is covetousness—the desire to have more than one currently has in the way of material goods, and especially money. The tenth commandment takes us beyond the outward dimension of moral life. It penetrates the recesses where envy, greed, and jealousy reside. Covetousness is the trigger for the constant, often unconscious competition between neighbors and friends, and often leads to unethical actions in the rush to get ahead in the economic game. As Nick Leeson put it, one can come to the point where "morals no longer matter."

The tenth commandment is very clear: "You shall not covet your neighbor's house. You shall not covet your neighbor's wife, or his manservant or maidservant, his ox or donkey, or anything that belongs to your neighbor" (Exod 20:17). When these words were written, the economy referenced was a barter economy and exchanging goods was the primary method for all transactions. Today we use money, a convenient way to

47. Jennings, *Business Ethics* (7th ed.), 63–68.
48. Ferrell et al., *Business Ethics*, 82.

purchase whatever goods we desire, rather than exchanging goods for
other desired goods. Thus we might "shorten" this commandment to
read: "You shall not covet your neighbor's money nor his ability to make
money, with which he obtains the goods that you desire."

When we express the commandment this way, we must acknowledge that money is not a neutral good, but that it has a spiritual power to
win our hearts.[49] Jesus recognizes the power of money when he says: "You
cannot serve both God and Money" (some translations read "mammon")
(Matt 6:24). Paul warns: "The love of money is the root of all kinds of
evil" (1 Tim 6:10). Why is this so? Richard Foster states:

> Money has many of the characteristics of deity. It gives us se-
> curity, can induce guilt, gives us freedom, gives us power, and
> seems to be omnipresent. Most sinister of all, however, is its bid
> for omnipotence.[50]
>
> Money has power all out of proportion to its purchasing
> power. Because the children of this world understand this, they
> can use money for noneconomic purposes. And use it they do!
> Money is used as a weapon to bully people and to keep them
> in line. Money is used to "buy" prestige and honor. Money is
> used to enlist the allegiance of others. Money is used to corrupt
> people. Money is used for many things; it is one of the greatest
> powers in human society.[51]

Because of the power of money to attract us and to act as a god in our
lives, we need to learn "how to possess money without *being* possessed *by*
money."[52] Foster suggests that the best way to break the power of money
in our lives is to give it away. Certainly giving away money and the things
that money can buy is the very opposite of covetousness.

David Gill notes: "Covetousness insults God by making an idol of
the coveted object and by rejecting God's provision in our lives as inadequate. Covetousness enslaves the coveter and blocks God's communication to our interior—our conscience, our spirit, and our heart."[53] Rather
than desiring what belongs to someone else, we need to develop gratitude
for what we have and appreciation for what our neighbors possess.[54] We

49. Foster, *Money, Sex and Power*, 26.

50. Foster, *Money, Sex and Power*, 28.

51. Foster, *Money, Sex and Power*, 54.

52. Foster, *Money, Sex and Power*, 46.

53. Gill, *Doing Right*, 312.

54. Gill, *Doing Right*, 310.

need to remember that we are stewards, not owners, and that "The earth is the Lord's, and everything in it, the world, and all who live in it" (Ps 24:1). Foster notes:

> Being aware of God's ownership can free us from a possessive and anxious spirit. After we have done what we can to care for those things which have been entrusted to us, we know they are in bigger hands than ours. . . . God's ownership of everything also changes the kind of questions we ask in giving. Rather than, "How much of my money should I give to God?" we learn to ask, "How much of God's money should I keep for myself?" The difference between these two questions is of monumental proportion.[55]
>
> When we have a spirit of thanksgiving we can hold things lightly. We receive; we do not grab. And when it is time to let go, we do so freely. We are not owners, only stewards. Our lives do not consist of the things we have, for we live and move and breathe in God, not things. And may I add that this includes those intangible "things" that are often our greatest treasures— status, reputation, position. These are things that come and go in life, and we can learn to be thankful when they come and thankful when they go.[56]

Paul told the Philippians: "I have learned to be content whatever the circumstances. I know what it is to be in need, and I know what it is to have plenty. I have learned the secret of being content in any and every situation, whether well fed or hungry, whether living in plenty or in want. I can do everything through him who gives me strength" (Phil 4:11–13).

THINKING IT THROUGH: ENRON CORPORATION

Since Enron is a case of accounting fraud, none of the proponents of the ethical theories discussed in chapter 1 would justify the actions of Enron's officers. These managers made decisions to hide Enron's debt and engage in other fraudulent actions in order to keep Enron's stock price up so that they could sell their own stock holdings before the price crashed. Neither would any of the ethical theories condone a decision whereby top management was able to sell their stock while the employees were forbidden to engage in the same financial activity. Finally, no ethical theory would

55. Foster, *Money, Sex and Power*, 42.
56. Foster, *Money, Sex and Power*, 49.

support the environment of fear that was established through Enron's employee evaluation process which required a large proportion of the employees to be dismissed after each evaluation period.

To be honorable in business, the Christian worldview stands strongly against any fraudulent or deceitful actions. Proverbs 13:5 states that "the righteous hate what is false" and Rev 21:27 notes that "anyone who does what is shameful or deceitful" will not enter the New Jerusalem. Treatment of others to their financial (or any other) disadvantage is also forbidden by the Christian worldview, both because of the Golden Rule (Matt 7:12) and by virtue of the fact that all humans are created in the image of God and therefore all are his children. For the Christian, however, the Enron example also illustrates the ease with which the temptation to acquire more money, fame, and/or power for oneself can lead to unethical behavior, even when the stated company, and perhaps personal values, are respect, integrity, communication, and excellence.

Chapter 10

What If I Am Far from Home?

International Ethical Challenges:
Bribery, FCPA, and Child Labor

Ethics and religion must not stay at home when we go to work.

—ACHILLE SILVESTRINI, CARDINAL OF THE ROMAN CURIA,
MAY 20, 2004

IN 1972 LOCKHEED WAS almost bankrupt due to cost overruns on government contracts in the prior years. To recover financially, Lockheed needed to sell its planes, ideally to Japan's All Nippon Airways, who, at that time, was the largest potential purchaser of new aircraft. But Lockheed needed to move quickly in completing a sales contract if it wanted to beat out its primary competitor, McDonnell Douglas, who also wanted to sell planes to All Nippon Airways. Lockheed sought the services of Yoshio Kodama to secure the contract with All Nippon Airways for the purchase of Lockheed's Tri-Star Jets. Kodama was not new to Lockheed; he had worked for them in the late 1950s to secure jet aircraft contracts with the Japanese air force. He had used bribes to secure contracts at that time, and he chose to do so again. Kodama asked for and received about nine million dollars to "ensure the sale," and allegedly gave the funds to

Kukeo Tanaka, the Prime Minister of Japan. At the close of negotiations, Lockheed obtained over $1.3 billion in contracts.

In 1975, after investigations by a US Senate committee, Lockheed pled guilty to concealing payments to the prime minister and other officials (by writing them off as "marketing costs"). During the investigation Carl Kotchian, president of Lockheed, maintained that the payments were not wrong because they had been made in accordance with "Japanese business practices" and had been requested by the prospective buyers and not initiated by Lockheed. In addition they did not violate any US laws. Kotchian, who was principally responsible for negotiating the deal, was forced to resign by Lockheed's board of directors. The Japanese canceled their billion dollar contract with Lockheed and Tanaka received a four-year prison sentence.[1]

THE FOREIGN CORRUPT PRACTICES ACT (FCPA)

The Lockheed story illustrates the position advanced by many when dealing outside their home country—that it is ethically acceptable to follow local customs in determining whether or not a particular action is ethical. Lockheed's argument that they broke no United States laws through their actions cannot be advanced today with respect to bribery, because due to *their* actions in Japan, the US government passed the Foreign Corrupt Practices Act (FCPA) in 1977. This Act makes it "unlawful for certain classes of persons and entities to make payments to foreign government officials to assist in obtaining or retaining business" or to use any instruments of interstate commerce to further "any offer, payment, promise to pay, or authorization of the payment of money or anything of value to any person, while knowing that all or a portion of such money or thing of value will . . . influence the foreign official in his or her official capacity to . . . act in violation of his or her lawful duty, or to secure any improper advantage in order to assist in obtaining or retaining business for or with, or directing business to, any person." The provisions of the Act apply to all US companies that issue securities, and, since 1998, to all foreign firms doing business within the United States. The law further requires that publicly listed firms must keep adequate accounting records and have

---

1. Velasquez, *Business Ethics* (4th ed.), 245–47.

internal control systems sufficient to ensure that the transactions of the organization are accurately recorded.[2]

This is the act referred to in Walmart's code of ethics, introduced in chapter 1, which stated that no bribes were to be paid when conducting the company's business or presenting the company's interests. It is interesting to note that as Lockheed wrote off their bribes to "marketing costs," Walmart wrote theirs off to "legal fees." Such actions provide some evidence that each company experienced a level of uncertainty regarding the ethics and legality of their actions, no matter what they later argued in court. But still the question remains: What and whose ethics should one follow when away from home? Are all actions ethical unless there is a law to prohibit the contemplated behavior?

GLOBAL BUSINESS: OPPORTUNITIES AND CHALLENGES

The globalization of business has created an unending opportunity for challenging interactions among people of different cultures, customs, and norms. Some of these interactions occur on brief business trips to locations outside one's home country; sometimes managers are sent on more lengthy assignments. Some of the interactions occur in the "home" country as more and more companies bring individuals from all over the world into their respective corporate headquarters. All of these interactions require cultural understanding, sensitivity, and openness.

For example, in the United States a simple "thank you" is expected when one receives a compliment. Other cultures would classify this response as uncouth and vain, as their culture demands that a word of praise be gently declined. The rather stiff and distant way Anglo-Saxons greet others seems to give lie to their expressions of welcome. Their reluctance to touch someone else is often interpreted as an expression of superiority. In the United States people talk together at two-arms'-length distance while in Arab countries people stand two inches apart. If you step back, the other person may well be offended. In the United States people like a vigorous handshake. In other countries it may be very offensive. Americans, who are taught to remain calm in discussions, tend to interpret the typical loud exchanges of views between Latins as angry and are amazed to see people who sounded like sworn enemies laughing

2. US Dept. of Justice, Foreign Corrupt Practices Act.

together once the discussion is over. Eye contact means very different things for an Anglo-Saxon and a Hispanic. A person who avoids eye contact in North America is quickly classified as dishonest. In the Hispanic setting, it is rude to look a superior in the eyes.

The very direct way of working on business deals in the United States often shocks others. The American way of "getting down to business" quickly conveys the impression that Americans do not care about people, only about money. Americans are in a hurry to make a deal, but in many countries, negotiating a contract is a lengthy process. In much of Asia one must first establish a personal relationship before bringing up the business matter. The use of drinks, including alcohol, is practically a ritual in many countries. Among the Slavs even an insignificant errand must be preceded by a lengthy social conversation and often the partaking of food. Included in the relationship ritual in many cultures is the expectation of exchanging gifts—a practice that is seen as cementing the relationship in some cultures but as bribery in others.

Embedded in the above described examples may be ethical challenges. Managing for ethical conduct is challenging enough when one operates in a common culture. The number of challenges explodes when a manager faces a different culture and often a different language. Companies have been doing business around the world for many years—sometimes ethically, and sometimes not. In the past, when operating abroad, companies were criticized for operating with a double standard, acting ethically when at home but engaging in unethical activities, if they were profitable, when away from home. Today, however, with technological advances and the globalization of business, the luxury of acting one way in one location and differently elsewhere is gone. Reports of actions spin around the world with literally the speed of the Internet. YouTube, Twitter, and email inform the public of actions taken by companies and individuals as quickly as they occur, irrespective of the location. Hence all managers must consider ethics from a global business perspective in order to be ethical business people in today's world.

CULTURAL RELATIVISM VS. CULTURAL IMPERIALISM

Thus the question: What and whose ethics apply when one is away from home, in a different culture, and often away from the legal constraints that operate in most Western countries? Some argue, "When in Rome, do as the Romans do." This argument, termed *cultural relativism*, follows from the belief that no culture's ethics are to be preferred over any other culture's ethics.[3] If one adopts cultural relativism, logically one must accept as ethical whatever actions occur in the country in which one works. For example, when searching for cheap waste-dumping sites in the late 1980s, some European tanneries and pharmaceutical companies approached Nigeria, who agreed to accept the highly toxic polychlorinated biphenyls (PCBs). Local workers, who did not know what the barrels contained, unloaded them while wearing only flip flops and shorts, and placed the barrels near a residential area.[4] Did the fact that unloading such materials was done with the Nigerian government's permission make the actions of the European companies ethical?

On the other hand, some assume that business ethics contains absolute truths which require exactly the same standards and behavior in every culture. This argument, called *cultural absolutism*, is a form of ethical imperialism that stems from the belief that one's own culture's norms are the blueprint that everyone else must follow. Cultural absolutism refuses to recognize that genuine cultural traditions and beliefs may differ around the world.[5] One can end up in difficult and troubling situations if one acts on this belief. For example, using US-developed sexual harassment training for Muslim managers in their home country under the guise of "consistency in training" would be offensive. Muslim countries have strict cultural norms that define male/female interactions and the vocabulary and examples in such videos or cases would shock and embarrass the audience in a Muslim culture. The intended ethical message to avoid sexual discrimination and coercion would not be heard because of the culturally-insensitive medium used.[6]

NAVIGATING CROSS-NATIONAL CULTURAL DIFFERENCES

Donaldson and Dunfee argue against both extremes: cultural relativism and cultural absolutism. In their article "When Ethics Travel: The

3. Donaldson, "Values in Tension," 115.

4. Donaldson, "Values in Tension," 115–16.

5. Donaldson, "Values in Tension," 117–18.

6. Donaldson, "Values in Tension," 117.

Promise and Peril of Global Business Ethics,"[7] they propose a third path, which they call "Integrative Social Contracts Theory" (ISCT). This theory promotes the use of hypernorms and micro-social contracts to ethically navigate between cultural relativism and cultural absolutism when doing business away from home.

 Hypernorms are defined as "fundamental human rights or basic prescriptions common to most major religions. The values they represent are by definition acceptable to all cultures and all organizations."[8] Examples of hyper-norms include the prohibition of child labor; over-extended, unreasonable working hours; unsanitary and unsafe working conditions; discrimination; and obeying local laws which prohibit bribery. ISCT uses the term "consistent norms" to describe culturally specific values that are in compliance with hypernorms. Examples of consistent norms would be found in the preferred ethical actions identified in most corporations' ethical codes of conduct.

 Donaldson and Dunfee argue that outside of hypernorms are norms that operate in moral free space which may be inconsistent between cultures.[9] These norms may express unique cultural beliefs but they are still compatible with recognized fundamental rights. An example of such a unique cultural belief is the business practice in India of hiring family members of current employees in the same firm. In the United States such a practice is labeled nepotism and is usually forbidden by the organization's employment policies. In India such practices are in harmony with India's cultural values of extended family. They are defended because the family members of a good employee are known persons, identified as coming from a good family, and therefore also likely to be good employees.

 Outside of the moral free space are illegitimate norms, which are always by definition incompatible with hypernorms. An example of such an illegitimate norm is exposing workers to harm by a health or safety violation.[10] This practice would be considered unethical even if justified by local laws or customs.

 One may believe that identifying hypernorms is impossible in our culturally-diverse world. However, Daryl Koehn, in his article "East

---

7. Donaldson and Dunfee, "When Ethics Travel," 45–63.

8. Donaldson and Dunfee, "When Ethics Travel," 51.

9. Donaldson and Dunfee, "When Ethics Travel," 52.

10. Donaldson and Dunfee, "When Ethics Travel," 53.

Meets West: Toward a Universal Ethic of Virtue for Global Business," argues that everyone, everywhere seeks behaviors that promote their ability to live happy lives within their families and communities, and which use the natural human feelings of shame and friendship to develop common, good practices.[11] These universal commonalities may then form the basis for hypernorms. Examples of such commonalities include evidence that thoughtful people everywhere make the same ethical distinctions (e.g., people around the world recognize the difference between a bribe and a social gift), and that individuals act on what appears to be a universal virtue (for example, respect). Koehn recognizes, however, that the actual practice engaged in may be culturally specific. For example, in some cultures people bury the dead; others cremate the corpse; no culture puts the body on a rubbish heap.[12]

Trevino and Nelson argue that one tradition *is* found across all cultures and religious traditions, and that is the "golden rule." In Christianity it is expressed in the words of Jesus: "Whatsoever you wish that men would do to you, do so to them, for this is the law and the prophets" (Matt 7:12). But it is also present in some form in the other major world religions.[13]

> *Buddhism:* Hurt not others in ways that you yourself would find hurtful.
>
> *Confucianism:* Tsze-Kung asked: "Is there one word which may serve as a rule of practice for all one's life?" The Master said: "Is not reciprocity such a word? What you do not want done to yourself, do not do to others."
>
> *Hinduism:* This is the sum of duty: Do naught to others which would cause pain if done to you.
>
> *Islam:* No one of you is a believer until he desires for his brother that which he desires for himself.
>
> *Judaism:* What is hateful to you, do not to your fellow man. This is the entire Law; all the rest is commentary.

Trevino and Nelson identify two other standards, often quoted from the Old Testament, that are also universally accepted: "Thou shalt not

---

11. Koehn, "East Meets West," 714.

12. Koehn, "East Meets West," 705–7.

13. Trevino and Nelson, *Managing Business Ethics*, 413.

kill" (Exod 20:13) and "Thou shalt not steal" (Exod 20:15).[14] But outside of these universal standards, how does one evaluate specific actions as either ethical or unethical, particularly when operating in a culture different from one's own? How does one distinguish between actions that are solely an expression of a different culture, and actions which are unethical?

THE IMPORTANCE OF UNDERSTANDING CULTURE

Geert Hofstede offers six dimensions of cultural difference[15] to enhance our understanding of actions taken within a culture and assist us in evaluating whether or not a particular action is ethical or unethical. These dimensions are:

1. *Power distance*: The degree of inequality among people which the population of a country considers as normal.

2. *Individualism versus collectivism*: In an individualistic culture, everyone looks out for himself or herself; the emphasis is on the "I." In a collectivistic culture, individuals are integrated into strong, cohesive groups and the emphasis is on the group–"we" instead of "I."

3. *Masculinity versus femininity*: The extent to which a culture is conducive to dominance, assertiveness, and acquisition of things versus a culture which is more conducive to people, feelings, and the quality of life.

4. *Uncertainty avoidance*: The degree to which people in a culture prefer structured over unstructured situations.

5. *Long-term versus short-term orientation*: Long-term culture's values are oriented toward the future, like saving and persistence. Short-term culture's values are oriented toward the past and present, like respect for tradition and fulfilling social obligations.

6. *Indulgence versus restraint*. The extent to which members of a society try to control their desires and impulses.

The following examples illustrate two of these dimensions: individualism vs. collectivism, and long-term vs. short-term orientation.

---

14. Trevino and Nelson, *Managing Business Ethics*, 413.

15. Hofstede et al., *Cultures and Organizations*, 31, 38, 286.

In a collectivistic society, people are rewarded for working together and the valued qualities are solidarity, generosity, and acceptance. In such a society, financial resources are viewed as "ours" or "mine," but not "yours." An individual's financial need will take precedence over all other considerations, including others' resources, others' desires (such as the donor's wishes for the use of a gift of funds), or others' expectations.

David Maranz tells the story of three single men who were renting an apartment together. The plan was to give funds each month to one of the men so he could pay the electricity bill. On the described occasion, however, the fund-collector had a personal bill that needed to be paid before the due date for the electric bill, so he used the money he had collected from the others to pay his personal bill. Unfortunately, his friend who was expected to reimburse him did not pay. The electric bill came due but could not be paid because the collected money had been spent and the electricity was cut off.[16]

Was the man unethical when he used his apartment mates' monies to pay a personal bill? Not in his West African society. In his culture, the apartment mates did not consider their colleague to be either irresponsible or dishonest. His financial need took precedence over their expectations; his financial need had first claim on the available resources.

In a second example, a short-term-oriented culture focuses on immediate needs, which often results in resources being used immediately rather than saved for the future. This focus on immediate needs also changes the expectations for success. In a long-term focused culture, success is measured by the long-term effects of the project. In a short-term focused culture, long-term success is not necessary for the project to have met its goals.

An international aid organization gave an African friend of David Maranz several hundred dollars as seed money to establish a chicken business. The African had no experience in raising chickens, so he kept the baby chickens in the bedroom he rented. As the chickens grew, they required more and more food, so he asked David Maranz for a loan to buy food for the chickens, promising to repay the loan when the chickens were sold. Some of the chickens died and some he ate, but when the rest were grown, he gave some to the woman who made his meals, some to other people to pay off his outstanding debts, and some he sold. But he did not make enough money to pay back the loan from Maranz for the

---

16. Maranz, *African Friends*, 14.

chickens' food, and he did not have sufficient funds to buy more baby chicks. However, he considered the project to be a total success, as he had had a job for a few months and had been able to pay off some of his debts, while at the same time he had chicken to eat.[17]

Was the African friend unethical? The international aid organization expected success to be measured in terms of the establishment of a chicken farm with long-term sustainability. Does the fact that the African friend's actions did not meet the international aid organization's expectations make his actions unethical?

The lack of understanding of the culture in which one is working can sometimes lead to business failure. Walmart operated in Germany from 1997–2006. They entered the German market by acquiring two different German hypermarket chains which were highly unionized. In the United States, Walmart is not unionized, so it does not have experience working in a highly unionized environment. In Germany, the specificity of Walmart's corporate statement of ethics, prepared by the corporate office in Bentonville, Arkansas, ran counter to German cultural and legal codetermination rules. The German Works Council (similar to US unions) took Walmart Germany to court because their universal statement of ethics (exported to all Walmart organizations around the world) included regulations on raising and disclosing ethical concerns by employees, receiving gifts or gratuities, preventing harassment and inappropriate conduct, releasing statements on behalf of the firm to the media, accessing company personnel and medical records, and banning internal dating and romantic relationships. The Works Council believed these mandates should have been subject to their jurisdiction and not imported from the Walmart corporate office. For example, the Works Council saw the ban on internal dating and romantic relationships as interfering with the workers' private lives and therefore illegal.

Walmart appealed the initial judgment that went against them, but before final action could take place on the second judgment, Walmart sold its business operations in Germany. Till Talaulicar argues in his article that if Walmart had written their statement of ethics as more principle-based and less rule-based for all of its divisions around the world, it might have avoided the lawsuits and the accompanying bad publicity. However, lack of understanding about how specific rules would translate

17. Maranz, *African Friends*, 150–51.

across cultures contributed to Walmart's inability to achieve financial success in the German market.[18]

GUIDANCE FOR DOING BUSINESS AWAY FROM HOME

These examples illustrate the need for guidance when engaged in business overseas. Boatright recommends three categories of consideration for such situations: consideration for *human rights*; consideration for the *welfare for the people* of the host country, and consideration for *just actions* which do not disadvantage the host country or its citizens.[19]

With respect to *human rights*, Boatright confirms Donaldson's description of the basic human rights that should be honored. These include the rights to freedom of physical movement, ownership of property, freedom from torture, a fair trial, nondiscriminatory treatment, physical security, freedom of speech and association, minimal education, political participation, and subsistence.[20]

With respect to the *welfare for the people* in the host country, Boatright refers to De George's seven principles to identify what is meant by consideration of welfare:

1. Multinational Corporations (MNCs) should do no intentional direct harm. They are guests, not conquering armies, in the host country.

2. MNCs should produce more good than bad for the host country. MNCs should act so they cannot be charged with exploitation of the host country.

3. MNCs should contribute by their activity to the host country's development.

4. MNCs should respect employees' human rights. Employees should work in conditions which recognize their status as human beings.

5. MNCs should respect the local culture to the extent it does not violate moral norms.

18. Talaulicar, "Global Retailers," 47–58.
19. Boatright, *Ethics and the Conduct of Business*, 422–26.
20. Donaldson, *Ethics of International Business*, 81.

6. MNCs should pay their fair share of taxes and cooperate with the local government in developing equitable laws and other support-ing institutions.

7. MNCs should cooperate with the local government in developing and enforcing just background institutions.[21]

To practice *just actions*, a MNC should avoid taking unfair advan-tage or engaging in unfair competition when involved in global business. Unfair advantage, for example, may occur through accounting methods which record profits in the countries with the lowest tax rates. When operating in overseas markets, MNCs should observe the rules of the marketplace, which require honesty, trust, and fair dealing, as well as transparency of transactions.

One example of a good corporate citizen is Merck and Company, an international pharmaceutical manufacturer and distributor. Merck de-veloped a human version of a best-selling animal drug that was expected to kill the parasite that causes river blindness. River blindness (or On-chocerciasis) begins when the common blackfly bites the victim and thus transmits the Onchocerca volvulus parasite to humans. Blindness sets in when the adult worms release their offspring under the victim's skin, particularly in the iris and retina. Generally blindness occurs when the individual is an adult at the prime of their working life. Since the parasite lives near rivers, fear of river blindness leads many West Africans, where river blindness primarily occurs, to migrate inland away from the fertile river basins to poorer land, further impoverishing the economy of the country.

While the World Health Organization (WHO) had been working for some time on killing the blackfly larvae in their habitat as a method of controlling onchocerciasis, this did not stop those already infected from going blind. The development of the drug Mectizan by Merck provided a breakthrough for these individuals. But the population most vulnerable to onchocerciasis were also the least able to afford the medication due to high population growth rates, poor economic performance, income inequality, and corruption.

Because the drug was originally manufactured for use in killing parasites in animals, Merck had to decide whether to do additional re-search to discover if the drug would indeed kill the parasites that caused river blindness, as well as be safe for human use. Further, since there is no

21. De George, *Competing with Integrity*, 45–56.

river blindness in the United States or other highly developed countries, the actual use of the drug would be in locations where any economic recovery of research costs would be impossible. Finally, even if the drug successfully killed the parasites and was safe for human use, those who needed the drug were generally located in remote areas. This required a distribution system that could reach them, as they could not come to a central location to obtain the medication. The decision was difficult and fraught with risk. However, George W. Merck, son of Merck's founder, stated: "We try never to forget that medicine is for the people. It is not for the profits. The profits follow, and if we have remembered that, they have never failed to appear. The better we have remembered it, the larger they have been."[22]

In October 1987, Merck committed itself to donate Mectizan—as much as needed for as long as needed—with the goal to help eliminate river blindness. In order to make sure that the drug reached those most in need, Merck worked with a number of government and private organizations to distribute the drug. The distribution system Merck developed has been a model for other drug donation programs.

On their 2013 website, Merck noted:

> Twenty-five years later the results of this program speak for themselves. With the efforts of a variety of partners, including the donation of more than one billion treatments to more than 117,000 communities in twenty-eight countries in Africa, six countries in Latin America, and in Yemen, disease transmission has been interrupted—meaning no new cases have been identified—in four of the six affected countries in Latin America and nine regions in five African countries.[23]

PRIMARY INTERNATIONAL ETHICAL ISSUES

The most common ethical issues that arise when a multi-national corporation (MNC) operates overseas deal with wages, working conditions, the use of child labor, and bribery.

---

22. Weiss and Bollier, "Merck & Company," 72.

23. Merck homepage.

Wages, Working Conditions, and Child Labor

The issues of substandard working conditions, child labor, and low wages for those workers who create inexpensive products for consumption in highly-developed economies are familiar because their stories receive much publicity in today's media-connected world. Recent fires (2012) and building collapses (2013) in the garment factories in Bangladesh, both of which cost hundreds of workers' lives, highlight the ineffective oversight of production by many multinational corporations.

The issue of poor working conditions and low wages has been with us for decades. Public attention, however, was drawn to the issues when well-known companies moved their manufacturing overseas in order to obtain lower production costs. The use of foreign contractors and the task of managing them is a constant challenge for companies, especially since in most cases the local contractors are not employees of the MNC but are independent companies owned and operated in a foreign country. In some cases the laws of the local country are lax, but in other cases, even adequate laws are ignored in the name of attracting foreign investment which results in local jobs. In some cases, such as the building collapse in Bangladesh in 2013, accusations of bribery by the building's owners, engaged in for the purpose of bypassing construction approvals, have been made.[24] Sometimes MNCs use their own employees to monitor these contractors in order to be certain the working conditions are satisfactory. Critics claim, however, that doing so is a conflict of interest, and demand that monitoring be done by an independent, external monitoring system. Sometimes, even if the monitoring is done by outside parties, the local contractor is aware that the monitor will arrive on a particular day, and accordingly manages the factory on that day to meet the standards, even if at other times the working conditions are substandard.

Nike, Inc. is a high-profile company that was targeted early on for the conditions in their overseas manufacturing facilities. Nike uses between 900 and 1000 suppliers in fifty countries annually, a huge manufacturing network that requires extensive monitoring. Recently Nike chose to move beyond traditional monitoring procedures and developed a grading system that incorporates more than just the factor of low-cost into their decision as to whether to sign on with a particular supplier. Through this grading system Nike attempts to reduce its exposure in countries where the working conditions may be risky, such as Bangladesh. At the time of

24. Yardley, "Report on Deadly Factory Collapse."

the 2012 fire, Nike noted that only eight of the 896 factories it worked with were located in Bangladesh.[25]

Other companies have attempted to correct matters in a more hands-on manner. Levi Strauss discovered that in Bangladesh it was using two contractors who appeared to employ underage workers. This is against Levi Strauss's code of conduct. No birth certificates were available but the children appeared to be under the age of fourteen, the international standard for a reasonable working age. To fire the children risked significantly diminishing the family income and probably would result in the children turning to prostitution or begging to make up the lost wages.

Levi Strauss came up with a unique solution. The contractors agreed to hire a physician to examine the children who appeared to be underage. Those children who were determined to be under the age of fourteen were removed from the production line and sent to school, even though they were still paid their factory wages by the contractors. In addition, Levi Strauss covered the cost of the children's uniforms, tuition, and books for school. When the underage children reached the age of fourteen, they were offered back their original factory jobs.[26]

Closely related to substandard working conditions and child labor is the problem of low wages. How do we know when wages are low? Actual numbers are not necessarily comparable across all economies, so what sounds low to those in a highly-developed economy may actually be sufficient in another economic situation.

Wage-setting in developed countries relies on the market (with constraints, such as minimum wage laws). Thus if an individual chooses to take a job at a comparably low wage, we accept their choice in the name of individual freedom. But in developing countries, there may not be a viable labor market and there may not be a minimum wage law. Even in some cases where there is a local minimum wage, critics argue that it is not a "living wage" and that the multinational company who pays the local minimum wage is, in fact, exploiting the workers of the host country. In some countries, especially when workers are not permitted to organize, there may not be a free labor market at all. Finally, from the host country's perspective, if the employment were not available at all its citizens might be forced into prostitution or begging to survive, and thus the host country may be quite happy for any jobs, even at very low wages.

25. Bustillo, "Nike's Game Plan."
26. Haas, "Ethics in the Trenches," 12–13.

This possibility focuses on the very incentive the MNC had in moving its factories to the developing country in the first place. If, indeed, the wages in the host country were to rise to a level comparable to the wages in a developed country, the multinationals would have no incentive to move their factories to the developing country. Would the developing country then be better off or worse off? From an economic standpoint, low labor costs provide the competitive advantage for many developing countries. Does that make low wages ethical?

As noted above, De George argues that a multinational company should avoid exploitation of the citizens of the host country. It is relatively easy to argue that minimum working conditions, particularly relating to health and safety, must be maintained, irrespective of local laws and customs. Putting workers in buildings which are unsafe and lack fire escape doors is wrong, even if these buildings meet local construction standards. Locking workers into overheated or unheated factories and refusing to allow them any breaks to care for basic physical needs is clearly exploitation. Such exploitation is ethically and morally wrong because these workers are children of God, created in the image of God, and entitled to the basic rights that support life as identified at creation and in the sixth commandment.

But what about the matter of wages? In defining an appropriate wage, what is "right"? What is "just"? Thomas Donaldson attempts to answer these questions by suggesting there are two types of ethical conflict: *the conflict of relative development* and *the conflict of cultural tradition*.

The concept of the *conflict of relative development*[27] highlights issues of wage differentials which may occur because of varying levels of economic development between the home country and the host country. The manager should ask: Would the practice be acceptable at home if my country were in a similar stage of economic development? If the answer is "yes," the practice is probably ethical in the host country. Paying lower wages which are fair in the host country (even if they are not "fair" in the home country) recognizes the difference in economic development. This may sound reasonable for determining wages, but in some instances, such as dealing with health and safety issues, the host country's standards may be inadequate at any level of economic development. Certainly the 2013 building collapse in Bangladesh where 1,127 people were killed is

---

27. Donaldson, "Values in Tension," 128.

an example of poor construction, irrespective of what local laws may have permitted or the wages paid to the workers.

Second is *the conflict of cultural tradition*.[28] Examples of this conflict include gift-giving in Japan and the role of women in Saudi Arabia. In both cases, the countries involved are economically well-developed, but their strongly-held religious and/or cultural beliefs make it unlikely that the cultural differences will disappear. For the Japanese, whose culture emphasizes group belonging and respect, gift-giving is a sign of acceptance into the group. To the Westerner, whose culture emphasizes individual responsibility and action, gift-giving may appear to be a bribe. To respect Japanese culture it may be necessary for companies to tolerate more gift-giving in Japan than they would elsewhere. Motorola is one company who faced and dealt with this problem in a creative way. For Motorola, in Japan only, limited gift giving and receiving is acceptable under specific guidelines: cost limits, gifts to be given only at certain times of the year, and any gift to an employee of Motorola must be displayed in and remains with the office after the recipient departs.[29] Recognizing these situations as ones where the cultural perception must be considered, Donaldson recommends that the manager consider creative solutions while at the same time asking: Is it possible to conduct business successfully in the host country without undertaking the practice? Is the practice a violation of a core human value? If the answer is "no" to both questions, the action is probably ethical.

However, problems can arise, even with these two principles, as each country and each situation brings unique challenges. Multinationals can abuse their power by exploiting their superior position in an imperfect market and by taking more than their fair share. International business can be further complicated by corruption at the local level, and by the need of the lesser-developed economic society for jobs at any "price." In such situations, what may be seen by developed countries' standards as unacceptable working conditions are considered by the host country as preferable to a situation where there are insufficient jobs for its citizens who need work.

Sometimes the multinational company has the clout and wealth to demand that unethical practices cease and may successfully change the climate in which business operates in another country. But sometimes

28. Donaldson, "Values in Tension," 129.

29. Moorthy et al., *Uncompromising Integrity*," 232–36.

even a major corporation does not have sufficient clout to change the economic climate of another country when they operate away from home.

For example, Google understandably was interested in entering the market in China in 2006 with the launch of Google.cn, as China represented an emerging economy with a huge population of potential Internet users. But Google's lack of understanding, not only of Chinese culture but more importantly, of the Chinese political and institutional environment, meant that Google's stated corporate objective of "the need for information crosses all borders" came into direct conflict with Chinese censorship. In this schizophrenic situation, Google appeared to be complicit with China's censorship policies—exactly the opposite position of Google's stated corporate policies. Google was forced to self-censure and erase links that the Chinese government disapproved of in order to obtain an Internet Content Provider (ICP) license for their operations in China. The tension of seeking profits at the cost of compromising its principles led to the eventual pull-out of Google from China in 2010.[30] As Tan and Tan ask:

> Why would Google thrust itself so suddenly into the international spotlight with a decision as controversial as pulling out of a market entirely? The rational might stem from the inherent tension between "what is profitable business" and "what is ethical conduct." The two standards are not necessarily contradictory, but they pose serious challenges to MNC management teams when they are not perfectly congruent—a state that is very rare in dynamic international business environments. . . . To enter [China], it is almost mandatory for the MNC to become complicit in the state's control of information and Internet freedom.[31]

As Lee et al. stated: "Both the Chinese government and Google ended up testing each other's baseline."[32]

Bribery

When discussing business activity in the international arena, usually bribery is the first topic that asserts its dominance. Even though officially

30. Schmidt et al., *Google: How Google Works*, 143–51.

31. Tan and Tan, "Business Under Threat," 475.

32. Lee et al., "Searching for Internet Freedom," 407.

all countries have agreed that bribery is illegal and the US Foreign Corrupt Practices Act (FCPA), as discussed above, prohibits US corporations from engaging in bribery, almost every business person who works internationally can tell a story where either a bribe was offered or demanded. The technical distinction between bribery (when the firm initiates the payments) and extortion (when an official demands a payment to complete an action) is usually lumped together under the general term "bribery."[33] For ease of discussion, we will do the same and lump all payments of this type under the common term.

Boatright defines bribery as: "A payment made with the intention to corrupt. More specifically, the payment is made with the intention of causing a person to be dishonest or disloyal or to betray a trust in the performance of official duties."[34] In the Walmart de Mexico example provided in chapter 1, bribery was undertaken with the intent to circumvent various zoning policies. The bribe was to facilitate the local officials' decision to fail to perform their official duties in the manner expected by the general population, as well as by their superiors.

Based on Boatright's definition, certain kinds of payments are legally permitted and are not considered bribes, such as "facilitating payments" or "grease payments." These small sums are paid to lower-level officials to lubricate the bureaucracy and get things done. That is not to say that there are no laws against "grease payments" in the countries that expect them. It is just that they are seldom enforced, and under the legal definition of bribery are not considered to be bribes, as there is no intent to corrupt or to ask the individual to betray a trust or be dishonest.[35] However, many question whether the legal definition of bribery is sufficient for moral purposes.

There is a third troubling bribery category, known as agent's fees. Agents are often used when a firm is unfamiliar with a country's conventions, rules, and regulations. In many Middle Eastern countries, companies must use agents because the culture requires that the company doing business must be properly introduced. Agents are generally used to bring firms and government officials together, and to assist a firm in entering a market without violating local rules or customs. In some instances, however, agents have been used as a conduit to provide bribes to officials,

33. Peach and Murrell, "Establishing and Maintaining an Ethical Posture."
34. Boatright, *Ethics and the Conduct of Business*, 432.
35. Boatright, *Ethics and the Conduct of Business*, 432.

thus keeping the company and the bribed official at arms' length.[36] Such actions are illegal under the FCPA. The use of agents in the Walmart de Mexico case may have permitted individuals to claim that they were not bribed by Walmart directly, but it did not lessen the guilt of Walmart once the bribes were disclosed.

The economic issues at stake when bribery occurs relate to the fact that the bribe inhibits the development of fair and efficient markets. When there is bribery, open access to all competitors on equal terms is missing. Resources will not be allocated to where the market demands they be placed; they will be moved to where the money (i.e., the bribe) directs they be placed. "When bribery occurs, prices are invariably higher than they would be in a competitive market. Higher prices also create a disincentive for domestic and foreign firms to invest in the further development of a nation's economy."[37]

For Christians, bribery is generally condemned because it is seen as dishonest and an attempt to gain favor through the misuse of money. Defining bribery as acting with an intent to corrupt the individual or to ask that individual to betray a trust or to be dishonest or disloyal, makes it clear that to engage in bribery is not an act a Christian should undertake. To do so would dishonor the inherent dignity of the person as granted at creation and would violate Christian commands to seek justice and love mercy.[38] It also resonates with what we know about God's character. God is very clear that he does not accept bribes (Deut 10:17) and if we wish to mirror the acts of God, then we too will not offer or accept bribes (Exod 23:8; Deut 16:18–20). When God makes such definitive statements, the accompanying stated issues are justice, the concern for impartiality, and the fact that the bribe may pervert both qualities.

But what about the facilitating payments? Some argue that facilitating payments are expected because the government officials who receive them are paid low wages. The culture anticipates that the officials will supplement their salaries by such facilitating payments. Often these facilitating payments are equated with tips given to waitresses in many Western societies. They, too, receive low wages because of the cultural expectation that they can "make it up" through earning tips because of the excellent service they provide.

36. Boatright, *Ethics and the Conduct of Business*, 434.

37. Boatright, *Ethics and the Conduct of Business*, 433.

38. Adeney, *Strange Virtues*, 150.

Adeney suggests that in such circumstances:

> A moral distinction may be made on the basis of whether a
> person has the freedom to give or not to give. If a small gift is
> freely given to obtain better service and there is no fear or threat
> involved, it is possible to consider it a tip. Presumably the ser-
> vice would be given in any case, but would probably take a little
> longer. The tip speeds up the process and benefits both parties.
> Little or no harm is done to the poor who either do not need
> the service or can obtain it with a little more time. On the other
> hand, if fear or force is involved, or if the expected delays are ex-
> treme, the freedom that characterizes a gift or a tip is removed.
> A gift or a tip is never compulsory.[39]

John Noonan Jr. argues that in his opinion, the Old Testament has
a double standard with respect to bribery. In the Old Testament there
is a recognition that a poor person may give a gift to stave off injustice,
while the rich may give a gift to exploit others.[40] Noonan maintains that
in Scripture the powerful and the powerless are not judged by the same
abstract absolute, but are judged by the relationships and intentions of
their situation (see Prov 15:27; 17:8; 17:23; 18:16; 21:14; 22:16). Proverbs condemns those who accept bribes in order to do wrong, but it also
warns those who give gifts that they do not always work.

Adeney suggests the use of Roman Catholic moral theology as a
third way to look at bribery. He notes that prima facie moral rules and
principles cover those situations that occur because our world is far from
perfect. Prima facie rules, which include prohibitions against killing, lying, working on Sabbath, and divorce, ought to be absolutes. But because
our world is fallen, we may break these absolutes (i.e., divorce to end
physical or emotional abuse). When we do, we recognize that an evil has
occurred and the act has been done regretfully, but it has been done to
prevent an even greater evil. This requires the actor to understand that
breaking moral rules is always serious, and when we do break absolute
moral rules for whatever reason, there will be personal and social rami-
fications. Adeney considers putting bribery in the prima facie category.
He states:

> Our individual actions cannot always overcome evil that is a
> structural part of a situation. Many Christians have told me

39. Adeney, *Strange Virtues*, 151.

40. Noonan, *Bribes*, 696–98.

stories of instances where they paid a small bribe to avoid what they understood as a far greater evil. Were they without sin in doing so? Perhaps not. The prima facie category does not absolve the lawbreaker from guilt. It only allows us to recognize our weakness in the face of a sinful world. Sometimes we are not wise enough or strong enough to act well in situations of ambiguity. Sometimes we cannot see any good course of action. Sometimes the law we break seems insignificant in the face of the enormity of our situation. If so, we dare not claim innocence. Nor may we rescind or denounce our action. It throws us on the mercy of God.[41]

THE LOCAL ENTREPRENEUR

In their case study about Motorola, Peach and Murrell tell the story of Motorola's decision to delay the opening of a plant in a country where the local officials wanted a bribe before they would issue the operating permit required to open the plant. It was tempting to pay the bribe rather than experience what would be an expensive delay in beginning production. However, Motorola chose to wait. The word spread that Motorola was unwilling to pay the requested bribe and, ultimately, the required permits were issued.[42]

It is one thing to be a major company like Motorola and have the financial resources to wait out the local officials who seek "facilitating payments." But what if you are a local businessperson who does not have the clout of the multinational corporation nor the financial resources to wait months until the local official issues the permit? Should the local entrepreneur be held to the same ethical standard as the multinational?

Richard De George thinks that often they should not be because the local entrepreneur may not have the same options available as the MNC.[43] Ahner agrees:

> The challenge of business in the face of bribery and corruption is to work toward convincing locals of the benefits of playing by the rules of good business. Perhaps there is a special role here for multi-national corporations who have greater resources, more power, and easier access to independent credit. Some

41. Adeney, *Strange Virtues*, 155–56.

42. Peach and Murrell, "Establishing and Maintaining an Ethical Posture."

43. De George, "Entrepreneurs, Multinationals," 271–80.

degree of ethical commitment to fair exchange is the basis for a free-market economy to prosper. In some markets there is no way of avoiding payment of bribes, except by exiting the market. In fact, many companies will not even attempt to do business in a country ruled by corruption and bribery. Again, it is the common people who suffer most.[44]

The local entrepreneur does not have the option of not operating in a country which is engaged in unethical practices, because it is his/her own country. The local entrepreneur also does not have the same resources, power, or wealth to stand up to local corruption that the multinational does. The multinational may be a desirable entity in the eyes of the government because it will bring jobs, taxes, and other benefits to the country, while the local entrepreneur may be too small to be seen as beneficial to the local officials. In many ways, the multinational corporation and the local entrepreneur do not operate in the same situation, and thus their responses may not be able to be the same. To immediately fault the local entrepreneur may show one's lack of understanding of the specific situation.

For example, when apartheid was the law in South Africa, local white entrepreneurs would have broken the law if they had disobeyed the apartheid law. Does this mean that the white local entrepreneurs should have closed their businesses, perhaps by leaving the country, and thus left South African local business to those who were unethical? It cannot be assumed that all white entrepreneurs who obeyed the law in South Africa in those days were necessarily unethical people because they chose not to disobey the laws of the country. Likewise, multinational corporations have taken a stance against the use of child labor in countries like Bangladesh or Pakistan where the use of child labor is common. In this case, the use of child labor is not mandated by law, but by the social structure of the country. Does this mean that a local entrepreneur in Bangladesh who uses his family to run his business, including his children, is an unethical person? If the wages are not even living wages, what choice does he have, in order to remain in business, if he cannot hire his children and instead must pay higher wages to his employees? If the result is bankruptcy for his business, might that leave the entrepreneurial activity to those who are unethical and use the social structure to support their activities?

44. Ahner, *Business Ethics*, 200.

Perhaps all these instances are occasions where the doer is thrown on the mercy of God. The cautionary words of Jesus in Matt 7:1–5 seem to have special application:

> Do not judge, or you too will be judged. For in the same way you judge others, you will be judged, and with the measure you use, it will be measured to you. Why do you look at the speck of sawdust in your brother's eye and pay no attention to the plank in your own eye? How can you say to your brother, 'Let me take the speck out of your eye,' when all the time there is a plank in your own eye? You hypocrite, first take the plank out of your own eye, and then you will see clearly to remove the speck from your brother's eye.

THINKING IT THROUGH: THE LOCKHEED CORPORATION

Since the passage of the Foreign Corrupt Practices Act (FCPA) in 1977, no ethical theory would argue in favor of breaking the law which prohibits bribery of foreign officials by public companies that have a presence in America. However, breaking the FCPA continues to occur, as was noted in the Walmart case discussed in chapter 1. Further, any search of the terms "corporate bribery" on the Internet will bring up other recent examples, such as Alstom, Siemens, and Avon.

For the utilitarian, the question often rests on whether the payment, particularly the facilitating payment which is not considered illegal under the FCPA, provides the best solution to a business problem for the greatest number of stakeholders (i.e., employees, stockholders, customers). Sometimes, particularly in cases where a US company has become an international organization, the international employees of the US firm will consider their own potential promotions or bonuses that might accrue if they are able to provide additional profits for the US organization and its stakeholders through bribery or facilitating payments. The utilitarian may also take into consideration the position of the local government and local laws with respect to facilitating payments (and bribery), and whether or not these laws are enforced.

Kant's position would consider whether or not one's actions with respect to either bribery or facilitating payments further "corrupted" the local officials, thus creating a business climate in which no one would wish to do business. The issue of trust would be high in the Kantian perspective, as would one's duty to be personally honest and trustworthy. A follower of Kant's theory would not be concerned as to whether local enforcement of anti-bribery laws was in place, but would focus on one's duty with respect to acting with integrity.

The Christian worldview would certainly mirror Kant's position. In addition, the Christian would consider Scripture's prohibition on bribery and would take into account whether or not the bribe would influence a favorable decision on the part of the other party with respect to the business transaction. It is probable that the Christian would not pay a requested bribe or a facilitating payment if there was any hint that the request for money was more than a "tip" as defined by a Western country's definition.

Chapter 11

What Difference Does a Christian Make?

What Is the Value Added by Being a Christian Business Person?

We do not act rightly because we have virtue or excellence, but rather we have these because we have acted rightly.

—ARISTOTLE

GOOGLE, A NAME SYNONYMOUS with g-mail, Google Drive, Google Docs, Google Chrome, and even the verb *googling*, was founded in 1998 by Larry Page and Sergey Brin. It enjoyed an eight-year run as the number one place to work in the United States, per *Fortune*, between 2009 and 2017.[1] While *Fortune*'s number one placement ended in 2018, Google was still high on *Forbes* list, coming in at number three that year.[2]

Why is Google considered to be the best place to work in the United States? Employees cite the great work environment which includes challenges, rewards, great bosses, and perks like an on-site fitness center, an on-site medical facility, and college tuition reimbursement to employees.[3] Google's stated mission is "to organize the world's information and

1. Fortune, "100 Best Companies."
2. Forbes, "America's Best Employers."
3. Fortune, "100 Best Companies."

make it universally accessible and useful,"[4] and clearly its employees (over 72,000 in 2018), resonate with that mission.[5]

In their book *Google: How Google Works*, Schmidt and Rosenberg describe Google's employees as "quite a different type of employee."[6] Their employees have unlimited access to Google's information and computing power, they are encouraged to take risks (and are not punished if the subsequent project fails), and they are encouraged to work on their own ideas on company time. They are noisy employees, letting management know if they disagree. They are roving employees—shifting jobs if they get bored. They are creative employees, using both technical and business knowledge. Google calls them "smart creatives" and considers that they represent cutting edge employees in the Internet Century.[7]

While recognizing that the employees like the perks Google offers, Schmidt and Rosenberg argue that the culture of Google is closer to the university model and the Stanford dorm room where the company started than a traditional corporation. While the employees have access to everything needed for cultural, athletic, and academic success, the offices are crowded and messy, like a dorm room, but designed that way to encourage creativity and teamwork with their colleagues.[8] "Google is renowned for its fabulous amenities, but most of our smart creatives weren't drawn to us because of our free lunches, subsidized massages, green pastures, or dog-friendly offices. They came because they wanted to work with the best smart creatives."[9]

What type of employee is a "smart creative" and how does Google search for them? When making hiring decisions, Google uses peer-based committees rather than individual hiring decisions, believing that hiring by a peer-based process focuses on a fit for the company rather than on a fit for a specific manager.[10] They look for passionate people who will "ramble" about whatever they are passionate about.[11] They seek people who can handle change and are interested in constantly learning.[12] They

4. Google Company, "Google's Mission."

5. Forbes, "America's Best Employers."

6. Schmidt et al., *Google*, 17.

7. Schmidt et al., *Google*, 17.

8. Schmidt et al., *Google*, 35.

9. Schmidt et al., *Google*, 99.

10. Schmidt et al., *Google*, 98.

11. Schmidt et al., *Google*, 101.

12. Schmidt et al., *Google*, 102.

call these people "smart generalists."[13] They seek people who are well-rounded, engaged with the world, and interesting.[14] They use the "LAX test" as the barometer. Would the interviewer, caught in a six-hour flight delay at LAX, enjoy conversing with the applicant during the delay? Would the interviewer consider it as time well spent or time wasted?[15] Finally, they are looking for people who have "ambition and drive, team orientation, service orientation, listening & communication skills, bias to action, effectiveness, interpersonal skills, creativity, and integrity."[16]

The adjectives used above—creative; passionate; well-rounded; interesting; ambitious; good communicators; action-oriented; good interpersonal skills; seeking challenges; team and service oriented; possessing integrity;—are qualities every employer wants. Every employee seeks to bring these qualities to the job in order to reap the available monetary and status rewards promised by great companies. But what more might these highly-talented employees bring to either Google, or any other employer, if they are Christians? What value would being a Christian add to employees who already possess the very desirable qualities noted, and are already seen as "smart creatives"? What difference does a Christian employee make in the business world? When an employer is looking for the very best, does the Christian, who follows and imitates Christ as completely as is humanly possible, offer more than even the list sought by Google, who has been known for years to be the best employer in the United States?

To begin to answer that question, let's consider the following eight qualities a Christian brings to the business world above and beyond what he or she offers in terms of natural talents and abilities.

A CALLING; A CAREER; A JOB

Timothy Butler, business psychologist at Harvard Business School, notes that there are three words related to careers that are sometimes used interchangeably, although they have very different meanings. The first is "vocation or calling," the second is "career," and the third is "job." Butler points out that vocation or calling is "what you do in life that makes a

13. Schmidt et al., *Google*, 104.

14. Schmidt et al., *Google*, 105.

15. Schmidt et al., *Google*, 106.

16. Schmidt et al., *Google*, 106.

difference for you, that builds meaning for you, that you can look back on in your later years and see the impact you've made on the world."[17] A career is a particular line of work, which may change from time to time during one's lifetime. A job, the third word, describes what one is doing at the moment for a specific employer. For a Christian, one's first vocation or calling is the call to a relationship with God and with the world around us. Thus the Christian's work mirrors his/her relationship with God and results in creativity and productivity similar to God's creativity and productivity as demonstrated in creation (see John 1:1–3). It also mirrors Christ's redemptive work by bringing justice, healing, reconciliation, compassion, kindness, humility, and patience to the workplace (see Col 3:12).[18] Christians see their business career as a calling from God to make a difference in the world, not just a job.

Michael Novak, in his book *Business as a Calling: Work and the Examined Life*, describes a calling as "the God-given ability to do the job, and (equally God-given) enjoyment in doing it because of your desire to do it."[19] He further notes that "half of the pleasure from the business calling derives from a sense that the system of which it is a part is highly beneficial to the human race. . . . The other half is personal—finding purpose and meaning in what one does."[20]

Gene Ahner, in commenting on Novak's position in his book *Business Ethics: Making a Life, Not Just a Living*, states:

> It allows us to embrace our life of work deliberately and consciously as something noble and God given. It allows us to position our striving and achieving in the broadest context of contributing to the progress and prosperity of all peoples. It allows us to see that our creation of an ever-widening array of goods and services is the human extension of God's work in the creation of our universe. It also holds us accountable for what we do with our God-given talent and desire.[21]

To see one's work as a calling from God, as serving God, moves it out of the usual view of work in today's world. John Knapp, professor and founding director of the Frances Marlin Mann Center for Ethics and

---

17. Butler and Waldroop, "Is Your Job Your Calling?"

18. TOW Project, "Calling & Vocation."

19. Novak, *Business as a Calling*, 19.

20. Novak, *Business as a Calling*, 15.

21. Ahner, *Business Ethics*, 15.

Leadership at Samford University, notes that many today see work as something to endure in order to feed and clothe the family and pay the rent.[22] The Christian who sees work as a calling from God will view their gifts, talents and abilities as God-given and therefore useful and needed by God to bless the people of the world.[23] This attitude gives a purpose for one's life beyond existing or serving only one's own interests. Instead, the Christian holds a perspective on work that brings out one's best, even in times of apparent drudgery and difficulty. The Christian views one's work as a calling with purpose and hope—a calling to use one's talent to work for God through assigned tasks which are bigger than they are, and which God has provided, day-by-day, for them to do. The Christian does not see himself or herself only working for money. Rather, they are working for God, to make a difference in the world and to glorify God. As Col 3:23 states: "Whatever you do, work at it with all your heart, as working for the Lord, not for me, since you know that you will receive an inheritance from the Lord as a reward. It is the Lord Christ you are serving."

Jeff Van Duzer, dean of the School of Business and Economics at Seattle Pacific University, noted that in business one serves as God's agent:

> The call to business is not neutral. It is not meaningless. It is a noble calling—a calling to participate at the very heart of God's work in the world. It is a calling to serve as God's hands and feet in feeding a hungry world and in bringing healing to the broken. It is an invitation to be commissioned as God's agents to further God's desire for human flourishing everywhere. And it comes with a reminder that the work we do in business matters *now*. It is part of the future kingdom breaking into the present reality.[24]

CREATING LIFE-GIVING GOODS AND SERVICES

Second, because Christians frame their "creation of . . . goods and services [as] the human extension of God's work in the creation of our universe,"[25] the goods and services they create will be life-giving products.

If one's employment is in a decision-making position, the choices of what products or services to create and offer to the market are almost

22. Knapp, *How the Church Fails Businesspeople*, 33.

23. Stackhouse, "Foundations and Purposes," 14.

24. Van Duzer, *Why Business Matters to God*, 199.

25. Ahner, *Business Ethics*, 22.

unlimited. The Christian will choose products and services that not only match the mission and resources available to the organization, but which will also support life—not death—for humans, for creatures, and for the environment. The Christian will reflect God's image in that as God's creation and redemption lead to life, so the businessperson's creativity will support the life God has created. If the Christian is not in a position where the decisions of what to produce or create are theirs to make, Christians will choose to offer their talents to those organizations that support life and life-giving products and services.

VanDuzer comments:

> Rather than simply adding to a community's stockpile of available goods, Christians in business will need to look for opportunities where the service or product that they provide may be used to heal or restore. In other words, a business should seek to serve its community by providing not only additive products but also products that reach back and help to redeem broken situations. For example, a business could provide services that would help clean up polluted waterways and toxic dumps. It could provide aesthetically pleasing designs for urban renewal projects. It could produce vaccines for diseases that are decimating communities, make available Internet access to economically oppressed communities or publish books that will increase understanding between communities torn apart by racial hatred, and so on.[26]

In supporting life, Christians in management positions not only seek to create life-giving products and services, but also seek to affirm life for the organization's employees. Christian managers promote activities that reignite the sense of mission and purpose into the work of others through empowerment and the infusion of creativity into the job.[27]

GUIDED DECISION-MAKING

Third, for the Christian, life is not a closed circuit. They do not consider themselves to be alone when faced with difficult and troubling decisions. Their strength and their ethics come from Scripture rather than solely from professional standards or the law, and their decisions will be guided by texts such as Mic 6:8.

26. Van Duzer, *Why Business Matters to God*, 114.
27. Van Duzer, *Why Business Matters to God*, 97, 114.

> He has told you, O mortal, what is good; and what does the
> LORD require of you but to do justice, and to love kindness,
> and to walk humbly with your God? (Mic 6:8 NRSV)

For the Christian, this text calls for justice that goes beyond the law, to actions that consider and protect the legitimate rights and interests of others.[28] To love kindness (or as some translations state, mercy,) means to be helpful, forgiving, generous, patient, compassionate, and sympathetic.[29] Loving kindness requires one to set aside their own interests for another's sake.[30] To walk humbly with God requires a connection with God that permits one to ask God for help to see oneself as God sees them. This results in a realistic perspective so that one can acknowledge failures and accept counsel from others.[31]

Sometimes, however, making the difficult, ethical decision is complicated because ethical conundrums often involve a conflict between principles. For example, most of us do not have to restrain ourselves from picking up a gun and shooting another fellow human being. But suppose that a drug-driven man, armed with a gun, knocks at the door and asks: "Is my wife here?" He wishes to know that answer because it is his intention to kill her. The wife may actually be in my house. What answer should I give? Some would say: "You must tell the truth. The Bible forbids lying." But telling the truth is equivalent to delivering the woman up for possible death. Is it truly God's will to deliver someone to an individual who is determined to kill her? The Bible also commands that we defend the innocent, and it supports the sacred concept of life. Which has priority? Life or truth?

When ethical principles conflict, the Christian looks to the example of Jesus. When his actions on the Sabbath were challenged by the theologians of his time, Jesus made it clear that people are more important than institutions. He said: "The Sabbath was made for man, not man for the Sabbath" (Mark 2:27). In the above hypothetical confrontation with the drug-crazed man, it is very likely that Jesus might say that truth was made for man, not man for truth. By that he would mean that a human life is more important than an abstract principle. This is the first rule when facing conflicts between principles—to ask what consequences

28. Knapp, *How the Church Fails Businesspeople*, 102.

29. Knapp, *How the Church Fails Businesspeople*, 104.

30. Knapp, *How the Church Fails Businesspeople*, 107.

31. Knapp, *How the Church Fails Businesspeople*, 108.

come to people who are made in the image of God. If we told the man where to find his wife, we might help him commit a crime—something which is unacceptable. In this case, the man is not entitled to know the truth because he would use it to harm another person—again, an unacceptable action.

Christians know that breaking a moral principle leads to inner agonizing—did I make the right choice? They therefore seek the guidance of the Holy Spirit through prayer in coming to the best decision. Sometimes it seems as if the choices are actually between the lesser of two evils rather than between something clearly good versus something clearly wrong. For example, Dietrich Bonhoeffer, the German Protestant leader who dared to defy Hitler and in fact joined a plot to kill the dictator, went through deep anguish before he made his decision. In such situations, Christians will remember the example of Jesus, maintain a prayerful attitude, and seek clarity, while relying on guidance from God through prayer and wise counsel from others.

They also recognize that being Christians, seeking to act with justice and loving kindness, does not automatically ensure that all their decisions are necessarily the best ethical choices. Often the results of a decision cannot be seen at the time the decision is made and thus the results must be left in God's hands. One cannot assume that even after seeking God's guidance, one will always make what appears at the moment to be a superior ethical decision. Knapp discusses this possibility and argues that in today's high-pressured world of business, difficult ethical decisions require "time for reflection and discussion with others—not an easy thing to do in today's time-pressed workplaces."[32] When possible Christians should take the time to reflect on the long-term rather than the immediate results of a decision. Unfortunately, it is not always easy to see the long-term. As Knapp comments:

> The short answer [to why being a Christian does not automatically qualify one to make a superior ethical decision] is that a Christian ethic of love and responsibility is not only about what we do; it is about who we are called to be in relationship to God. It defines our primary vocation as disciples seeking to be more like Christ—people of integrity (wholeness) at work and in every other area of life. A Christian ethic also points us to ultimate reasons for acting morally, providing a firmer ground

32. Knapp, *How the Church Fails Businesspeople*, 111.

and greater motivation than can be derived from reason and experience alone.[33]

Developing such a motivation and foundation takes time, intention, and prayerful consideration of the tasks at hand. As James Gustafson stated:

> This "loving" perspective is likely to color the things Christians value and approve of in their perception, interpretation, and choices in the world. That which restores and brings life and joy is to be preferred to that which destroys and brings death and suffering and pain, for example. Not only in his rational discriminations, but in his moral sensitivities, the Christian is likely to be sensitive to oppression and injustice, to physical and mental suffering. Christians are likely to interpret not only what is the case, but what ought to be the case in light of the valuations that are determined by the perspective or posture of their faith.[34]

IMPACT WITHOUT WORDS

Fourth, Christians live with God's grace and acceptance in their lives, which means they will have a huge impact on others whether or not they ever witness in words.

Normally, businesspersons approach situations where there are strong differences of opinion with fear and distrust and armed with persuasive tactics as if about to do battle. In contrast, the Christian in a situation potentially filled with conflict will seek to resolve differences by practicing the gifts of the Spirit (Gal 5:22–23) and thus seek to create space where honest listening and gracious speaking can occur.

InsureMe, a Colorado company that connects insurance shoppers to insurance professionals nationwide in order to find the most competitive rates, is no stranger to awards. In 2006 they received the Leadership Award from *Leadership Excellence*—an award given for having one of the top leadership development programs in the country. Also in 2006 they received the Working Mother Best Small Company Award from *Working Mother Magazine*. In 2007 they received Colorado's Top Philanthropic Award from the Association of Fundraising Professions. In 2009, for the fourth year in a row they were selected by the Society for Human

33. Knapp, *How the Church Fails Businesspeople*, 112.
34. Gustafson, *Theology and Christian Ethics*, 114.

Resource Management and the Great Place to Work Institute, Inc., as one of the nation's Top 25 Places to Work.

In 2008 the annual Colorado Ethics in Business Award was given to Robin Paquette, the chief operating officer of InsureMe, because he gave "the employees of InsureMe a greater sense of purpose and develop[ed] a values-based culture where employees are motivated by teamwork and accountability rather than fear."[35] According to Mike Taylor, managing editor of *ColoradoBiz* magazine, "The award is given to individuals who have a winning business strategy that is carried out in an ethical manner." Tim McTavish, president and CEO of Insure Me, stated: "For Robin, ethics in business has always been a given. The values he espouses in his personal and professional life—love, integrity, leadership and innovation—are now a deep-seated part of InsureMe."[36]

Robin Paquette based InsureMe's core values—love, integrity, leadership, and innovation—on the Golden Rule: "Do unto others as you would have them do unto you" (Matt 7:12). But, as he said in an interview with the author, "These are, of course, just words until they are observed and/or manifested in actions." One instance where these words became actions was in the middle of negotiations with one of InsureMe's competitors. As Paquette explained: "During the drafting, review, and finalization of the legal language of the contract, I changed and re-drafted some language concerning profit sharing that clearly, if left as the competitors had drafted it, would have been, in the long term, to InsureMe's favor." After making the changes and submitting them to the competitor for final approval, Paquette did not hear back from the competitor for several days. When the competitor finally responded, it became clear that they were so shocked that Paquette would clarify the language in the document to *their* advantage (and to InsureMe's disadvantage), that they had had their lawyers try to figure out what InsureMe was up to. Finally, "they correctly concluded that there was no hidden strategy. We were living our company values [which] included being fair and just to our closest competitors. As a side note, this generated some very interesting conversations between the competitor's CEO and me with regard to following Christ, ethics, and the treatment of people." As one might expect, the competitor maintained a "long and mutually prosperous relationship with InsureMe." But for Paquette, the financial advantage the

35. Cision PRWeb homepage.

36. Reed, "InsureMe Earns Ethics in Business Award."

relationship brought was second to the fact that the competitor changed his consideration of ethics and values in business, and ultimately wove Christ-centered values toward employees into his own company.[37]

The Christian principles Robin Paquette espouses show more clearly through his actions than any words he might say. Words may follow actions, but the power of the words is only reflective of the power of the actions already manifested.

USING POWER FOR SERVICE RATHER THAN FOR CONTROL

Fifth, Christians use power for service rather than for control. Most management textbooks describe power as "a key component of effective leadership" and recommend it as the tool the leader can use "to affect other people's behavior and get them to act in certain ways."[38] The primary types of power generally suggested as tools for the leader are: legitimate power (i.e., position power); coercive power (i.e., the ability to punish the offender); reward power (i.e., the ability to give or withhold rewards, such as pay increases); expert power (i.e., the power based on specialized knowledge or skill); and referent power (i.e., power based on personality and coworkers' respect and loyalty).

For the Christian however, power is not to be used to get others to act in a prescribed or desired way. Rather it is to be used for the benefit of others—to empower *them* rather than to empower oneself. Duane Elmer, professor of International Studies at Trinity Evangelical Divinity School, explains: "Power, when grounded in biblical values, serves others by liberating them. It acknowledges that people bear the image of God and treats them in a way that will nurture the development of that image. In so doing, we honor their Creator."[39]

Kent Hanson, an attorney in southern California, tells a story of a family who moved across the United States to California to establish a business, only to have the husband and father die suddenly shortly after the move. The wife and daughters subsequently purchased a house "for sale by the owner" with a wraparound deed of trust, an arrangement where the seller would see that his lender was paid. Being inexperienced

37. Paquette, email correspondence to author, November 13, 2013.

38. Jones and George, *Essentials of Contemporary Management*, 332.

39. Elmer, *Cross-Cultural Servanthood*, 170–71.

and grief-stricken, they did not go through escrow but made the purchase of the house directly with the seller.

After making the down payment and monthly payments for several months, the family had a visit from another man who indicated that he was the actual owner of the house and that since he had not been receiving his rental payments, he decided to visit his tenant. Unfortunately for the widow, the actual tenant was the man who had sold the house to her and her daughters, but instead of sending the money to the real owner, he took the widow's down payment and rental payments and skipped the country. The widow sought out Hanson for legal help, while recognizing that under California law she and her family would probably be evicted as they had no rights against the owner.

The owner was a professor at a nearby Christian university. He originally purchased the house as an investment, with the intention of selling it when he reached retirement age. When he came to Hanson's office to meet with the lawyer and the widow, he produced the proper papers indicating that indeed he was the owner of the property. Without a doubt, he had both legitimate power and coercive power in his hands.

However, instead of acting in accordance with his rights under the law and the power he held over the widow, the owner said to the lawyer's client: "I am not going to throw you out of the house. You're a widow. You know I have an obligation to you . . . to see that [you] do not lose the roof over [your] head." The lawyer was dumbfounded and responded: "In my experience, sir, that is not the reaction of most property owners in your situation." The owner responded: "Isn't that what a Christian is supposed to do?" Accordingly, he proposed a lease-purchase plan in which what the widow had already paid was applied toward the purchase of the home. His decision cost him and his wife a lot of money, but when asked about his actions years later, he merely responded "Oh, that?" and said nothing more.[40]

Jesus said: The meek shall inherit the earth (Matt 5:5). Jonathan Wilson, professor of theology at Carey Theological College, calls meekness "power under control." He argues that meekness is "the disposition of one who has power and who could act on the basis of that power but restrains or directs that power in such a way that the act of power is properly proportioned to the circumstances and the proper telos [end]."[41]

40. Hanson, *Grace at 30,000 Feet*, 52–54.

41. Wilson, *God's Good World*, 226.

The Christian professor acted with meekness. He had the power, but he chose to use it to serve the widow and her family, to bring the situation to what he perceived, as a Christian, to be the proper end. What he did looks crazy to most people. He lost money on a deal where both he and the widow had been defrauded by another. He was not at fault; he, too, was an innocent party. But he saw a better end to the story than merely serving himself. He chose an end where he played a part in redeeming the widow's world, thus following the example of the meekness exhibited by Jesus.

Wilson brings this meekness, this power under control, to directly challenge the businessperson.

> In its everyday expression, meekness characterizes the person who could dominate a committee by his knowledge, human insight, and rhetorical skills, but holds back so that a community is formed and the committee becomes not an extension of one person's ego, but a place where all people and their gifts have room to flourish, and human communing become a reality. Meekness is the gifted vocalist who could soar above all the other voices in the choir and thrill us with the timbre, range, and versatility of her voice restraining herself to blend in with the other voices so that the choir may be heard as the uniting of diversity in pursuit of musical excellence. In neither of these cases is meekness a substitute for or an obstacle to excellence. Rather, meekness in all circumstances depends on discernment of the proper telos. This is the excellence of life in creation-being-redeemed.[42]

Often Christians may be tempted to use their power "for good"—at least for the good as they perceive it. This is especially tempting when that "good" acts in a manner that may be perceived to be in direct service to the church or by extension, to the service of God. When faced with such a situation, Henri Nouwen cautions:

> What makes the temptation of power so seemingly irresistible? Maybe it is that power offers an easy substitute for the hard task of love. It seems easier to be God than to love God, easier to control people than to love people, easier to own life than to love life. Jesus asks, "Do you love me?" We ask, "Can we sit at Your right hand and Your left hand in Your kingdom?" (Matt 20:21). Ever since the snake said, "The day you eat of this tree your eyes will be open and you will be like God, knowing good and evil"

---

42. Wilson, *God's Good World*, 227.

(Gen 3:5), we have been tempted to replace love with power. Jesus lived that temptation in the most agonizing way from the desert to the cross. The long painful history of the church is the history of people ever and again tempted to choose power over love, control over the cross, being a leader over being led. Those who resisted this temptation to the end and thereby give us hope are the true saints.[43]

Jon Paulien, dean of the School of Religion at Loma Linda University, challenges Christians to exhibit a "foot-washing mindset" as they enter the world where usually the powerful rule. The term "foot-washing mindset" refers to the service-oriented actions which Jesus exemplified by washing his disciples' feet just prior to the Last Supper (John 13:1–5). To avoid being overcome by the temptation to use power in any and all of its forms in business requires that one maintain a deep relationship with God and a constant handle on meekness—that is, power under control.

SUPPORT THE FAMILY AND FAMILY LIFE

Sixth, Christians will support the family and family life and will hold high standards for sexual ethics.

A discussion of sexual harassment is now standard fare in all management textbooks, and sexual harassment is noted to be both unethical and illegal.[44] As discussed in chapter 4, sexual harassment can take several forms, including "quid pro quo," and the "hostile work environment." These same textbooks provide a list of actions that managers can take to eradicate sexual harassment in the workplace, such as developing a policy forbidding sexual harassment, providing training for employees so sexual harassment is recognized, and identifying the penalties for engaging in sexual harassment.[45] Often the discussion of sexual harassment spills over to harassment of people in general because they are different from each other due to race, ethnicity, background, and gender. However, the primary focus of textbook discussions usually relates to gender differences and the issues that arise because today all jobs are equally open to all people.

---

43. Nouwen, *In the Name of Jesus*, 59–60.

44. Jones and George, *Essentials of Contemporary Management*, 111.

45. Jones and George, *Essentials of Contemporary Management*, 111–13.

From a Christian perspective, treating all as created in the image of God and thus as one's brothers and sisters is a standard demanded by the creation story. But when business brings men and women together in the workplace, special ties can develop between people who are engaged in assignments that raise the creative juices and ultimately result in special teamwork relationships bound together by the thrill of achievement. As a result, workplaces can become places of romantic opportunity—both for single employees and for those already married. In addition, western culture sometimes glorifies the excitement of an illicit affair in Hollywood movies, as well as through various websites such as Ashley Madison, a website designed for cheaters, which was hacked in July 2015, much to the dismay of many of the users of its services.

The Christian takes seriously the seventh commandment which forbids adultery, as well as other biblical texts that stress the importance of loyalty to one's spouse (Prov 5:18; Mal 2:14–16). The Christian knows that what Hollywood and the Internet portray as excitement is not a true token of love, and in the end, brings shame and, if the participants are exposed, horror at being discovered.

In business, many activities are undertaken without regard to the effect they have on the family. Long hours, significant extended travel, and, in some cases, a requirement to live for an extended period of time in separate locations for the benefit of the organization are commonly expected, especially if one wishes to advance in rank or salary. Sometimes the organization's social activities, such as Christmas parties and similar events, are designed to exclude spouses and other family members because it is expected that the activities will not pass the "family-friendly" test.

Christians in business will make arrangements for business activities with the intent of strengthening the family and family ties. David Gill, as noted in chapter 4, writes that "undermining and attacking a marriage covenant is first and foremost an offense against God."[46] Gill urges Christians to "do whatever you can to support fidelity, loyalty and commitment" with respect to covenanted, committed relationships.[47] He further argues that because the Christian views all people as made in the image of God, they understand that human beings must not be used in any way. Gill concludes: "This perspective gives us a rich, holistic texture

46. Gill, *Doing Right*, 223.
47. Gill, *Doing Right*, 233.

for managing our sexuality—nothing like the superficial sexual mythology of our decadent era."[48]

A BALANCED LIFE

Seventh, Christians seek wholeness, a balanced life. This means choosing to rest as well as work while also seeking to integrate one's work life into one's worship life, thus creating one whole.

In their book *Church on Sunday, Work on Monday*, researchers Laura Nash and Scotty McLennan note that the business people they interviewed felt they were living in two worlds—the world of work where daily pressures ruled, and the world of religious life where doing right and having faith reigned supreme. Unfortunately these worlds never came together. As Nash and McLennan state: "The changing world of business poses problems their religious upbringing never touched on."[49]

Yet in the beginning, God demonstrated that humans were created for work and rest and worship. In the creation story God gave humans work to do when he said: "Be fruitful and increase in number; fill the earth and subdue it. Rule over the fish of the sea and the birds of the air and over every living creature that moves on the ground . . . [and] the LORD God took the man and put him in the Garden of Eden to work it and take care of it" (Gen 1:28; 2:15).

Today humans are expected to be available for work 24/7. "Going home" from work is a thing of the past, as everyone is available at any time due to the reach of technology. In fact, some businesses encourage employees to "work from home"—further confusing the concept of what is work and what is separate from work. To find balance when 24/7 expectations fill our lives is very difficult.

As noted, in the garden God set a balance for work and rest and worship. God worked for six days in the creation of the world, and on the seventh day he rested (Gen 2:2). God refers to this resting when he spoke the fourth commandment from Mt. Sinai:

> Remember the Sabbath day by keeping it holy. Six days you shall labor and do all your work, but the seventh day is a Sabbath to the LORD your God. On it you shall not do any work, neither you, nor your son or daughter, nor your male or female servant,

48. Gill, *Doing Right*, 233.

49. Nash and McLennan, *Church on Sunday*, 7.

> nor your animals, nor the alien within your gates. For in six days
> the LORD made the heavens and the earth, the sea, and all that
> is in them, but he rested on the seventh day. Therefore the LORD
> blessed the Sabbath day and made it holy. (Exod 20:8–11)

Thus God set out for humankind a model for the balanced life—a life
balanced by work, rest, and worship—as he both demonstrated and commanded. Jonathan Wilson argues that this balance is not something only
for the original state of the world, but it has important meaning for those
of us caught in the 24/7 world of today:

> The call to Sabbath rest is located in both creation and redemp-
> tion. In Exodus 20:8–11, we are called to Sabbath because
> after creating, God rests on that seventh day. In Deuteronomy
> 5:12–15, the call to Sabbath is rooted in God's deliverance of
> Israel from Egypt, where the people of God were enslaved and
> toiled for others. This change from the Exodus call for Sabbath
> to the Deuteronomy call beautifully reflects the dialectic of the
> kingdom. We cannot simply root Sabbath in the Genesis story
> of God's work of creation. We must also situate it in God's work
> of redeeming creation. This second story is essential to both a
> commitment to keep Sabbath faithfully and a full understand-
> ing of Sabbath. That is, Sabbath not only grounds us in the rec-
> ognition of God's work of creation as a gift and blessing; it also
> resists, subverts, and overthrows the claims of other powers in
> our lives.
>
> If we have only the call to Sabbath from Exodus, then we
> may very well find ourselves thinking, "That's well and good
> for the original state of creation, but now we live in a world of
> competition and survival of the fittest. We can't afford to take a
> day off." But the call of Deuteronomy teaches us that even in the
> midst of possible enslavement to other powers and the toil of a
> fallen world, we are called to rest in God.[50]

Abraham Joshua Heschel notes that the Sabbath is the first occasion
when God called something holy. He calls the Sabbath a palace in time;
a moment in time, not an object in space. It is a reminder that "the world
has already been created and will survive without the help of man."[51]

The balanced life confirms that humans are not valued or defined
by their work—their activities for six days a week. They are valued and
defined by God through his work of creating them and redeeming them.

50. Wilson, God's Good World, 253.

51. Heschel, Sabbath, 13.

As Van Duzer clearly states: "A Sabbath reminds us that we are not the sum of what we produce and that our worth is not found in our instrumental value, as a tool in service of profit, but rather in our innate nature as children of God."[52]

TAKING THE LONG VIEW

Eighth, Christians take the long view—the New Testament end-time perspective. This means that when Christians engage with clients and employees, they engage not only for today, but for eternity.

In his 2015 Gordon-Conwell Advent Devotional, Dr. Jeffery Arthurs notes that the New Testament speaks often of the "imminent" return of Christ. "That doesn't mean that Christ's return is going to happen *soon* (necessarily), only that it is *next* in the order of events—like a second string quarterback who knows that he will enter the game if the starting quarterback gets hurt. He doesn't know when this will happen, only that it is next. Nothing need intervene. All is in readiness."[53] That's the long view. The next big thing is the Second Coming of Christ, the Second Advent, and eternity.

When describing heaven and eternity, Scripture speaks of some intriguingly possible administrative roles for people with business talents and interests. For example, Rev 7:15 mentions those who have come out of great tribulation who "are before the throne of God and serve him day and night in his temple." This might imply humans who are members of a governing council. Revelation 14:4 speaks of those who "follow the Lamb wherever he goes," which may envision a retinue that cares for the needs of the Lamb as he travels. Revelation 3:21 promises to "those who overcome, I will give the right to sit with me on my throne," a promise made to those of the church of Laodicea who have heard the voice of the Lord and opened the door so that he may come in and eat with them. Perhaps those who overcome will have a presence at the seat of authority. In the parable of the talents, the kingdom of heaven is described by a story where the master finds upon his return that his faithful servants have doubled the talents of money which he gave to them when he left for his journey. To those faithful servants the master says: "Well done, good and faithful servant! You have been faithful with a few things; I will put

52. Van Duzer, *Why Business Matters to God*, 72.
53. Arthurs, "Day 24—Meditation."

you in charge of many things. Come and share your master's happiness" (Matt 25:21, 23). This commendation may imply management activities for the faithful servants in the world to come.

Jeff Van Duzer argues that because God created the material world and called it "very good," and because God has called Christians to work in this world, he will, in some mysterious way, "adopt and transform our purified work for divine purposes in the new heaven and the new earth."[54] While Christians work on earth, Van Duzer suggests that they recognize that

> in the long run we know that God will secure what we are striving for. This gives Christians who run their businesses as tools in God's hands reason to approach each day's endeavors with optimism, hope and conviction. In addition to giving us hope, knowing the end of the story also assures us that our work has meaning. In a sense, we can find our own work on the last pages of God's great story.[55]

Whether or not one wishes to go as far as Van Duzer does in arguing that we are moving from a garden toward the New Jerusalem and that "the end is a place that adopts the city-building work of humanity (including much of the work of business) and holds it in God's overflowing love,"[56] one must acknowledge that the skills and the character that we develop in this life will go with us to the next. Likewise, how we use our influence for others, to make their lives flourish while we were on earth, will follow us to eternity. So will the relationships that we develop and nurture—they will be relationships which we will continue forever. The Christian businessperson knows this, and as a result develops his or her business with the end in mind.

THE CHRISTIAN'S CONCEPT OF SUCCESS

In view of the obstacles to integrity that exist in the marketplace and the challenges to act ethically when engaged in business, we must consider what a Christian means by success. There are two basic views of success. One is described by Laurence Shames in his book *Hunger for More*, in the

---

54. Van Duzer, *Why Business Matters to God*, 95.

55. Van Duzer, *Why Business Matters to God*, 97–98.

56. Van Duzer, *Why Business Matters to God*, 97.

chapter entitled "A Sickness Called Success."[57] This concept of success is essentially an adversarial concept. It thrives on greed. It craves for more things. In the inner city it results in killings for sneakers, jackets, and gold-rimmed car wheels. In the suburbs, success is also a killer by causing dysfunctional families and heart attacks, which are the results of efforts to keep up with others. It is an expression of pride. Success is understood as being better or best. While it is certainly acceptable to experience satisfaction from achievements, to feel that to be successful means to be better than others will never truly satisfy, because that success is always threatened by the success of others.

Jesus' idea of success is totally different. Success is the experience of faithfulness and service. It comes in a community mode of living. It is the result of helping others find happiness and fulfillment. It is the success described by Jesus in Matthew 5. The word used by Jesus to refer to those who are successful is a Greek word that means not only *happy* but *lucky*. People who seek the success described by Jesus are lucky because they will find happiness and fulfillment. They are lucky because they are simple in spirit; they are satisfied with what God gives them. They are lucky because they are willing to admit that they make mistakes. People who are willing to accept blame are easy to live with. They are lucky because they are meek; they are not compelled to assert themselves arrogantly to safeguard a shaky self-esteem. Because they are meek, they can be peacemakers. They do not find any thrill in crushing others.

They are pure in heart. Their words can be trusted. Their words of appreciation are genuine; their motives are sincere; they can look at persons of another gender with a clear glance. They are willing to be persecuted for righteousness' sake; they are willing to espouse unpopular causes when justice and truth are involved. They are not seduced by the longing for upward mobility.

This does not mean that Christians condone mediocrity. Jesus appeals continually to ideals and excellence in whatever one does as a basic characteristic of anyone who wants to live according to the ethics of the Lord. There is no inconsistency in seeking true success and aspiring to positions of responsibility and leadership. The difference is the path that is used to reach the top. Some people climb on the shoulders of people they have crushed. Christians climb while being sensitive and helpful, and they are rewarded for this spirit.

57. Shames, *Hunger for More*, 119–37.

They can give a satisfactory answer to Jesus' searching question: "What good will it be for a man if he gains the whole world and yet he forfeits his soul? What will a man give in exchange for his soul?" (Matt 16:26). The word soul in Greek means life. What Jesus is asking is whether it is worth it to succeed if it costs one all the joys that life should bring and the immense happiness of a relationship with God.

THE STONE CATCHERS

Bryan Stevenson is the founder of Equal Justice Initiative, a legal practice located in Montgomery, Alabama, that is focused on defending those in US society who are poor and/or wrongly condemned. In his book *Just Mercy*, he recalls a particularly stressful and exhilarating day in court when he was fighting for the release of two men who had been jailed for decades.

As he left the courthouse he saw an older black woman sitting on the steps, apparently waiting for him. He thought she might be a member of one of the men's families, but he wasn't sure. She called out to him as he went by, so he stopped to speak with her. In response to his inquiry she said she was not a family member but was at the courthouse as a stone catcher. When Stevenson looked confused, she explained that her sixteen-year-old grandson had been murdered fifteen years before. In her grief, she came to the courtroom to watch his killers' trials. Although the killers were found guilty, she did not find the relief from her grief that she was seeking and had expected.

Seeing her weeping, a woman in the courtroom came over to sit with her, assuming that one of the boys who was sentenced was her child. The grandmother explained that no—the defendants had murdered her grandson. She then again burst into tears. The women sat together for well over an hour. As the grandmother told Stevenson, "It felt good to finally have someone to lean on at that trial, and I've never forgotten that woman. I don't know who she was, but she made a difference."[58] As a result of that experience, the grandmother had been coming to the courthouse for years to be someone others could lean on.

The grandmother recalled the biblical story of the woman taken in adultery (John 8:3–11) who was brought to Jesus by the teachers of the law, with the expectation that he would condemn her for her behavior.

58. Stevenson, *Just Mercy*, 308.

Instead, Jesus bent down and wrote on the ground with his finger. As the teachers' questions continued, Jesus finally stood up and said: "If any of you is without sin, let him be the first to throw a stone" (John 8:7). The grandmother noted that in her years of visiting the courthouse, she saw stones being thrown by judges who threw "people away like they're not even human, people shooting each other, hurting each other like they don't care. I don't know, it's a lot of pain. I decided I was supposed to be here to catch some of the stones people cast at each other."[59] She continued: "I heard you in that courtroom today. I've even seen you here a couple of times before. I know you's a stonecatcher, too."[60]

At times Christians in business will be stone catchers—acting with justice and mercy in a world where often the results of business activities are like stones being thrown at supervisors, colleagues, employees, customers, vendors, stockholders, the public, anyone in general, with or without naming specific individuals. In these instances, the Christian who wishes to answer the first question asked in heaven: "Were you honorable in business?" in the affirmative must act as that grandmother did—as a stone catcher.

Since the Christian knows the end of the story, he or she will today "engage in business with a sense of hope and meaning."[61] They will look forward to whatever God has in mind for eternity for those who have spent their lives serving their fellow humans through "enabling the community to flourish and providing opportunities for employees to engage in meaningful and creative work."[62]

THINKING IT THROUGH: GOOGLE CORPORATION

As noted above, Google's mission is "to organize the world's information and make it universally accessible and useful."[63] Their purpose is to create products that both make the web better *and* make the user's experience on the web better. They are clearly seeking, in the utilitarian sense, to bring the greatest good (information) to the greatest number of people. But Google's website also reflects Kant's philosophical position. In

59. Stevenson, *Just Mercy*, 308.
60. Stevenson, *Just Mercy*, 309.
61. Van Duzer, *Why Business Matters to God*, 97.
62. Van Duzer, *Why Business Matters to God*, 152.
63. Google, "Google Mission."

Google's "Ten Things We Know to Be True," a statement of the company's philosophy, number 6, says: "You can make money without doing evil."[64] In their commentary on that portion of Google's vision statement, they promise that as they advertise on their website, they will do so in a way that does not "compromise the integrity of our search results. We will never manipulate rankings. . . . Our users trust our objectivity and no short-term gain could ever justify breaching that trust."[65] Schmidt and Rosenberg broaden the meaning of this philosophy when they state that "don't-be-evil" is also the way the employees and management at Google check their moral compass whenever they make a decision.[66]

The moral compass for the Christian, however, isn't a vision statement. It is the character of God. As noted in chapter 1, God describes his character as: compassionate and gracious, abounding in love and faithfulness (Exod 34:6–7), and exercising justice and righteousness (Jer 9:23–24). The Christian businessperson can exhibit God's *compassion and graciousness* when they seek to practice empathy for those who are suffering or seen as unpromising. Such empathy make take the form of caring for one's employees who may be suffering health or family problems, or hiring someone who has a criminal past in order to offer them a chance to succeed in society, or by taking a chance on a new graduate who applies for an open position while lacking work experience.

Love and faithfulness are the foundation of trust that is indispensable to business dealings. A Christian businessperson will be true to his or her commitments regardless of the consequences. A Christian's customer or supplier may be certain that his or her business partner is fully reliable at all times and that his or her honesty does not suffer lapses.

Justice requires that the Christian businessperson will respect the law and will not attempt to find legal loopholes in order to dodge one's responsibilities. Coupling *justice with righteousness* means that the Christian businessperson will always give equal pay for equal work and will not allow a glass ceiling to determine hiring or promotions. The Christian will not prepare fraudulent or ambiguous reports in order to increase the organization's profits. The Christian will mirror God's transparency in all of their dealings with others, so that they are not afraid to have their work scrutinized. For the Christian businessperson, upward mobility will not

---

64. Google, "Ten Things."

65. Google, "Ten Things."

66. Schmidt et al., *Google*, 64–65.

be their primary motivation, especially if it comes through scheming or playing office politics. They will find fulfillment through service, and will remember that they work for God and from him they expect their reward (Col 3:23–24).

To engage in business with God's character as one's moral compass is to be honorable in business. Job describes his experience: "When I went to the gate of the city and took my seat in the public square . . . I rescued the poor that cried for help and the fatherless who had none to assist him; the man who was dying blessed me; I made the widow's heart to sing for joy; I was eyes to the blind and feet to the lame. I was the father to the needy; I took up the case of the stranger. I broke the fangs of the wicked and snatched the victims from their teeth" (Job 29:7–17). To cause the hearts of those with whom one comes in contact to "sing for joy" is the result of engaging with one who has chosen to be honorable in business.

Appendix

Divine Help for Individuals Seeking God in a Sinful World

As noted in chapter 1, Adam and Eve chose to eat of the Tree of the Knowledge of Good and Evil and the result, as described by Van Duzer, "tore a hole through the whole fabric of the 'good' creation."[1] In response to the choice of humankind and acting on his goodness and love, God countered their choice with his action to provide help for those who seek to remain faithful to him. Specifically God gives such individuals revelation, prayer, the Holy Spirit, a new mind, the Christ-like spirit of love, the church, and the eschatological hope to encourage them throughout their earthly life and to provide hope for a better world to come. These divine helps for individuals seeking God in a sinful world are described below.

REVELATION

Satan led Eve into sin by maligning God. The serpent claimed that God kept from his creatures what was indispensable for their happiness. To remedy the tragedy of sin, God provided knowledge concerning himself and his will, as throughout history he sent prophets and other inspired writers to reveal himself. The knowledge provided by God is contained in the Bible. In that book God's ways and will are made known through events of history, through laws, through direct rebukes of evil acts, and through praise for justice and mercy. Because in the garden the serpent attempted to discredit God and distort his character, in the Bible people

1. Van Duzer, *Why Business Matters to God*, 55.

report about their journey with God, what they learned about him and the meaning of their encounters with God. They freely express their frustrations and their joys. In those writings Christians and Jews find the road to a close relationship with God.

The stories in the Bible are much more than bedtime stories. They show us how men and women faced and acted in difficult ethical situations, and they also let us know, in many cases, how God reacted to those decisions. They provide guidance and encouragement because we see a God who understands and forgives the person who recognizes a mistake and is willing to learn from him. The practical application of the divine world view is greatly clarified by these accounts.

God revealed himself most fully in the incarnation of the Son, who took upon himself the human condition. Human beings did not only hear about God but they saw him. Unbelievably he did not appear in the glory of a royal court but in the stench of a stable. He did not belong to the social or economic elite of his people, but grew up in the home of a poor family. He was not identified with intellectual circles; he spoke with an accent and had no formal education. He touched the lowest rungs of mankind, the social outcasts, the slaves, even the criminals when he died on the cross. Even in these seemingly unfavorable circumstances he lived such a life that he could gently scold his disciples when they asked to see the Father. "Anyone who has seen me has seen the Father," he said to Philip. "How can you say, 'Show us the Father'?" (John 14:9).

This revelation of God is called the gospel. Gospel means *good news*. It is good news because it reveals a God who is very different from the image that most people have of him. It is he who takes the initiative in the reconciliation. It is he who gladly forgives those who were actually his enemies in their hearts. It is he who prepares a place for us, so that we can be with him. It is he who wants us to call him "Father," and who calls us children. Thus the right relationship between God and man is restored. Humans are no longer under the condemnation of the law because of their rebellion.

PRAYER AND THE HOLY SPIRIT

Prayer is the great weapon of the Christian. It is the time when he or she opens the heart to God as to a friend. No thought is considered too improper to be presented. On several occasions in the Bible, men and women freely express their disappointment with the way God acts. Prayer is an expression of complete openness and trust.

But prayer is not the presentation of our plans to God and asking him to make them succeed. Too many people consider prayer as a means to manipulate God and extract favors from him. It is striking to see how in our prayers, material concerns occupy a much greater place than spiritual aspirations. Too often prayer reveals a very self-centered mind.

True prayer is asking God to make his will known to us and give us the assurance that we have completely surrendered our lives to him. Often it is a request to open our eyes to our true spiritual condition and the changes that we should make. In that context, we can truly cast our burdens upon the Lord and let him work out the solution. When a Christian has placed himself in the hands of God, he should stop worrying because God is faithful. "Therefore I tell you, whatever you ask for in prayer, believe that you have received it, and it will be yours" (Mark 11:24). While this promise is a puzzle for most Christians, we must remember that many in history have learned to depend totally upon God's answers to their prayers and have not been disappointed.

Prayer must be considered in the context of the action of the Holy Spirit. In Romans 8, we are told that it is the Holy Spirit that "translates" our human petitions and presents them to the Father. Through him we hear the divine answer. It is also the Spirit that leads us into all truth (John 16:3). If we resist his entreaties, he will convict us and make us face the reality of our willfulness and the judgment that is coming. A true Christian life is prayer-filled and Spirit-filled.

A NEW MIND

With the new relationship with God comes a total change of mind. "Do not conform anymore to the pattern of this world but be transformed by the renewing of your mind. Then you will be able to test and approve God's good, pleasing, and perfect will" (Rom 12:2–3). "You are all sons of God through faith in Christ Jesus, for all of you who are baptized into Christ have clothed yourselves with Christ. There is neither Jew nor Greek, slave nor free, male nor female for you are all one in Jesus Christ" (Gal 3:26–28). All human relationships are restored to their original beauty. It is with this new mind that the business person approaches his or her work. For a Christian, feelings of contempt or superiority toward others that lead to discrimination cannot be harbored. With this new mind comes also a new set of priorities. The mad rush toward the top of the ladder, even if it means crushing others in the attempt, loses its appeal. Greed is replaced with a willingness to accept one's fair share of material prosperity. The spirit of community dislodges the self-centered mode of living.

THE CHRIST-LIKE SPIRIT OF LOVE

No passage of Scripture is more beautiful and more puzzling than 1 Corinthians 13. While it makes our hearts resonate with its splendid ideals, it frustrates us because it seems to be so clearly impractical in the marketplace. As we dream of the perfection of love, we are more aware than ever of the rough environment in which we must operate. We tend to assume that the command of love prohibits the determination and cool-headed efficiency that success requires.

In his book, *Love Within Limits*,[2] Lewis Smedes reminds us that it is vital to notice that the love of which the Bible speaks is not a soft, warm feeling, but the power that enables us to seek our neighbor's good in all circumstances. Love is not resignation but the supreme expression of a Christian's freedom to choose the proper course of action, independent of anger or thirst for revenge. This love is not the result of mental discipline but a divine gift. The extent of that love is clearly expressed in what Jesus said: "Love each other as I have loved you" (John 15:12). It becomes a fruit of the Spirit because it is the natural result of the activity of the Spirit in a heart.

Because it comes from God, love does not lead us to accept the evil we suffer. To suffer evil takes courage, but to accept evil is cowardice. While Jesus in the Sermon on the Mount teaches that we should not act in the spirit of the tribunal and ask for a tooth for a tooth and an eye for an eye, he also does not tell us that we must blissfully trust everybody. Jesus acted in the light of his knowledge of the hearts of men, and advised his disciples to be as shrewd as serpents and as innocent as doves. He warned them not to throw their pearls to the pigs. He used the strongest language to denounce the hypocrisy of the religious leaders of his people. He said to the adulteress that while he did not condemn her, she should leave her life of sin. Jesus used tough love at times.

2. Smedes, *Love Within Limits*, 51–61.

We must not, Smedes states, abandon our rights when it would jeopardize the rights of others or destroy our self-esteem. Love, therefore, makes us capable of loving ourselves while loving others. It heals our moral blindness and makes us able to see the point of the other person and to recognize his or her rights. It gives us the strength to seek justice if those rights have been denied. It is the power that gives us the courage to take risks and blow the whistle if necessary.

Love is kind, we are told, but to be kind calls us not only to affirm but also to criticize what can be improved. A teacher who does not honestly show how a paper could be improved is not a good teacher. A manager who does not suggest how a worker can perform at a higher level is not a kind manager. Because of love, a business person is free from anger, fear, contempt, and resentment when he or she deals with others. One can be calm when others lose their self-control; patient when others are unreasonable; positive when others are despondent. There are few places where Christian love is more indispensable than in the office or in the marketplace.

THE CHURCH

Throughout the ages God tried to reveal himself through humans. Before the incarnation of Jesus, he attempted to use a people, the Jews, whose wisdom and prosperity would draw others to glorify God. After the cross he turned to a spiritual body, the church, where humans would reflect the spirit of their creator and help dissipate the false notions about God.

There have been many discussions on the proper role of the church in society. Some say that its duty is to pray while staying disengaged from the world. On the other hand, the social gospel tends to picture the church as the "organized conscience of society" which must permeate the world to transform it according to the will of Christ.

While those concepts can be justified, without question one of the main reasons for the existence of the church is that it must be a laboratory where people can see a demonstration of the spirit of the gospel and learn how to live that totally new lifestyle. "Do everything without complaining or arguing," Paul says, "so that you may become blameless and pure, children of God, without fault in a crooked and depraved generation, in which you shine like stars in the universe" (Phil 2:14–15). The church is the place where one should be able to discover the unity of the Spirit that transcends that of the unity of ideas and ways. "Make every effort to keep the unity of the Spirit through the bond of peace . . . until we reach unity in the faith and in the knowledge of the Son of God and become mature, attaining to the whole measure of the fullness of Christ" (Eph 4:13).

The church is a unique institution founded on a commitment to a person, not to an idea. It has a radical openness of membership. No one is excluded because of physical problems. The unclean, the lepers, are made to feel welcome. It is not limited to the learned. "Blessed are the poor in spirit," said Jesus in the Sermon on the Mount (Matt 5:3). The boundaries of race should not be considered. Gentiles are admitted as well as Jews. Even if there are stains in the past, they are not constantly brought back to memory. The fallen Mary Magdalene was welcomed by Jesus. In the church you should never be judged by your associations. Matthew was not shunned because his friends were tax collectors.

The church is a place where mutuality is rediscovered. It is neither a club nor an organization. It is a body. As Paul states clearly in Romans 12, in the church everyone is important. His or her talents are indispensable to the health of the whole body. "Just as each of us has a body with many members, and these members do not all have the same function, so in Christ we who are many form one body, and each member belongs to all the others. We have different gifts according to the grace given us" (Rom 12:4–6).

Few of the teachings of the gospel have been overlooked as much as this one. Too many church communities seem to act on the assumption that it is their role to make everyone conform to a certain unique pattern of thinking and acting. They reject mercilessly those who do not fit into their models. They ostracize those who dare to ask questions and distrust those who suggest new avenues of service. Paul tells us that the church is strong because of its variety of gifts, not because of the absolute conformity of its members.

One has not discovered the meaning of the church when he or she still speaks about it and says "they." The only way of talking about the church is the first person plural, "we." The church becomes an agent of reconciliation. While sin is hated there, sinners are loved. It should be both a fortress where one finds protection from temptations and a hospital where one finds healing. If the church is what it should be, it will be the place where those who have lost their self-esteem regain it and those who feel abandoned find a family.

THE ESCHATOLOGICAL HOPE

Even before God pronounced the three curses on Adam and Eve, he gave a promise of redemption in his denunciation of the serpent (Gen 3:15). Thus God immediately gave evidence of his desire to restore what had been lost through the initial choice of mankind.

For the early Christians, the expectation of the coming of the Lord was a very positive motivation for doing good works. "The night is nearly over; the day is almost here. So let us put aside the deeds of darkness and put on the armor of light. Let us behave decently as in the daytime" (Rom 13:12–13). The Christian lives continually as if the Lord were to come that same day. Yet many days have passed and the Lord has not returned. In Matthew 24 and 25, Jesus told many parables on the perils of having to wait for the return of the Master. Whether it is the false confidence of the superintendent who thinks that he is in charge for a long time, the routine of women who are grinding grain, or the weariness of the young women waiting for the bridal procession, it is difficult to remain poised for the greatest event of history when there is a delay.

The purpose of the delay is to allow time for all people to make an intelligent choice for God (2 Pet 3:9), although many use the time to act as if there is to be no redemption or restoration (2 Pet 3:3–4). Herein lies the ethical challenge—to live as if the promised restoration was just on the horizon while still acting as God's children every day in one's business and community relationships. The medieval temptation to withdraw from the world in order to be righteous must be rejected by the example of Christ, who observed that his followers were in the world but not of the world (John 17:15–16). His prayers for his followers are a powerful example of the certainty of the promises of divine help for God's followers until the promised redemption is a reality.

Bibliography

ACFE. "The Fraud Triangle." Association of Certified Fraud Examiners. www.acfe.com/fraud-triangle.aspx.

————. "Report to the Nations: 2018 Global Study on Occupational Fraud and Abuse." https://www.acfe.com/report-to-the-nations/2018/.

Adeney, Bernard. *Strange Virtues: Ethics in a Multicultural World*. Downers Grove: InterVarsity, 1995.

Ahner, Gene. *Business Ethics: Making a Life, Not Just a Living*. Maryknoll: Orbis, 2007.

Ajala, Emmanuel Majekodunmi. "The Influence of Workplace Environment on Workers' Welfare, Performance and Productivity." *African Symposium* 12 (2012) 141–49.

Amabile, Teresa. "How to Kill Creativity." *Harvard Business Review* 76 (1998) 77–87.

Aristotle. *Nicomachean Ethics*. 2nd ed. Translated by H. Rackham. Loeb Classical Library. Cambridge: Harvard University Press, 1934.

Arthurs, Jeffery. "Day 24—Meditation on 1 Thessalonians 5:1–11." *2015 Gordon-Conwell Advent Devotional*. Email distribution, December 22, 2015.

Associated Press. "For Some Whistle-Blowers, Big Risk Pays Off." *New York Times*, November 29, 2004. https://www.nytimes.com/2004/11/29/politics/for-some-whistleblowers-big-risk-pays-off.html.

————. "Polartec Moving 150 Jobs from Mass. to Tennessee." *Telegram* (Worcester, MA), August 9, 2016. http://www.telegram.com/news/20160809/polartec-moving-150-jobs-from-mass-to-tennessee.

Awan, Abdul Ghafoor, and M. Tafigue Tahir. "Impact of Working Environment on Employee's Productivity: A Case Study of Banks and Insurance Companies in Pakistan." *European Journal of Business and Management* 7 (2015) 329–45.

Barnett, John H., and Marvin J. Karson. "Managers, Values, and Executive Decisions: An Exploration of the Role of Gender, Career Stage, Organizational Level, Function and the Importance of Ethics, Relationships, and Results in Managerial Decision-Making." *Journal of Business Ethics* 8 (1989) 747–71.

Barstow, David. "The Bribery Aisle: How Wal-Mart Got Its Way in Mexico." *New York Times*, December 17, 2012. https://www.nytimes.com/2012/12/18/business/walmart/bribes/teotihuacan/html.

————. "Vast Mexico Bribery Case Hushed Up by Wal-Mart After Top-Level Struggle." *New York Times*, April 21, 2012. https://www.nytimes.com/2012/04/22/business/at-wal/mart-in-Mexico-a-bribe-inquiry-silenced-html.

Birchard, Bill. "Herman Miller's Design for Growth." *Strategy & Business*, issue 59, summer 2010. https://www.strategy-business.com/article/10206.

Boatright, John R. *Ethics and the Conduct of Business*. 6th ed. Upper Saddle River, NJ: Prentice-Hall, 2009.

"Bowe v. Colgate-Palmolive—Appeals Court Overrules." Last modified December 29, 2009. http://law.jrank.org/pages/24545/Bowe-v-Colgate-Palmolive-Appeals-Court-Overrules.html.

Brill, Steven. *Tailspin: The People and Forces behind America's Fifty-Year Fall—and Those Fighting to Reverse It*. New York: Knopf, 2018.

Bustillo, Miguel. "Nike's Game Plan for Policing Its Suppliers: Try to Avoid Bangladesh and Other Risky Cities." *Wall Street Journal*, November 29, 2012.

Butler, Timothy, and James Waldroop. "Is Your Job Your Calling?" Interview with Alan M. Webber. *Fast Company*, January 31, 1998. https://www.fastcompany.com/33545/your-job-your-calling-extended-interview.

Carroll, Archie B., and Ann K. Buchholtz. *Business & Society: Ethics, Sustainability, and Stakeholder Management*. 9th ed. Stamford, CT: Cengage Learning, 2015.

Catalyst. "Fortune 500 Executive Officer Top Earner Positions Held by Women." Last updated December 10, 2013. https://www.catalyst.org/knowledge/women-executive-officer-top-earners-fortune-500-0.

Ceres. "The Ceres Roadmap for Sustainability: A Strategic Vision and Framework for Sustainable Corporations in the 21st Century Economy." Last modified August 8, 2018. https://www.ceres.org/roadmap-assessment.

Cision PRWeb. Cision PRWeb homepage. Last modified August 8, 2018. www.prweb.com.

Clark, Heather, and Jim Barry. "Business Ethics and the Changing Gender Balance." In *Current Issues in Business Ethics*, edited by Peter W. F. Davies, 134–52. New York: Routledge, 1997.

Computer Ethics Institute. "The Ten Commandments of Computer Ethics." http://computerethicsinstitute.org/publications/tencommandments.html.

Conti, Katheleen. "Manufacturing Poised for a Comeback at Ex-Polartec Plant as Incubator Leases Space for Startups." *Boston Globe*, June 11, 2018. https://www.bostonglobe.com/business/2018/06/10/manufacturing-making-comeback-former-polartec-plant/YjCB14mr4dro65Vde1yJKN/story.html.

Cressey, Donald R. *Other People's Money: A Study in the Social Psychology of Embezzlement*. Glencoe, IL: Free Press, 1953.

De George, Richard T. *Business Ethics*. 2nd ed. New York: MacMillan, 1986.

———. *Business Ethics*. 6th ed. Upper Saddle River, NJ: Pearson/Prentice Hall, 2006.

———. *Competing with Integrity in International Business*. New York: Oxford University Press, 1993.

———. "Entrepreneurs, Multinationals, and Business Ethics." In *International Business Ethics*, 271–80. South Bend, IN: University of Notre Dame Press, 1999.

Department of Justice, Office of Public Affairs. "McNeil-PPC Inc. Pleads Guilty in Connection with Adulterated Infants' and Children's Over-the-Counter Liquid Drugs." *Justice News*, March 10, 2005. https://www.justice.gov/opa/pr/mcneil-ppc-inc-pleads-guilty-connection-adulterated-infants-and-childrens-over-counter-liquid.

De Pree, Hugh. *Business as Unusual*. Zeeland, MI: Herman Miller, 1986.

DiTomaso, Nancy. *The American Non-Dilemma: Racial Inequality Without Racism*. New York: Russell Sage Foundation, 2013.

Dole, Charles E. "Pinto Verdict Lets US Industry Off Hook." *Christian Science Monitor*, March 14, 1980. www.csmonitor.com/1980/0314/031435.html.

Donaldson, Thomas. "Ethics in Cyberspace: Have We Seen This Movie Before?" *Business and Society Review* 106 (2001) 273–91.

———. *The Ethics of International Business*. New York: Oxford University Press, 1989.

———. "Values in Tension: Ethics Away from Home." In *Harvard Business Review on Corporate Ethics*, 113–38. Boston: Harvard Business School Press, 2003.

Donaldson, Thomas, and Thomas W. Dunfee. "When Ethics Travel: The Promise and Peril of Global Business Ethics." *California Management Review* 41 (1999) 45–63.

Dowie, Mark. "How Ford Put Two Million Firetraps on Wheels." *Business and Society Review* 23 (1977) 46–55.

———. "Pinto Madness." *Mother Jones*, September/October 1977. www.motherjones.com/politics/1977/09/pinto-madness/.

Drum, Kevin. "Why We Sue." *Mother Jones*, August 25, 2010. www.motherjones.com/kevin-drum/2010–08/why-we-sue/.

Economist. "Why the Gun Lobby Is Winning." *Economist*, April 4, 2015. https://www.economist.com/united-states/2015/04/04/why-the-gun-lobby-is-winning.

Eichelberger, Curtis, and Charles R. Babcock. "Football-Ticket Tax Break Helps Colleges Get Millions." *BloombergBusiness*, October 25, 2012. www.bloomberg.com/news/articles/2012–10-25/got-college-football-tickets-take-a-tax-break.

Eichenwald, Kurt. "He Blew the Whistle, and Health Giants Quaked." *New York Times*, October 18, 1998. https://www.nytimes.com/1998/10/18/business/he-blew-the-whistle-and-health-giants-quaked.html.

Elmer, Duane. *Cross-Cultural Servanthood*. Downers Grove: InterVarsity, 2006.

Equal Employment Opportunity Program. "EEO Terminology." Last reviewed on August 15, 2016. https://www.archives.gov/eeo/terminology.html.

Eveleth, Rose. "Forty Years Ago, Women Had a Hard Time Getting Credit Cards." January 8, 2014. Smithsonian.com. www.smithsonianmag.com/smart-news/forty-years-ago-women-had-a-hard-time-getting-credit-cards-180949289/.

Fairchild, Caroline. "Number of Fortune 500 Women CEOs Reaches Historic High." *Fortune*, June 3, 2014. http://fortune.com/2014/06/03/number-of-fortune-500-women-ceos-reaches-historic-high/.

"Family Honor." Wikipedia.com. Last modified July 21, 2018. https://en.wikipedia.org/wiki/Family_honor.

Federal Glass Ceiling Commission. "Good for Business: Making Full Sense of the Nation's Human Capital; Executive Summary." Washington, DC: U.S. Department of Labor, 1995. https://www.dol.gov/oasam/programs/history/reich/reports/ceiling/pdf.

Ferrell, O. C., et al. *Business Ethics: Ethical Decision Making and Cases*. 10th ed. Stamford, CT: Cengage Learning, 2015.

Fink, Steven. *Crisis Management*. New York: American Management Association, 1986.

"Fire Destroys Malden Mills: December 11, 1995." Massmoments.org. https://www.massmoments.org/moment-details/fire-destroys-malden-mills.html.

Forbes. "America's Best Employers." Forbes.com. Last modified August 8, 2018. https://www.forbes.com/best-employers/list.

Fortune. "The Fortune 100 Best Companies to Work For." https://web.archive.org/web/20180201001616/https://www.greatplacetowork.com/best-workplaces/100-best/2017.

Fortune. "100 Best Companies to Work For 2017." Last modified August 8, 2018. https://www.greatplacetowork.com/best-workplaces/100-best/2017.

Fortune Editors. "These Are the Women CEOs Leading Fortune 500 Companies." *Fortune*, June 7, 2017. http://fortune.com/2017/06/07/fortune-500-women-ceos/.

Foster, Richard J. *Money, Sex & Power: The Challenge of the Disciplined Life*. San Francisco: Harper & Row, 1985.

Friedman, Milton. "The Social Responsibility of Business Is to Increase Its Profits." *New York Times Magazine*, September 13, 1970.

Garcia, Ahiza. "Only 9 Hispanic CEOs at Top 500 Companies." *CNN Money*, September 9, 2015. http://money.cnn.com/2015/09/09/news/hispanic-ceo-fortune-500-companies/.

Gelles, David. "Want to Make Money like a C.E.O.? Work for 275 Years." *New York Times*, May 25, 2018. https://www.nytimes.com/2018/05/25/business/highest-paid/ceos-2017.html.

Gill, David W. *Becoming Good: Building Moral Character*. Downers Grove: InterVarsity, 2000.

———. *Doing Right: Practicing Ethical Principles*. Downers Grove: InterVarsity, 2004.

Gioia, Dennis. "Pinto Fires and Personal Ethics: A Script Analysis of Missed Opportunities." *Journal of Business Ethics* 11 (1992) 379–89.

Goffman, Erving. *The Presentation of Self in Everyday Life*. New York: Doubleday, 1959.

Google Company. "Google's Mission Is to Organize the World's Information and Make It Universally Accessible and Useful." Google Company. Last modified October 6, 2015. https://web.archive.org/web/20151006094316/www.google.com/about/company/.

———. "Ten Things We Know to Be True." Google Company. Last modified October 17, 2017. https://www.google.com/about/philosophy.html.

Gourley, Bruce T. "American Theocracy: Who Is Trying to Turn America into a Theocracy?" Last modified April 20, 2018. www.brucegourley.com/chistiannation/theocracy.htm.

"Great Place to Work." Great Place to Work. Last modified August 8, 2018. http://reviews.greatplacetowork.com.

Griner, David. "18 Bullish Stats about the State of U.S. Advertising." *Adweek*, September 25, 2017. https://www.adweek.com/agencies/18-bullish-stats-about-the-state-of-u-s-advertising.

Gustafson, James. *Theology and Christian Ethics*. Cleveland: United Church Press, 1974.

Haas, R. D. "Ethics in the Trenches." *Across the Board* 31 (1994) 12–13.

Hanson, Kent. *Grace at 30,000 Feet and Other Unexpected Places*. Hagerstown, MD: Review and Herald, 2002.

Haynes, Barry. "An Evaluation of the Impact of the Office Environment on Productivity." *Facilities* 26 (2008) 178–95.

Herman Miller. Herman Miller homepage. Last modified August 7, 2018. www.hermanmiller.com.

Heschel, Abraham Joshua. *The Sabbath: Its Meaning for Modern Man*. New York: Farrar, Straus and Giroux, 1951.

Hoffman, W. Michael, and Mark S. Schwartz. "The Morality of Whistleblowing: A Commentary on Richard T. De George." *Journal of Business Ethics* 127 (2015) 771–81.

Hofstede, Geert, et al. *Cultures and Organizations: Software of the Mind.* 3rd ed. New York: McGraw Hill, 2010.

Holmes, Stanley. "The Affair That Grounded Stonecipher." *Bloomberg*, March 8, 2005. https://www.bloomberg.com/news/articles/2005/03/07/the-affair-that-grounded-stonecipher.

International Labour Organization. "Safety and Health at Work." Last modified August 7, 2018. http://www.ilo.org/global/topics/safety-and-health-at-work/lang--en/index.htm.

Jackman, Michael, ed. *Macmillan Book of Business and Economic Quotations.* New York: Macmillan, 1984.

Jennings, Marianne M. *Business Ethics: Case Studies and Selected Readings.* 7th ed. Mason, OH: South-Western Cengage Learning, 2012.

———. *Business Ethics: Case Studies and Selected Readings.* 8th ed. Stamford, CT: Cengage Learning, 2015.

Jimenez, Ralph. "New Rash of Fires Presses Lawrence." *Boston Globe*, September 21, 1992. https://www.newspapers.com/newspage/440054653/.

Joint Committee on Taxation. "Report of Investigation of Enron Corporation and Related Entities Regarding Federal Tax and Compensation Issues, and Policy Recommendations." February 2003. http://www.jct.gov/s-3-03-vol1.pdf.

Jones, Gareth R., and Jennifer M. George. *Essentials of Contemporary Management.* 6th ed. New York: McGraw Hill, 2015.

Joy, Bill. "Why the Future Doesn't Need Us." *Wired*, April 1, 2000.

Kantor, Jodi, and Megan Twohey. "Decades of Sexual Harassment Accusations against Harvey Weinstein." *New York Times*, October 5, 2017. https://www.nytimes.com/2017/10/05/us/harvey-weinstein-harassment-allegations.html.

Kell, John. "McDonald's CEO Exit Erodes Diversity among Fortune 500 Execs." *Fortune*, January 29, 2015. http://fortune.com/2015/01/29/mcdonalds-ceo-exit-lessens-diversity/.

Kidder, Rushworth M. *How Good People Make Tough Choices: Resolving the Dilemmas of Ethical Living.* New York: Fireside, 1995.

Kile, J. "Aaron Feuerstein." *Moral Heroes* (blog). November 19, 2010. http://moralheroes.org/aaron-feuerstein.

Kim, David, et al. "Modernism, Christianity, and Business Ethics: A Worldview Perspective." *Journal of Business Ethics* 90 (2009) 115–21.

Kinnaman, David, and Gabe Lyons. *Good Faith: Being a Christian When Society Thinks You're Irrelevant and Extreme.* Grand Rapids: Baker, 2016.

Knapp, John C. *How the Church Fails Businesspeople (and What Can Be Done about It).* Grand Rapids: Eerdmans, 2012.

Koehn, Daryl. "East Meets West: Toward a Universal Ethic of Virtue for Global Business." *Journal of Business Ethics* 116 (2013) 703–15.

Koehn, Nancy. "Great Men, Great Pay? Why CEO Compensation Is Sky High." *Washington Post*, June 12, 2014. www.washingtonpost.com/opinions/great-men-great-pay-why ceo-compensation-is-sky-high.html.

Koh, Yoree, and Rachel Feintzeig. "Can You Still Date a Co-worker? Well, It's Complicated; Some Employers Are Starting to Review Their Rules and Are Now

'Drawing a Hard Line in the Sand.'" *Wall Street Journal* (online), February 6, 2018. ProQuest.

Kroll, Andy. "Cloak and Data: The Real Story behind Cambridge Analytica's Rise and Fall." *Mother Jones*, May/June 2018. https://www.motherjones.com/politics/2018/03/cloak-and-data-cambridge-analytica-robert-mercer/.

Lacayo, Richard, and Amanda Ripley. "Time Persons of the Year 2002: The Whistleblowers." *Time*, December 30, 2002.

Larmer, Robert. "Whistleblowing and Employee Loyalty." In *Taking Sides: Clashing Views in Business Ethics and Society*, edited by edited by Lisa H. Newton et al., 184–89. 12th ed. New York: McGraw Hill, 2013.

Lee, Jyh-An, et al. "Searching for Internet Freedom in China: A Case Study on Google's China Experience." *Cardozo Arts & Entertainment Law Journal* 31 (2013) 405–34.

Leeson, Nick. *Rogue Trader: How I Brought Down Barings Bank and Shook the Financial World*. Boston: Little, Brown, 1996.

Leiner, Barry M., et al. *Brief History of the Internet*. n.d. www.internetsociety.org/internet/what-internet/history-internet/brief-history-internet/.

Lemon, W. Morley, and Wanda A. Wallace. "Ethical Issues Facing Internal Auditors and Their Profession." *Research on Accounting Ethics* 6 (2000) 189–203.

Leung, Rebecca. "The Mensch of Malden Mills." 60 Minutes, July 3, 2003. www.cbsnews.com/news/the-mensch-of-malden-mills/.

Levitt, Theodore. "The Morality (?) of Advertising." *Harvard Business Review* 48 (1970) 91–92.

Lewis, Michael. "Faking It: The Internet Revolution Has Nothing to Do with the Nasdaq." *New York Times Magazine*, July 15, 2001.

———. *Next: The Future Just Happened*. New York: Norton, 2001.

Lowndes, Leil. "Dangerous Office Liaisons." *Legal Assistant Today* 11 (1993) 64–71.

Lucas, Edward. *Cyberphobia: Identity, Trust, Security and the Internet*. New York: Bloomsbury, 2015.

Lucas, Suzanne. "How Much Does It Cost Companies to Lose Employees?" *Moneywatch*, November 21, 2012. www.cbsnews.com/news/how-much-does-it-cost-companies-to-lose-employees/.

Maranz, David. *African Friends and Money Matters: Observations from Africa*. SIL International Publications in Ethnography 37. Dallas: SIL, 2001.

McGregor, Jena. "Median CEO Pay for the 100 Largest Companies Reached a Record $15.7 Million in 2017." *Washington Post*, April 11, 2018. https://www.washingtonpost.com/news/on-leadership/wp/2018/04/11/median-ceo-pay-for-the-100-largest-companies-reached-a-record-15-7-million-in-2017-html.

McKinnon, John D. "Web Freedom's Role in Sex Trafficking." *Wall Street Journal*, July 12, 2016.

McLean, Bethany, and Peter Elkind. *The Smartest Guys in the Room*. New York: Penguin, 2003.

McMillan, Michael. "Retaliation against Whistle-Blowers: No Good Deed Goes Unpunished." *Enterprising Investor* (blog). CFA Institute. October 24, 2012. http://blogs.cfainstitute.org/inestor/2012/10/24/whistle-blowing-no-good-deed-goes-unpunished/.

Merck. Merck homepage. Last modified August 8, 2018. www.merck.com.

Miceli, Marcia P., and Janet P. Near. *Blowing the Whistle: The Organizational and Legal Implications for Companies and Employees*. New York: Lexington, 1992.

Microsoft. "Internet Information Services." Last modified October 26, 2015. http://media.corporate-ir.net.

Moberg, Dennis J. "When Good People Do Bad Things at Work." *Issues in Ethics* 10 (1999) 7–10.

Mochizuki, Takashi and Sarah E. Needleman. "Pokemon Game Jolts Nintendo." *Wall Street Journal*, July 12, 2016.

Monsma, George N., Jr. "Biblical Principles Important for Economic Theory and Practice." In *On Moral Business: Classical and Contemporary Resources for Ethics in Economic Life*, edited by Max L. Stackhouse et al., 38–45. Grand Rapids: Eerdmans, 1995.

Moorthy, R. S., et al. *Uncompromising Integrity: Motorola's Global Challenge.* Schaumburg, IL: Motorola University Press, 1998.

Moser, Douglas. "Polartec Moving Operations South, Hundreds Will Lose Jobs." *Eagle Tribune*, December 11, 2015. http://www.eagletribune.com/news/polartec-moving-operations-south-hundreds-will-lose-jobs/article_8955a7c2-9fd5-11e5-9ba3-4fb1a3e6644a.html.

Mullaney, Tim. "Why Corporate CEO Pay Is so High, and Going Higher." *CNBC Explains* (blog), May 18, 2015. https://www.cnbc.com/2015/05/18/why-corporate-ceo-pay-is-so-high-and-going-higher.html.

Muller, Wayne. *Sabbath: Finding Rest, Renewal, and Delight in Our Busy Lives.* New York: Bantam, 1999.

Murphy, Patrick E. *Eighty Exemplary Ethics Statements.* Notre Dame: University of Notre Dame Press, 1998.

Nash, Laura, and Scotty McLennan. *Church on Sunday, Work on Monday: The Challenge of Fusing Christian Values with Business Life.* San Francisco: Jossey-Bass, 2001.

"National Business Ethics Survey (NBES) 2013." Ethics and Compliance Initiative. https://connects.ethics.org/ecihome/research/nbes/nbes-reports/nbes-2013.

Newsweek. "Mea Culpa, Sort Of." *Newsweek*, September 27, 1971.

Noonan, John T. *Bribes: The Intellectual History of a Moral Idea.* New York: McMillan, 1984.

Nouwen, Henri. "Adam's Peace." *Signs of the Times* 116 (1989) 9–11.

———. *In the Name of Jesus.* New York: Crossroad, 1989.

Novak, Michael. *Business as a Calling: Work and the Examined Life.* New York: Free Press, 1996.

Ollukkaran, Bindu Anto, and Rupa Gunaseelan. "A Study on the Impact of Work Environment on Employee Performance." *Namex International Journal of Management Research* 2 (2012) 71–85.

O'Reilly, Brian. "Agee in Exile." *Fortune*, May 29, 1995. http://archive.fortune.com/magazines/fortune/fortune_archive/1995/05/29/203144/index.htm.

Pacelle, Mitchell. "Enron's Creditors to Get Peanuts." *Wall Street Journal*, July 11, 2003.

Patagonia. Patagonia homepage. Last modified August 8, 2018. www.patagonia.com.

Pava, Moses. "Developing a Religiously Grounded Business Ethic: A Jewish Perspective." *Business Ethics Quarterly* 8 (1998) 65–84.

Peach, E. B., and K. L. Murrell. "Establishing and Maintaining an Ethical Posture in a Global Multi-cultural Environment: Motorola, a Case Study." Presented at the Academy of Management Annual Conference, Chicago, August 9, 1999.

Petersen, Melody. "Health Net Tried to Block Employee Whistleblowers, SEC says." *Los Angeles Times*, August 16, 2016. http://www.latimes.com/business/la-fi-health-net-whistleblower-20160816-snap-story.html.

Peterson, Andrea. "Google Is Tracking Students as It Sells More Products to Schools, Privacy Advocates Warn." *Washington Post*, December 28, 2015. www.washingtonpost.com/news/the-switchw/2015/12/28/google-is-tracking-students-as-it-sells-more-products-to-schools-privacy-advocates-warn/.

Pettinger, Anne. "Jim Alderson: A Whistleblower's Odyssey." *Montana State University Mountains & Minds Magazine*, November 27, 2007. www.montana.edu/news/mountainsandminds/article/html?id=9280.

Philbrick, Nathaniel. *Mayflower: A Story of Courage, Community and War*. New York: Penguin, 2006.

Pierard, Richard V. "Where America Missed the Way." *Journal of the American Scientific Affiliation* 29 (1977) 18–21.

Rae, Scott B., and Kenman L. Wong. *Beyond Integrity*. 3rd ed. Grand Rapids: Zondervan, 2012.

Ragins, Belle Rose, et al. "Gender Gap in the Executive Suite: CEOs and Female Executives Report on Breaking the Glass Ceiling." *Academy of Management Executive* 12 (1998) 28–42.

Reed, Lori. "InsureMe Earns Ethics in Business Award." *PRWeb*, March 10, 2008. https://www.prweb.com/releases/2008/03/prweb753974.htm.

RIAA. "About Piracy." Recording Industry Association of America. Last modified August 8, 2018. http://www.riaa.com/resources-learning/about-piracy/.

Roach, Ronald. "High-Tech Cheating." *Black Issues in Higher Education* 15 (1998) 26–28.

Rose, Barbara. "Stonecipher's Partner Quits at Boeing." *Chicago Tribune*, March 19, 2005. http://articles.chicagotribune.com/2005/03–19/business/0503190259 1 debra-peabody-harry-stoncipher-boeing-spokesman-john-dern.

Rosen, Jeffrey. "The Eroded Self." *New York Magazine*, April 30, 2000. https://www.nytimes.com/2000/04/30/magazine/the-eroded-self.html?scp=1&sq=the+eroded+self+rosen&st=nyt.

Rubin, Paul H. "More Money into Bad Suits." *New York Times*, November 15, 2010. www.nytimes.com/roomfordebate/2010/11/15/investing-in-someone-elses-lawsuit/more-money-into-bad-suits.

Ruch, Dick. *Leaders & Followers*. Holland, MI: Star, 2002.

Samuelson, Robert J. "Delinquency of the CEOs." *Washington Post*, July 13, 2006. http://www.washingtonpost.com/wp-dyn/content/article/2006/-7/12/AR2006071201871_pf.html.

Sandberg, Sheryl. *Lean In: Women, Work, and the Will to Lead*. New York: Knopf, 2014.

Satariano, Adam. "What the G.D.P.R., Europe's Tough New Data Law, Means for You." *New York Times*, May 6, 2018. https://www.nytimes.com/2018/05/06/technology/gdpr-european-privacy-law.html.

Schmidt, Eric, et al. *Google: How Google Works*. New York: Grand Central, 2014.

Schwartz, Mark S. "Developing and Sustaining an Ethical Corporate Culture: The Core Elements." *Business Horizons* 56 (2013) 39–50.

Shames, Laurence. *The Hunger for More: Searching for Values in an Age of Greed*. New York: Times, 1989.

Shea, Virginia. *Netiquette*. San Rafael, CA: Albion, 1994.

Shulevitz, Judith. *The Sabbath World*. New York: Random House, 2010.

Singer, Natasha. "What You Don't Know about How Facebook Uses Your Data." *New York Times*, April 11, 2018. https://www.nytimes.com/2018/04/11/technology/facebook-privacy-hearings.html.

Smedes, Lewis B. *Love within Limits*. Grand Rapids: Eerdmans, 1989.

Smith, Elliot Blair. "Wal-Mart Sets New Policy on Ethics." *USA Today*, January 28, 2005.

Smithsonian. "The Passenger Pigeon." Smithsonian Institute. https://www.si.edu/spotlight/passenger-pigeon.

Spinello, Richard A. "Information Integrity." In *Internet Ethics*, edited by Duncan Langford, 158–80. New York: St. Martin's, 2000.

Stackhouse, Max L. "Foundations and Purposes." Introduction to *On Moral Business: Classical and Contemporary Resources for Ethics in Economic Life*, edited by Max L. Stackhouse et al., 10–34. Grand Rapids: Eerdmans, 1995.

Statista. "Media Advertising Spending in the United States from 2015 to 2021 (in Billion U.S., Dollars)." *Statista: The Statistics Portal*. Last modified August 8, 2018. www.statista.com/statistics/272314/advertising-spending-in-the-US/.

Steiner, Peter. Cartoon. *New Yorker*, July 5, 1993, 61.

Stevenson, Bryan. *Just Mercy: A Story of Justice and Redemption*. New York: Spiegel & Grau, 2015.

Sykes, Timothy. "Exposing Convicted Penny Stock Manipulator Jonathan Lebed of the National Inflation Association's Latest Pump & Dump." *TimothySykes* (blog). January 18, 2012. https://web.archive.org/web/20130525105816/http://www.timothysykes.com/2012/01/exposing-convicted-penny-stock-manipulator-jonathan-lebed-of-the-national-inflation-associations-latest-pump-dump/.

Talaulicar, Till. "Global Retailers and Their Corporate Codes of Ethics: The Case of Wal-Mart in Germany." *Service Industries Journal* 29 (2009) 47–58.

Tan, Justin, and Anna Tan. "Business under Threat, Technology under Attack, Ethics under Fire: The Experience of Google in China." *Journal of Business Ethics* 110 (2012) 469–79.

Thomas, C. William. "The Rise and Fall of Enron." *Journal of Accountancy* 193 (2002) 41–48.

Timberg, Craig, and Elizabeth Dwoskin. "How Years of Privacy Controversies Finally Caught Up with Facebook." *Washington Post*, July 26, 2018. https://www.washingtonpost.com/technology/2018/07/26/how-years-privacy-controversies-finally-caught-up-with-facebook/?utm_term=.524b405e54b5.

Toossi, Mitra. "Labor Force Projections to 2022: The Labor Force Participation Rate Continues to Fall." *Monthly Labor Review*, US Bureau of Labor Statistics, December 2013. https://doi.org/10.21916/mlr.2013.40.

TOW Project. "Calling & Vocation: Overview." Theology of Work Project. https://www.theologyofwork.org/key-topics/vocation-overview-article.

Trevino, Linda Trevino, and Katherine A. Nelson. *Managing Business Ethics: Straight Talk about How to Do It Right*. 2nd ed. New York: Wiley, 1999.

———. *Managing Business Ethics: Straight Talk about How to Do It Right*. 6th ed. Hoboken, NJ: Wiley, 2014.

US Department of Justice. Foreign Corrupt Practices Act. https://www.justice.gov/criminal-fraud/foreign-corrupt-practices-act.

Useem, Jerry. "New Ethics . . . or No Ethics?" *Fortune*, March 20, 2000.

Van Duzer, Jeff. *Why Business Matters to God (and What Still Needs to Be Fixed)*. Downers Grove: IVP Academic, 2010.

Velasquez, Manuel G. *Business Ethics: Concepts and Cases*. 4th ed. Upper Saddle River, NJ: Prentice Hall, 1998.

———. *Business Ethics: Concepts and Cases*. 6th ed. Upper Saddle River, NJ: Pearson / Prentice Hall, 2006.

Von Drehle, David. *Triangle: The Fire That Changed America*. New York: Atlantic Monthly, 2003.

Waide, John. "The Making of Self and World in Advertising." *Journal of Business Ethics* 6 (1987) 73–79.

Walker, Brian C. "Profits with Purpose: Herman Miller Inc." *45 Social Entrepreneurs Who Are Changing the World*. March 25, 2016. https://web.archive.org/web/20160325183752/www.fastcompany.com/social/2008/profiles/herman-miller.html.

Wal-Mart, Inc. "Wal-Mart Annual Report, 2018, Notes to the Consolidated Financial Statements 10." Bentonville, AR. http://stock.walmart.com/investors/financial-information/annual-reports-and-proxies/default.aspx.

Wal-Mart, Inc. "Wal-Mart Statement of Ethics, 2013." Bentonville, AR. http://corporate.walmart.com/policies.

Washington State University. "The Internet & Copyright." Posted from stock.xchng, courtesy of Áron Balogh. https://ucomm.wsu.edu/the-internet-copyright/.

Weckert, John. "What Is New or Unique about Internet Activities?" In *Internet Ethics*, edited by Duncan Langford, 47–64. New York: St. Martin's, 2000.

Weise, Karen. "Judge Approves Merrill Lynch's $160 Million Racial Bias Settlement." *Bloomberg Businessweek*, December 6, 2013. https://www.bloomberg.com/news/articles/2013-12-06/judge-approves-merrill-lynchs-160-million-racial-bias-settlement.

Weiss, Stephanie, and David Bollier. "Merck & Company, Inc.: Having the Vision to Succeed." In *Readings and Cases in International Management: A Cross-Cultural Perspective*, edited by David C. Thomas, 71–74. Thousand Oaks, CA: Sage, 2003.

Whirlpool. Whirlpool Corporation home page. Last modified August 8, 2018. www.whirlpoolcorp.com.

Wilbanks, Charles. "Ex-Enron CEO Jeff Skilling to Leave Prison Early." *Moneywatch*, June 21, 2013. www.cbsnews.co/news/ex-enron-ceo-jeff-skilling-to-leave-prison-early/.

Wilkens, Steve. *Beyond Bumper Sticker Ethics: An Introduction to Theories of Right & Wrong*. Downers Grove: InterVarsity, 1995.

Wilson, Jonathan. *God's Good World: Reclaiming the Doctrine of Creation*. Grand Rapids: Baker Academic, 2013.

Woodruff, David. "Herman Miller: How Green Is My Factory." *Business Week*, September 16, 1991.

Wrenn, Bruce, et al. *Scriptural Foundations for Marketing*. Berrien Springs, MI: Andrews University Press, 2013.

Yancey, Philip. "Confessions of a Racist." Part 2. *Christianity Today*, January 1, 2000. www.christianitytoday.com/ct/2000/januaryweb-only/13.0b.html?start=2.

———. *Soul Survivor: How My Faith Survived the Church*. New York: Doubleday, 2001.

Yardley, Jim. "Report on Deadly Factory Collapse in Bangladesh Finds Widespread Blame." *New York Times*, May 22, 2013. http://www.nytimes.com/2013/05/23/

world/asia/report-on-bangladesh-building-collapse-finds-widespread-blame.
html.

Yeoman, Barry. "Why the Passenger Pigeon Went Extinct." *Audubon*, May-June 2014.
www.audubon.org/magazine/may-june-2014.

Zacharek, Stephanie, et al. "Time Persons of the Year 2017: The Silence Breakers." *Time*,
December 18, 2017. https://time.com/time-person-of-the-year-2017-silence-
breakers/.

Zobel, Hiller B. "In Love with Lawsuits." *American Heritage* 45 (1994) 58–66.

Index

A

absolutes, 211–12
absolutism, cultural, 195
accessibility, 143
accountability, 42, 135, 225
accounting fraud
    conflict of interest and, 184–86
    Enron case story on, 175–79,
    186, 189–90
    as part of financial fraud,
    179–81
    root cause of, 187–89
    triangle of conditions leading
    to, 181–84
    whistle-blowing and, 161, 171
    See also financial reports/
    statements
accusations. *See* whistle-blowing
actions/behavior
    Christian business person's,
    224–26
    conflict of interest, 184–85
    decision-making and, 17, 19,
    23–24
    environment and, 44–46, 50, 55
    the fall after creation and, 33,
    241
    global business ethics and, 194,
    202, 211–12
    influence of culture on, 112–13,
    115–16
    law/ethics and, 106–7

    marketing/advertising and,
    151–52
    quality/safety and, 100, 102,
    110–11
    service-oriented, 226–29
    technology/values and, 134–37
    whistle-blowing as/for. *See*
    whistle-blower; whistle-blowing
    workplace relationships and, 93
    worldview and, 4, 30
    See also code of conduct;
    misconduct
Adam and Eve
    anonymity issues and, 134
    environment and, 45–48
    the fall after creation and, 34–36
    God's response to, 241, 247
    rights/freedoms and, 60
    worldview and, 5
Adeney, Bernard, 211
adultery, 92, 93
advance fee fraud, 180
advertising
    about, 143–45
    need for integrity in, 150–53
    Nestlé case story on, 140–42,
    154–55
    power of greed and, 153–54
    psychological appeals in,
    147–48
    responsibility in, 148–50
    Scripture/puffery and, 145–47
African American CEOs, 87

268 INDEX

employee rights (continued)
    biblical use of, 72–74
    concept of rights in, 58–60
    dignity of work and, 68–71
    Malden Mills case story on,
        56–58
employees
    Enron case story on, 177–79
    environment and, 43, 52, 54
    Google on valued qualities of,
        216–18, 237–38
    InsureMe case story on, 225
    monitoring activity of, 64
    from overseas, 66
    quality/safety and, 110
    value-added qualities of Chris-
        tian, 218–34
    whistle-blowing and, 160
employer directives, reasonable, 160
employment
    employee rights and, 59, 61
    global business ethics and, 205
    whistle-blowing and, 157
end-time perspective, 233–34
Enlightenment, 25
Enron Corporation
    case story on, 175–79, 189–90
    conflict of interest and, 185–86
    whistle-blowing and, 158, 165,
        171
Enron Finance Corporation, 179
entrepreneur, local, 212–14
environment. See resources, environ-
    mental; workplace environment
Equal Credit Opportunity Act (1974),
    81
Equal Employment Opportunity
    Commission (EEOC), 88
Equal Justice Initiative, 236
equal liberty principle, 22
equality of opportunities, 22–23, 83
Erbitux (ImClone), 187
Ernst & Young (EY), 170
error, moral, 34
espionage, industrial, 163
ethical conflicts, 206–7, 222–23. See
    also decision-making
ethics

about Christian, 1
computer, 122–23
culture/law and, 106–8, 114–16
love and situational, 49–50
of safety, 101–3
spirit of, 107–8
theories of. See philosophy, ethi-
    cal theories of
See also codes of ethics
ethics lapse, 100
ethics program, corporate, 168
Ethics Resource Center (ERC), 160
ethnicity, discrimination and, 85
E-trade, 118
Eve. See Adam and Eve
evidence, decision-making and, 25
evil, existence of
    decision-making and, 17, 223
    environment and, 55
    the fall after creation and, 33–35
    global business ethics and,
        211–12
    law/ethics/culture and, 115
    love and, 244
exaggeration in advertising, 144, 146
excellence, 235
exchange, product, 149
expectations, 164, 179
expertise
    marketing/advertising and, 143
    rise of Internet and, 120–21
    technology/values and, 124–27
    whistle-blowing and, 172
exploitation
    global business ethics and, 205,
        206, 207
    marketing/advertising and,
        152–53, 154
    workplace romance and, 92
exposure, hazardous, 62–63
extortion, 209
Exxon Valdez oil spill, 49–50

F

Facebook
    discrimination and, 83–84

G

gender bias, 84
General Data Protection Regulation
  (GDPR-Europe), 131
General Mills case (Cheerios), 144
generally accepted accounting principles (GAAP), 176
German Works Council, 200
gift-giving in cultures, 207
gifts (talents)
  creation perspective and, 32
  dignity of work and, 68–69
  discrimination and underused,
  85
  long-view of, 233–34
  technology/values and, 138
gifts/gratuities, 152, 186, 211. *See also*
  tips (gratuity)
Gill, David, 8, 30–32, 93–95, 102, 128,
  145–46, 188, 230
Gioia, Dennis, 98–101, 108, 110, 112,
  114–15
"glass ceiling," 85–87
Glass Ceiling Act (1991), 86
Global Anti-Corruption Policy, 15
global business. *See* business,
  international
God
  a balanced life and, 231–33
  Christian and character of,
  238–39
  decision-making and, 17, 23,
  25–33
  discrimination and, 79–80
  environment and, 44–47,
  52–53, 63
  global business ethics and, 210,
  212, 214
  help for seeking, 241–47
  marketing/advertising and, 145,
  151
  name of, 30–31
  on relationships, 92–95
  technology/values and, 134–35,
  138
  workplace rights and, 60, 68–71,
  72
  worldview and meeting, 1–4
Goffman, Erving, 135

Golden Rule, 21, 79, 102, 190, 197,
  225
Goldman Sachs Group, Inc., 158, 187
good and evil, 17
Good Faith (Kinnaman & Lyons), 116
Good Manufacturing Practices
  (cGMP), current, 113
Good Samaritan (parable), 137
good will, 55
"good/just cause," 59, 61
Goodman, Shira, 87
goods and services. *See* products/
  services
Google: How Google Works (Schmidt
  et al.), 217
Google LLC case stories, 208, 216–18,
  237–38
Google products/services, 130, 216
Gordon-Conwell Advent Devotional,
  233
gospel, 242
gossip, office, 91
governance for sustainability (Ceres),
  42
government. *See* laws/legislation
government fraud, 157–58, 159
government regulator, 157, 164
graciousness, 28, 238
"grease payments." *See* "facilitating
  payments"
Great Man theory, 67
Great Place to Work Institute, Inc.,
  225
greed
  covetousness and, 187
  environment and, 37, 55
  fair compensation and, 67–68
  marketing/advertising and, 144,
  148, 153–54
  rights/freedoms and, 72
  Walmart case story on, 12
  worldview and, 3, 4
"Green Companies," 42
growth/development, economic, 53
guidance, moral, 51, 201–3, 221–24
guilt, global business ethics and, 212
gun lobby, 62
Gupta, Rajat, 187

possessiveness. *See* greed; ownership
postmodernism, 25
power
    abuse of, in global business, 207
    of culture in product safety, 112
    for service vs. control, 226–29
    of technology, 124, 131
    types of, 226
power distance in cultures, 198
pragmatism, 107
prayer, 223, 242–43
predatory pricing, 143
Pregnancy Discrimination Act (1978), 81
prejudice, 83
pressure in fraud triangle, 179, 181–82, 186, 187
price fixing, 143
pricing, 142–43
prima facie moral rules, 211–12
Princeton Theological Seminary, 136
privacy agreements, 130
privacy issues, 121, 129–32, 163
privacy rights, 63–64
privacy vs. safety, 130–31
privilege, rights/freedoms and, 59
problem, non-sharable financial, 181–82
product liability, 104–6
productivity, 63
products/services
    advertising, 149
    creating life-giving, 220–21
    defective, defined, 105
    environment and, 42, 52, 55
    marketing, 142–43
    misuse of, 104
    non-delivery (fraud) of, 180
    quality/safety of. *See* quality/safety of products
profanity, 30, 89
Profile Bread case (Continental Baking Company), 145
profiling, online, 135–36
profit, 52, 153, 179
profit sharing plan, 41, 64
promise keeping/breaking, 20, 92

promotion in marketing/advertising, 143
promotions, workplace, 85–86, 91, 92, 230
property rights (tangible/intangible), 60, 72, 124–28
prophets (biblical) for guidance, 51
protection, legal, 164, 171
Protestant perspective, 4
psychological appeals, 144, 147
public interest, 158. *See also* disbelief, public; recognition, public
puffery in advertising, 146–47

Q

qadosh, 71, 151
quality/safety of products
    ethics and, 101–3
    Ford case story on, 97–100, 116–17
    influence of culture and, 111–13
    law/ethics/culture and, 106–8, 114–16
    organizational culture and, 108–11
    vs. privacy, 130–31
    role of American law in, 103–6
    See also safety, workplace/personal
qui tam case, 157
quid pro quo harassment, 89, 229
Quorum (company), 156

R

racial inequality without racism, 84
racism, 84
Rae, Scott B., 51, 53
Rajaratnam, Raj, 187
rationality, 20, 149
rationalization in fraud triangle, 181–83
Rawls, John, 21–23

Rosen, Jeffrey, 135–36
Rosenberg, Jonathan, 217, 238
"roving leadership," 40
Rowley, Coleen, 161
Ruch, Richard H., 40
rulership, biblical, 5, 44–45
rumors, harmful, 133

S

Sabbath, 29, 46, 69–70, 231–33
Sabbath (Heschel), The, 70
Sabbath: Finding Rest, Renewal,
    and Delight in Our Busy Lives
    (Muller), 70–71
Sabbath World (Shulevitz), The, 136
safety, workplace/personal
    employee rights and, 61–63
    environment and, 43
    ethics of, 101–3
    global business ethics and, 196
    whistle-blowing and, 164, 167
    See also quality/safety of
    products
Samford University, 220
Samuelson, Robert J., 68
Sandberg, Sheryl, 83
Santa Clara University, 136
Sarbanes–Oxley Act (2002), 168, 171
Saul (biblical king), 167
scams, 118–21, 138–39
Scanlon plan (profit sharing), 41
Schilling, John, 157
Schmidt, Eric, 217, 238
Schwartz, Mark S., 163–68
science, decision-making and, 25–26
Scott, H. Lee, 14
scripts, theory of, 100
Scriptural Foundations for Marketing
    (Wrenn), 149–50
Scripture
    decision-making and, 21, 25,
    33–34, 221–22
    on discrimination, 79–80
    on employee work rights, 65,
    67–74
    on environment, 44–47, 51–52

fraudulent actions and, 190
global business ethics and, 210,
    211, 214
marketing/advertising and,
    145–46, 149–50, 151–52
misuse of, 82
product quality/safety and,
    101–2
on relationships, 92–95
revealing God, 241–42, 245–47
on taking long view, 233
technology/values and, 127–28,
    134–35
whistle-blowing and, 166–68
worldview and, 1–5
See also Ten Commandments
Seattle Pacific University, 45, 220
SEC (Securities and Exchange Com-
    mission, U.S.), 118–20, 170, 171
Second Coming of Christ, 233, 247
security, 121, 167
segregation, 84
self-centeredness, 34–35
self-esteem, 31
self/self-interest, 3, 30, 184. See also
    greed
Sermon on the Mount, 19–20, 51, 73,
    244, 246
service, 226–29, 235
services. See products/services
sex in advertising, 147
sex trafficking, Internet, 133–34
sexual favors, 89
sexual harassment
    about, 87–90
    family/family life and, 229
    office romance vs., 90–91
    Scripture related to, 92–95
    whistle-blowing and, 163
sexual interest (romantic), 90–92
sexual material, 89
Shames, Laurence, 234–35
Shea, Virginia, 122
Shipman, Todd, 177
short-term vs. long-term orientation,
    198–200, 233–34
Shulevitz, Judith, 136
Siemens, 214

T

Y

Z

CPSIA information can be obtained
at www.ICGtesting.com
Printed in the USA
BVHW040206020520
579077BV00005B/422